M. F. Smith & As

Total Business Solutions

STRATEGIC THINKING FOR INFORMATION TECHNOLOGY

Bernard H. Boar

Director, Enterprise Strategies
M. F. Smith & Associates, Inc.

John Wiley & Sons, Inc.
New York • Chichester • Brisbane • Toronto • Singapore • Weinheim

For Diane, Jessica, and Debbie—
With Love Always

Copyright © 1997 by AT&T
Published by John Wiley & Sons, Inc.
All rights reserved. Published simultaneously in Canada.

Library of Congress Cataloging-in-Publication Data

Boar, Bernard H.
 Strategic thinking for information technology / Bernard H. Boar.
  p. cm.
 Includes bibliographical references and index.
 ISBN 0-471-15881-X (pbk. : alk. paper)
 1. Information technology—Management. 2. Strategic planning.
I. Title.
T58.64.B62 1996
658.4′038—dc20   96-27114
                     CIP

Printed in the United States of America

10 9 8 7 6 5 4 3 2

On Strategy

What everyone knows is what has already happened. What everyone knows is not called wisdom. What the *aware* individual knows is what has not yet taken shape; what has not yet occured.

. . . The multitudes know when you win but they do not know the basis. Everyone knows the form by which I am victorious, but no one knows the form by which I ensure victory. The science of ensuring victory is a mysterious secret. Victory is not repetitious but adapts its form endlessly.

—Sun Tzu, *The Art of War*

Other Books by the Author

Abend Debugging for COBOL Programmers

Application Prototyping: A Requirements Definition Strategy for the '80s

Implementing Client/Server Computing: A Strategic Perspective

The Art of Strategic Planning for Information Technology: Crafting Strategy for the '90s

Practical Steps for Aligning Information Technology with Business Strategies: How to Achieve a Competitive Advantage

Cost Efffective Strategies for Client/Server Systems

About the Author

Mr. Bernard (Bernie) Boar is an accomplished author and consultant in the field of information technology. He has four published books on the critical topics of IT strategy and architecture entitled *Cost Effective Strategies for Client/Server Systems, Practical Steps to Aligning Information Technology with Business Strategy, The Art of Strategic Planning for Information Technology: Crafting Strategy for the '90s*, and *Implementing Client/Server Computing: A Strategic Perspective*. His book *Application Prototyping: A Requirements Definition Strategy for the '80s* is now recognized as the seminal work on the subject. Bernie has been published in *CIO Journal, Computerworld, Journal of Systems Management, Journal of Business Strategy, DMR*, and *The Journal of Systems Development*. He is a frequent speaker at leading industry conferences on IT strategy, IT management and distributed computing. He holds an MBA from the Baruch Graduate School of Business and a B.S. in Computer Science from the City College of New York. Bernie is a member of both the Strategic Planning Society and the Strategic Management Society. He has provided guest lectures at American Graduate School for International Business, the Stevens Institute of Technology, University of West Indies, University of Minnesota, Sydney Technology University, and Cornell University. Bernie serves as an information technology strategist, architect, and consultant for M. F. Smith & Associates, Inc. in Morristown, New Jersey. He can be reached at bboar@mfsmith.com.

Contents

Foreword

It was during my transcontinental flight home, after attending my final industry conference of the year, that it suddenly became clear what had been subliminally pestering me for some time. It had been my custom to select and attend presentations that included the word *strategy* in their title. I had attended, for example, seminars on "Middleware Strategy," "Object Strategy," "Data Warehousing Strategy," "Internet Strategy," "Operating System Strategy," "Year 2000 Strategy," and "Enterprise Information Technology Strategy for the Next Millennium." Though the presentations were normally quite informative, I always departed feeling that my expectations had just not been meet. I didn't know exactly what, but I did know that something very important and fundamental was missing from all those seminars.

The realization that occurred to me, while having dinner somewhere over the Midwest, was that, in almost all the cases, the seminars were, in reality, 90 percent technology and 10 percent strategy. Although the presenters titled their presentations with the attention-stealing and sacrosanct word *strategy*, in delivery, the presentations were unanimously technological perspectives as opposed to strategic synthesis. There was always an abundance of material about the technology under scrutiny but very little provocative or novel strategic thought.

This really should not have been such a discovery. Information technology (IT) professionals are enamored, not surprisingly, with information technology. The discipline of strategy is a distant, arcane, and often dry subject to those who have been raised on databases, telecommunication monitors, and five generations of programming languages. Most IT audiences would much prefer to listen to the latest gossip on the server operating system wars than think about how to relate information technology to sustainable competitive advantage for the business. So what was missing from all those information technology strategy seminars that I attended was, paradoxically, strategy.

This book is quite different than those seminars; it is 90% strategy and 10% technology. This is long overdue and welcomed. There are numerous studies, some dating as far back as 1980, that show a consistent and growing dissatisfaction with IT by the business leadership. This chronic disappointment is directly related to the persistent inability to use IT to build, compound, and sustain strategic advantage for the firm.

The need to think about and deploy information technology strategically becomes tantamount in the emerging information age. Information technology is no longer an unfortunate expense that supports the real purpose of the business. For most businesses, future success or failure will directly hinge on how well IT is deployed. The application of strategic thinking to IT is the business imperative of the latter part of the 20th century.

I therefore cannot recommend too strongly that you read and reread this book. There are endless resources available to acquire all the information you will ever need about each and every information technology of interest, but there is an absolute poverty of resources that can provide you with insightful and executable strategic advice. This book, especially Chapter 3, "Strategic Thinking," is a rare find. Don't ever forget, the most important information technology core competency is strategic excellence. The word of primary importance in the often-repeated phrase *information technology strategy* is *strategy*, and that is what you will find in this book.

William J. Gilbert

Professional Services
Enterprise Computing Division
NCR

Preface

John McGraw managed the NY Giants baseball team from 1901 to 1932. During his illustrious career, he managed 4,769 games and won 2,763 of them. Only the equally legendary Connie Mack has ever managed and won more baseball games.

At the end of his career, a young reporter asked Mr. McGraw if, having managed 4,768 games, he now finally knew and understood *the idea of the game*. The reporter had come to the great man in search of a profound insight. Mr. McGraw looked thoughtfully at the inexperienced reporter and promptly answered "*The idea of the game is to win*" and walked down the runway to manage his last game.

Mr. McGraw's answer was simple, yet profound, and when it comes to winning, business and baseball are very much alike. The idea of business, for those who are not confused, is also to win. In baseball, you win by scoring more runs; in business your win by growing market share, increasing stakeholder satisfaction, and earning profit margins. The measures of winning are certainly different but the fundamental idea of both games is the same; the idea is to win.

In business, even more so than baseball, what is particularly challenging is that while the objectives, market share, stakeholder satisfaction, profit margins, and so on remain relatively constant across time, how you accomplish those objectives changes dramatically and abruptly. Strategic actions that made you successful during one period of time will atrophy and, rather than creating advantage, will paradoxically create disadvantage during another period. In business, it is necessary to reinvent strategy to reposition yourself in harmony with swiftly changing times and circumstances. So the game of business is conducted in an environment where the metrics of success are held fairly constant but, due to the background dynamics and turbulence of the business playing field, the actions required to accomplish those objectives are subject to ceaseless revision.

The need to redefine strategy reaches its apex during a shift between economic *ages*. During different periods of time, the fundamental basis of societal wealth has varied widely. Within any age, with time and experience, the rules of the game crystallize and we have the opportunity to master the game. The periods between ages, however, are intervals of extreme strategic difficulty as we all muddle through trying to adapt and cope with novelty, upheaval, and discontinuity.

One can identify the following important historical ages:

1. *The Nomadic Age:* The basis of societal wealth was the hunting ability of the tribe. People were hunters and the hunting club (or similar crude weapon) was the icon of the age. The Nomadic Age equated winning with being a highly capable hunter.
2. *The Agrarian Age:* The basis of societal wealth was farmland. People were landowners, peasants, or farmers, and the plow was the icon of the age. The Agrarian Age equated winning with owning land and cultivating the soil for food.
3. *The Mercantile Age:* The basis of societal wealth was trade conducted by sailing-based trading companies. People were sailors and the great sailing merchant ship was the icon of the age. The Mercantile Age equated winning with being a successful shipping merchant.
4. *The Industrial Age:* The basis of societal wealth was land, labor, and capital. People were laborers and the defining icon was the gasoline engine. Winning equated to being a capitalist who could mass produce material products through the use of natural resources and factories. Most of us were born during this age and have taken it for granted.

In each age, fundamentally different strategies were required to prosper and the winners and losers changed radically. We have now entered another age, *The Information Age*. In this epoch, the basis of societal wealth is knowledge. People are knowledge workers and the defining icon is the microprocessor. Wealth and power are generated though the exercise of knowledge. Even those businesses that produce primarily physical goods find themselves ever more dependent on information.

The information age requires an information age strategy. For the first time in history, businesses will engage in *IT fighting*. The strategic and tactical conduct of business will primarily be dependent on exploiting information, thus elevating information technology to an authentic strategic asset. The weaponry of the information age will be information technology assets; not the land, labor, or capital that dominated our birth era. The battles will take place in the virtual world of bits, not the physical world of atoms. Those who harness information technology to build new advantages will win and those who do not will lose. More and more, strategy will focus on how to engage in IT fighting to win customers, grow markets, and create profits.

The purpose of this book is to synthesize the subjects of the information age, strategy, strategic thinking, and information technology so that companies can create a robust strategic response to the information age shift. The processes, competencies, technologies, and so on that enabled you to prosper in the industrial age will probably not be sufficient to succeed in this new epoch. Rather, you will need to understand what the information age really means, how to think strategically and, finally, how to deploy IT to engage in profitable IT fighting.

The following subjects will be covered:

- *Chapter 1: The Information Age*
  This chapter will provide a deep and far-reaching analysis of what the information age will mean to business. The synthesis will focus on the convergence of information forms (text, graphics, sound, image) and how this will change the nature of competition. Of primary importance will be the replacement of the marketplace by the marketspace. IT will ascend to a key strategic asset as it becomes the primary way to create products and services, add value to existing products and services, or engage in transactions and collaborations with suppliers and customers. The essence of the information age can be conveyed in the idea that in all other ages, business consisted of moving physical things, or atoms, while in the information age, business will focus on moving virtual things, or bits.

- *Chapter 2: Strategy*
  This chapter will explain what is meant by strategy. Topics covered will include strategy definition, sustainable competitive advantage, the dimensions of advantage, temporary competitive advantage, strategic frameworks, strategic thinking,

and the relationship of strategic ideas to strategic thinking. A shared appreciation of exactly what strategy means is a compulsory prerequisite to developing a collective response to the information age. All these ideas will be directly related to the information age.

- *Chapter 3: Strategic Ideas*
  This chapter will focus on the subject of how strategists think. It will be suggested that strategists think about pressing issues in terms of key strategic ideas across the strategic dimensions of time (past, present, and future), substance (the abstract to the solid), logic (linear and paradoxical), and cardinality (number of issues and ideas that can be concurrently synthesized). An analysis will be made of the most important strategic ideas that will be related to both the information age and information technology fighting. Having developed the means of strategic thought, we will be in a position to build a strategic IT response to the information age.

- *Chapter 4: Strategic Configurations of Power*
  This chapter will propose four actions that the IT organization must take to enable the business to succeed in the information age. These actions, which will enable the business to maneuver, are:
  - *IT Governance:* The definition of the roles and responsibilities of the IT function and the associated decision-making processes. Governance is a strategy to reduce friction.
  - *IT Architecture:* The definition of an enterprise architecture that will permit information, regardless of form, to move both within the company and between the company and its trading partners. Architecture is a strategy of leverage and maneuverability.
  - *IT Economy:* The definition of how goods and services are bought and sold both between the IT organization and its customers and within the IT organization. The internal economy is a strategy of alignment.
  - *Human Resource Architecture:* The definition of a set of human resource policies that will create an adaptive organization.
  These actions are implemented as strategic configurations of power. This places you in a state of potentiality to cope with the uncertainties of our era.

- *Chapter 5: Breeder Strategy*
  This chapter will address the perennial problem of what actions should be taken so that an organization will continuously *breed* new and successful strategic actions. A great deal of management attention is being devoted to the ideas of empowerment, participation, workplace democratization, power sharing, and the dispersion of strategic responsibility across the organization. The problem becomes, if everybody is responsible for strategy, how do we prepare them so that they are competent to develop innovative, prescient, and insightful actions?

- *Chapter 6: IT Organization Structure for the Information Age*
  The purpose of this chapter is to develop a methodology by which a information age organizational structure can be designed for the IT organization. Most people equate strategy to organizational structure; all they see or understand are the endless reorganizations. While in good strategic practice, structure follows strategy and should be one of the last strategic items addressed in the strategic plan development, everyone wants to know first, *How should we (re)organize?* Properly crafted, organization structure becomes a strategic configuration of power.

- *Chapter 7: The Anatomy of an IT Guru*
  The purpose of this chapter is to provide an analysis of the advice industry. The information age could almost just as well be called the advice age. Pundits, gurus, market researchers, consultants, academics, authors, and so on clamber for your attention and provide seemingly endless, and often contradictory, advice on what the besieged executive should or should not do. The advice industry may encounter a crisis at the turn of the century when the number of gurus exceeds the number of people requiring sage advice. This chapter will take a light look at the advice industry and analyze thought leaders from the perspectives of *The Thought Leader, The Ideas,* and *The Packaging of the Ideas.*

- *Chapter 8: Epilogue: The Way of the IT Warrior*
  This chapter will provide some final thoughts on the application of strategic thinking to the information age.

It is our proposition that success in the information age requires three things:

1. *Assessment:* A deep and far-reaching understanding of the information age so that you may fully comprehend the challenges being presented to you.
2. *Strategy:* Excellence in strategic thinking so that you may develop a set of winning strategic actions that position you for winning over your competitors who have already lost.
3. *Execution:* Commitment, will, and fortitude in execution so that you may overcome the barriers and obstacles to translating your strategic thinking into reality.

The idea that you must keep in mind is that you will be no longer be engaged in industrial age economies of scale fighting; you will be engaged in information age IT fighting. Success will go to those who master the collection, presentation, movement, storage, manipulation, and analysis of information in all its forms. Success will go to those make the great transition to conducting business in the marketspace rather than the marketplace.

This book will be of interest to middle and senior management both inside of and outside of the IT organization. It presents IT from a business perspective as opposed to a technological perspective, so it will be thoroughly readable even by those who are not members of the technology community. It is our view that in the information age, IT yields its maximum strategic value when analyzed as a business issue rather than a technical issue. The book will not be of interest to hands-on technical people who are engrossed in the bits, bytes, pixels, applets, widgets, and packets unless they are interested in understanding the greater strategic context of their work.

In the greatest book ever written on strategy, *The Art of War*,[1] Sun Tzu said:

> What everyone knows is what has already happened. What everyone knows is not called wisdom. What the aware individual knows is what has not yet taken shape; what has not yet occurred. The multitudes know when you win but they do not know the basis. Everyone knows the form by which I am victorious, but no one knows the form by which I ensure victory. The science of

[1]*The Art of War*, Sun Tzu, translated by Thomas Cleary, Shambhala Editions, Boston, MA, 1988.

ensuring victory is a mysterious secret. Victory is not repetitious but adapts its form endlessly.

The problem of being an IT strategist is like being a baseball scout. The problem is not to see the player before you but the player that will be. Everyone can judge the current abilities of the ballplayer; there is no mystery in reviewing the black and white statistics. The scout has a much more difficult task than knowing what everyone else knows; the scout has to foresee the player who has not yet taken shape and imagine the player's future performance. A scout has to be an aware individual.

We who are responsible for managing IT would do well to model ourselves more on baseball scouts than accountants. We must rise above the multitudes and create a form through which we will be triumphant in the information age. We must become aware individuals who fathom the science of ensuring victory.

Bernard H. Boar
East Brunswick, New Jersey
July 1996

Acknowledgments

I would like to recognize the support of the management team at NCR who provide an environment conducive to both serving the customer and personal growth. I would like to thank the numerous customers worldwide who provide the working laboratory for my research. Lastly, as is my custom, I would like to acknowledge the profound influence of the classic works of strategy on my views of how to formulate and execute contemporary IT strategy. There is steadfast strategic wisdom in the classical strategy works of Sun Tzu (*The Art of War*), Miyamoto Musashi (*The Five Rings*), Machiavelli (*The Prince*), and B. H. Liddell-Hart (*Strategy*).[1] I cannot too strongly emphasize that to be the best IT strategist possible, you must first be the best strategist possible. Studying these works will vastly magnify your ability to think and act with strategic astuteness. Then, like the great strategist of ancient times, *you will not wander when you move.*

---

[1]Appendix B and Appendix C provide a bibliography of these and other books on strategy. The quotations in this book from these four authors come from the listed references in the appendices and will not be individually cited.

1

The Information Age

WHAT'S HAPPENING?

A friend of mine, in a moment of unintended profundity, once said that there are two questions and only two questions that really matter:

1. Who turned on the lights?
2. What's happening?

The first question is a puzzle that has perplexed humanity since the dawn of civilization and the answer is best left to the efforts of gifted scientists, theologians, philosophers, cosmologists, astronomers, and each person's private beliefs. It certainly is not an inquiry that I am qualified to publicly answer.

The second question is addressable by me and is extremely important to those of us who are involved with information technology. What is happening, as illustrated in Figure 1.1, is that we are living through a time of extraordinary turbulence and transition. We are experiencing what has been referred to as destructive creation. What had been value creating for extended periods of time suddenly becomes obsolete and superior and novel replacements spurt forth. Change is occurring at an ever-accelerating pace and at the center of that change is information technology (IT).

An instructive example of the turbulence that brands our times is illustrated in the European telecommunications market. As illustrated in Figure 1.2, the European telecommunication companies, which had historically been stable and sedate state-run monopolies, are now in a state of uproar as change is being imposed on

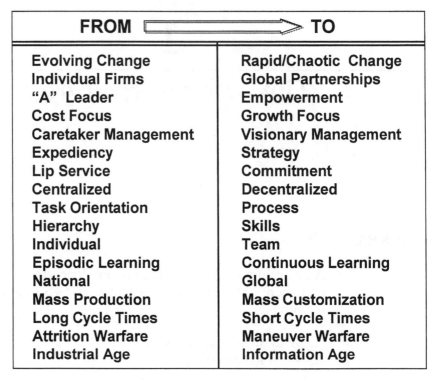

FROM	⟹	TO
Evolving Change		Rapid/Chaotic Change
Individual Firms		Global Partnerships
"A" Leader		Empowerment
Cost Focus		Growth Focus
Caretaker Management		Visionary Management
Expediency		Strategy
Lip Service		Commitment
Centralized		Decentralized
Task Orientation		Process
Hierarchy		Skills
Individual		Team
Episodic Learning		Continuous Learning
National		Global
Mass Production		Mass Customization
Long Cycle Times		Short Cycle Times
Attrition Warfare		Maneuver Warfare
Industrial Age		Information Age

Figure 1.1   Transition and turbulence. We live in a time of discontinuous and radical change.

them by suppliers, competitors, customers, and regulators. Specifically, the following factors are rapidly conspiring to alter anything and everything about their businesses:

- Globalization: Service requirements are shifting from national to global markets.
- National deregulation: The telecommunication companies are losing their state monopoly and ownership status.
- European regulation: New pan-European rules of business conduct are being defined by the European Union.
- Hyper-competition: Once protected markets are being entered by nimble European, global, and local competitors.
- Solutions: Customers are insisting on complete end-to-end services solutions.

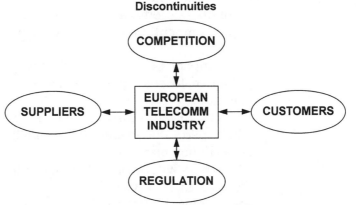

European Telecommunications Industry

- Globalization
- National Deregulation
- European Regulation

- Hyper-Competition
- Solutions
- Convergence
- Technological Discontinuities

- Powerful User Groups
- European Union
- Alliances

Figure 1.2   European telecommunications industry. The once tranquil European telecommunications industry is being buffeted by change initiated by customers, suppliers, competition, and regulators.

- Convergence: Customers are demanding new services that permit them to move and manage information regardless of form in an integrated manner.
- Technological discontinuities: Existing investments are becoming rapidly dated as customers require broadband communications.
- Powerful user groups: Customers are joining together into user groups to insist on new services and associated terms and conditions.
- European Union: A new political body governs political decisions and replaces the previous domestic regulation.
- Alliances: European telecommunication companies find it necessary to participate in new global alliances such as World Partners to offer global service to global clients. European telecommunication companies are dividing into competing camps.

European telecommunication companies find themselves in the challenging, perplexing, and demanding position of being both a supplier and internal user of telecommunication services during a period of unprecedented industry instability and transformation.

The situation is no less agitated in the United States. With the passage of the Telecommunications Act of 1996 in February, the following pro-competition provisions were put into law:

- The regional Bell Operating Companies and others will be permitted to enter the long distance business (a $70 billion market).
- The long distance carriers—AT&T, Sprint, MCI, and others— will be permitted to enter the local telephone service business (a $90 billion market).
- All carriers will be permitted to sell bundled services of long distance, local service, wireless service, internet service, and entertainment services (interactive TV, video on-demand, home shopping, etc.).
- Cable companies will be permitted to offer phone service.

With the growing sophistication of the Internet to also provide cheap phone service, the domestic telecommunications industry is best described as in a state of frenzied mutation.

What is behind much of the change, stress, and instability that we are all witnessing is the societal shift to the *information age* from the industrial age. As illustrated in Figure 1.3, there have been many different defining epochs for civilization. While forward movement within an epoch can be quite challenging, movement across epochs is always disruptive, demanding, unpredictable, and destabilizing because entrenched ways of conducting business and living are overthrown and new ways have to be discovered, refined, and institutionalized.

There are many synonyms for the popular designation *information age*. Table 1.1 itemizes what I believe to be the most commonly used 54 synonyms. These synonyms are derived by multiplying the nine richly descriptive adjectives (cyber, digital, infomedia, knowledge, virtual, networked, post-capitalist, post-industrial, and information) with the six subjects (age, corporation, economy, enterprise, era, and society). They all refer to the same phenomena, the shift to knowledge or information as the basis of society wealth

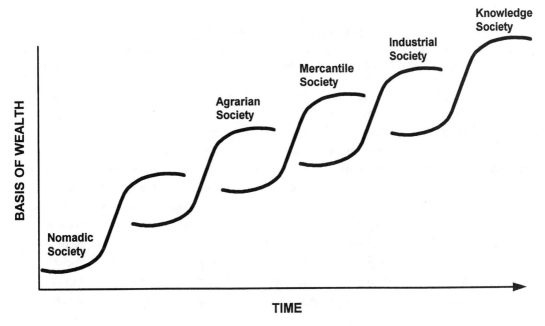

Figure 1.3   **The information age. Civilization evolves through well defined periods and we have now entered the information age.**

from land, labor, and capital but each places a different emphasize on what represents the essence of the shift. I use them interchangeably and will do so throughout this book. My choice of label is a function of the context and what I wish to highlight at the moment. For reasons that will become obvious later, I believe that the synonyms *virtual economy* and *digital economy* are the most meaningful descriptors for the age.

Of these 54 equivalent terms, a few appear more often than others and deserve some special stress because of the representative and potent ideas that they communicate:

- The Information Age: This is by far the most common designation, and implies the foundation notion that we are in a period of time where the utilization and exploitation of information in all its forms will be the basis for wealth generation. Networked, interactive, and interoperable multimedia (text, graphics, image, video, and sound) will dominate our business and personal lives.

Table 1.1
Information Age Synonyms

	Age	Corporation	Economy	Enterprise	Era	Society
Cyber	Cyber Age	Cyber Corporation	Cyber Economy	Cyber Enterprise	Cyber Era	Cyber Society
Digital	Digital Age	Digital Corporation	Digital Economy	Digital Enterprise	Digital Era	Digital Society
Infomedia	Infomedia Age	Infomedia Corporation	Infomedia Economy	Infomedia Enterprise	Infomedia Era	Infomedia Society
Knowledge	Knowledge Age	Knowledge Corporation	Knowledge Economy	Knowledge Enterprise	Knowledge Era	Knowledge Society
Networked	Networked Age	Networked Corporation	Networked Economy	Networked Enterprise	Networked Era	Networked Society
Virtual	Virtual Age	Virtual Corporation	Virtual Economy	Virtual Enterprise	Virtual Era	Virtual Society
Post-Capitalist	Post-Capitalist Age	Post-Capitalist Corporation	Post-Capitalist Economy	Post-Capitalist Enterprise	Post-Capitalist Era	Post-Capitalist Society
Post-Industrial	Post-Industrial Age	Post-Industrial Corporation	Post-Industrial Economy	Post-Industrial Enterprise	Post-Industrial Era	Post-Industrial Society
Information	Information Age	Information Corporation	Information Economy	Information Enterprise	Information Era	Information Society

- The Cyber Corporation: Corporations will be characterized by ubiquitous computing. Information will be collected, transported, stored, and processed throughout the corporation at the most opportune points. The business will become *informated.*
- The Digital Economy: The economy will be built on a foundation of electronic commerce. The marketplace will make a dramatic shift to the marketspace, products and services will be information-intensive, and the value chain for goods and services will be replaced by the information chain for goods and services.

- The Virtual Enterprise: Business will be conducted in cyberspace. Employees will work where and when it is convenient and be linked to each other through electronic means. The enterprise will become boundaryless as business partners electronically join the business as project-specific partners or as part of an extended alliance.
- The Networked Era: Business will shift from being hierarchical to being horizontal. Work will get done by electronically networked teams that focus on process as opposed to hierarchical bureaucracies that focused on tasks.
- The Knowledge Society: Wealth creation will be a function of the application of knowledge as opposed to the use of land, labor, and capital. The creation, processing, and dissemination of information will be the defining work of the majority of people.

Two of the synonym adjectives, post-industrial and post-capitalist, are of minimum utility in describing the information age. They tell us what it is not but they do not tell us anything about what it is. I rarely, if ever, use them as descriptive terms. Regardless of which term is used, when you hear or read any of them, it is best to think of all of them so that you get the richest impression of what is being communicated.

Figure 1.4 identifies some of the key distinctions between the ages illustrated in Figure 1.3. There are clear contrasts between each epoch in how society lived, worked, and created wealth. Each period could be characterized as follows:

- The Nomadic Society: Society was organized into tribes. The defining work was being a hunter, the dominant technology was crude hunting tools, and the icon of the era was the hunting club. The basis of wealth was a function of courage and the hunting ability of the tribe. Science did not exist and people were extremely superstitious.
- The Agrarian Society: Society was feudalistic. The defining work was being a farmer (land-based peasant), the dominant technology was manual farm equipment, and the icon of the age was the plow. The basis of wealth was farmland. Trade occurred in the village square.
- The Mercantile Society: The trading house was the form of business organization. The defining work was being a sailor,

Age Attribute	Nomadic Society	Agrarian Society	Mercantile Society	Industrial Society	Knowledge Society
Dominant Technology	Crude Hunting Tools	Manual Farm Equipment	Sailing Ships	Machines	The Computer
Icon	The Hunting Club	The Plow	The Great Sailing Ships	The Gasoline Engine	The Microprocessor
Science	Superstition	Civil Engineering	Marine Engineering	Mechanical Engineering	Computer Science
Output	Slaughtered Animals	Farm Food	Trade	Mass Consumer Goods	Knowledge
Energy Source	Fire	Animals	Wind	Fossil Fuels	The Mind
Basis of Wealth	Hunting Ability of Tribe	Farm Land	Sailing Ships	Land, Labor, and Capital	Information
What Makes the Difference	Courage	Muscle	Fleets	Economies of Scale	Intelligence
Defining Work	Hunter	Farmer	Merchant	Laborer	Knowledge Worker
What Are You Doing	Surviving	Eating	Trading	Automating	Informing
Organizational Form	Tribe	Feudalism	Trading House	Hierarchical Corporation	Networks
Means of Logistics	People	Animals	Ships	Airlines, Trains, Ships & Trucks	Network
Where is the Marketplace	Person-to-Person	Village Square	Town Stores	Shopping Malls	Cyperspace — The Marketspace

Figure 1.4   Comparative ages. The ways that people live, work, and create wealth is dramatically different in each age.

8

the dominant technology was the great sailing ship, and the icon of the age was the sailing ship. What made the difference in wealth creation was ownership or access to large fleets of merchant sailboats.

- The Industrial Society: The organizational form was the bureaucratic corporation. The defining work was a laborer, the dominant technology was machines, and the icon of the age was the gasoline engine. Wealth creation was a function of land, labor, and capital. What made the difference was economies of scale, and the output of this society was mass-produced consumer goods targeted for a statistical customer.

We have now entered the Information Society (or any of the other preferred 53 synonyms per Table 1.1). It has the following distinguishing characteristics:

- The dominant technology of the era is the computer. Computing intelligence is dispersed into anything and everything that can be improved by being smart.
- The icon of the era is the microprocessor. Inexpensive and programmable chips permit products to be customized and made dynamically and personally responsive to each user.
- The science of the era is computer science. No other technology has ever matched price/performance improvements for an equally extended time period.
- The output of the era is knowledge. Products and services are made attractive to consumers by making them information-rich.
- The basis of wealth is information. Information drives the creation of knowledge, which drives agile strategic actions that create both sustainable and temporary competitive advantage for the business.
- What makes the difference is intelligence, or the ability to apply information to create new information-intensive products and services.
- The defining work is the knowledge worker. Over half the work force is involved with collecting, processing, and communicating information.
- What you are doing is *informating* your business and personal life. Rather than automating labor, which was the focus of the industrial era, in the information age, the brain is being enhanced by providing information.

- Organizational structure is based on horizontal and flat networks. Information flows based on need to know, not bureaucratic and hierarchical order.
- The means of moving things is communications networks. Logistics is concerned with moving bits (electronic products) rather than atoms (physical products).
- The marketplace, where people gather to buy and sell products and services shifts from the physical marketplace (a mall or shopping center) to the marketspace (an electronic marketplace in cyperspace).

In maximizing your value in interpreting Figure 1.4 as a description of Figure 1.3, it should be kept in mind that the characteristics of prior ages do not necessarily ever disappear or suddenly vanish with the emergence of a new era. What happens is they gradually become obsolete or diminish in relative importance. For an extended period of time into the industrial age, wind and sail remained as critical as a means of logistics as did steam or combustion engine driven boats. Many of the characteristics of the industrial society will remain relevant in the information age; they will, however, take a secondary place as the information age attributes guide our way of living.

The information age marks a clear and decisive break from the preceding industrial society. It is a decisive break because the dominant logic of how you create wealth is irrevocably changed. This demarcation forces us to ask the complementary questions: How should business fully comprehend the information age and creatively respond to it, and what is the strategic role of information technology to successfully compete in the information age?

THE INFORMATION AGE

The label information age (together with all of its Table 1.1 synonyms) is used generously by all but ambiguously by many. It is normally far from clear exactly what the speaker or writer has in mind and the audience must make multiple private interpretive assumptions. This, of course, results in everybody nodding their heads in vigorous agreement while, in truth, everybody has given the phrase their own private spin and there is no substantive agreement whatsoever.

I believe that a robust interpretation of the phrase information age must include, at least, the aggregate of the following ideas:

- Information-based enhancements become the primary way to create new products and services and to embellish the value of existing products and services.
- People buy dynamic and variable nondiscrete combinations of information-based products. Value is created at the time of purchase through digitized customization.
- Customers are treated (marketed to, sold to, and serviced) as individuals, not as statistical averages.
- The marketplace become hyper-competitive. Consumers have almost complete access to product information, which creates, for the first time, a perfectly competitive market for goods and services.
- The hyper-competitive nature of the marketplace forces employees to engage in continuous lifetime learning.
- The majority of workers become information-centric knowledge workers. Information, as the focal point of life, permeates all aspects of our culture and way of living. Programmable multimedia makes the virtual marketplace interactive and entertaining.
- Knowledge about a product is often as, if not more, valuable than the product itself. The yellow pages become more profitable than some phone services, TV Guide becomes more profitable than some TV networks, and airline reservation systems become more profitable than the subject airlines. Three Internet search engines, Yahoo, Excite, and Lycos that provide assistance in finding information on the Internet, all had initial public offerings (IPO) in April 1996. Yahoo, which has yet to turn a profit, completed its first day of training at a valuation of one third that of Silicon Graphics Inc. As of May 13, 1996, all three had market prices above their IPO prices as follows:
  - Yahoo: IPO price of $13 and May 13 price of $30.25.
  - Excite: IPO price of $17 and May 13 price of $17.75.
  - Lycos: IPO price of $16 and May 14 price of $18.00.

  These companies are of value because they provide the customer with knowledge about the WEB.
- A broadly accessible information highway (currently personified as the Internet) permits global and interactive access to multimedia information.

- The convergence of information forms yields entirely new ways of working and living. Time and space constraints on markets collapse permitting people to live where they please, work with remote employers, and purchase products from local or distant providers as situationally desired.

The information age means, more than anything else, a radical shift in the basis of wealth. In the industrial age, products were physical; in the information age, products become virtual. In the industrial age, the focus of effort was the automation of labor; in the information age, the focus of effort is the creation and exploitation of knowledge. In the industrial age, information flow is physical and paper-based; in the information age, information flow is virtual and digitized. This results in the movement from manufacturing as the basis of societal wealth to knowledge as the linchpin of wealth. It results in the entire global economy becoming merged and information centric.

How might life be different as the information age takes full bloom? Consider the following possibilities:

- Upon waking up in the morning you log onto the Internet (or Commerce-net or Retail-net or Commercial-net) on your television (or is it a PC?). You are greeted by your avatar, which is a graphical image of your favorite singer. Your avatar informs you that all the appliances, security systems, and utility management systems on your home-net report that all is normal. Your software traffic agent automatically downloads to you videos of the major intersections that you cross on your way to work as well as traffic reports. It also informs you that it has put your electrical usage and communications services (phone, WEB, data) out for bid by competing service providers based on your seasonally adjusted usage patterns.
- On the way to the shower, you switch the net to your favorite radio station in Australia. Tonight, you have made plans to watch the rugby game from New Zealand after playing in an international interactive 3-D game tournament with your son.
- Before leaving for work, you update your food shopping agent. The agent notifies you of all sales, electronic coupons, and promotions consistent with your historical seasonal buying habits. The agent automatically shops all the local supermarkets within delivery distance and makes the appropriate

orders based on price, quality, sales, frequent purchaser discounts, and quantity. The charges are automatically debited to your charge account and your personal inventory of items bought year-to-date is updated. Your groceries are scheduled to be delivered to your house at your chosen time. Replenishment of standard purchases is simplified because your shopping agent knows exactly what you have used up by accessing your home food database. The home food database is updated by you by your wireless bar code scanning of food items as you finish using them. The notion of point of sale scanning has migrated to the home providing improved accuracy and convenience of reordering.

- Your lawn management subsystem notifies you on your home-net that the sensor readings from two sectors of your lawn indicate watering is necessary. With your approval, the system automatically schedules the sprinkler system for the amount of time needed and at a time consistent with local watering restrictions.

- You stop at the gas station and pay with your digital cash card. Besides debiting your card, the gasoline payments system automatically updates the gasoline inventory system and schedules the next replenishment based on dynamic usage. The same thing will happen on your way home when you stop at the mini-mart to pickup some odds and ends.

- While driving to work, you call your office, hands free, with your voice activated cellular phone. Your electronic secretary greets you. After appropriate security checks, and with your direction, it reads to you your e-mail, faxes, voice mail, and daily calendar. Based on your voice commands, your electronic secretary responds to each message in the manner you prescribe.

- The drive to work has become much more interesting since static and dull paper roadside billboards have become WEB driven electronic billboards. Advertising is sold in units of 30 seconds by day of year and time of day. Billboard mounted motion detection and identification cameras permits the billboard vendor to provide traffic demographics to advertisers that identify precise traffic volumes, types of cars, and number of drives.

- Driving is also much safer now that accidents have been informated. In the event of an accident sufficient to inflate the airbags, the car automatically makes a wireless 911 mayday call for assistance. A global positioning satellite system (GPS) identifies the exact location of the accident and provides coordinates to an imaging satellite to photograph the accident. The accident picture is sent to the emergency response units and ambulances to help them assess the magnitude of the accident and the amount of aid required. Traffic management systems are also notified which permits motorists to be informed in their vehicle navigation systems of the accident and traffic can be routed to alternate routes to reduce congestion at the accident scene. Wireless signals from emergency vehicles automatically set approaching traffic lights to red in both directions to minimize risk in crossing intersections. As patients are put on medical equipment and identified, their life sign measurements are sent to the emergency room to expedite receipt preparation and their medical histories are downloaded from the WWW to both the emergency vehicle and the emergency room.

- As you approach the garage gate of your office, your wireless ID card identifies you and the barrier gate is automatically elevated. The Corporate Locator Database is updated with your site presence, your administrative support person is notified of your arrival, and your PC is turned on and your e-mail is downloaded. Messages in foreign languages are automatically appended with a translation into your native language. Per your start-up script commands, a list of your voice mail and faxes is printed for your review when you arrive at your desk. As was the case with the garage door, the electronic building door also opens automatically in response to the wireless ID.

- Your day is full of meetings but you never leave your desk. All the meetings are done through video-conferencing and each person can see at their screen what you point to on your screen. A complete log of each meeting is kept and automatically archived. Copies of discussion materials are sent to each participant electronically at their request.

- During a break, you check in with your clothing software agent. You previously had your body laser-measured, your image digitized, and completed a questionnaire on what clothes you wanted. Your software agent also maintains an inventory of your prior purchases so that your historical preferences are retrievable. You are presented with a set of candidate business suits from clothing stores around the world. Your software agent, now a mannequin, models the clothing for you. You can alter the image to show how the clothes look from all perspectives or have your software mannequin replicate itself to show multiple views concurrently of the same or different pieces. You can change colors, cuts, and so on to meet your personal requirements before purchasing. The software mannequin also models matching shoes based on the exact digitized measurement of your feet. On request, the clothing agent will suggest and robe the software mannequin in accessories to match the base outfit. Your final specifications are passed electronically into the front of the clothing manufacturing process to prepare your customized clothing.

- Before returning to your next meeting, you log onto the decision-support network to get information on changing demographics in your markets. In response to a combination of voice and key entered commands, the desired demographics are located and graphed in a designated format to project sales. The graphics are automatically e-mailed to all participants in the next meeting.

- During lunch in the office cafeteria, you watch a video clip of the annual stockholders meeting on a large screen projection system. On the way back to your office, you pass by the wearable PC clothing fair but decide not to stop because the stuff still makes the wearer look like a Borg.

- Returning to your desk, your avatar acts as travel agent and assists you in booking your next trip. Deviations from policy are automatically noted and you digitally sign the electronic approval forms that are automatically routed for appropriate consent. All reservations and payments are managed electronically and your airline check-in, car rental, and hotel check-in will all done with your smart card.

- During a break, you call up the corporate digital library to review a new benefit announcement. The hypermedia-based announcement explains the new 401(k) option of investing your money in the Global Convergence Fund. You send some questions on a video message to the benefits administrator with a cut of the announcement attached.

- As your last acts of the day, you review logs of three meetings that occurred while you were on vacation. You send video mail to all participants with your comments. Just before logging off for the day, your journal search agent notifies you that it has found three research articles per your specification. Your cost of buying the material is reduced because you can just buy the market research segments of the complete reports that you are interested in. You tell the agent to fax the articles to you at home and copies of them to your project team by e-mail.

• On your way home, you stop at the mini-mart to pick up some odd and ends. Checkout for non bar-coded items such as fruits and vegetables is both quicker and more accurate since the point-of-sales system now includes voice recognition technology that can price such items based on their name being stated which eliminates the need to key enter the produce code. The traditional telephone has been replaced by a multi-function information appliance. You engage in a video call with your spouse and then, since the information appliance functions as a Web PC, you perform some quick e-mail that you had forgotten about. You pay with your digital cash card.

You are living and working digitally.

Table 1.2 illustrates how some professions will become information-enabled as the information age develops. Table 1.3 illustrates, conversely, that many jobs will be eliminated or reduced by the application of new information age technologies. This phenomenon is called *disintermediation*. Disintermediation means that a consumer can do a service directly for themselves through electronic channels and bypass a traditional intermediary service provider. Jobs that include words like agent, broker, or collector are in first-wave jeopardy. Figure 1.5 illustrates the growth of consumer home shopping revenue, which may be used as a surrogate measure of disintermediation. The key idea to consider in projecting the impact on jobs in the information age is to understand their informational nature and imagine how the job could be done more efficiently and effectively for the benefit of both the supplier and the consumer when information technologies such as broadband communications, wireless communications, mobile computers, advanced presentation information appliances, and interactive multimedia are used. In doing this, you must anticipate that many professions that do not superficially appear to be good candidates to be informated, are, in fact, very information-intensive. For example, as shown in Table 1.2, though certainly not an apparent or automatic first pick, farming is a very information-intensive business and will benefit substantially from information age technologies.

Table 1.2
Information Age Work

Information Age Profession	Enabling Information Technologies
Farmer	• Soil sensors will provide automatic monitoring of land. • Stock feed will automatically be customized to each animal based on reading bar-code on animal. • Weather forecasts will be collected through automated feeds from national and local university forecasting systems. • Irrigation systems will be automatically adjusted based on soil monitoring and predicted weather conditions. • Productivity of farm animals will be point-of-delivery collected and available for extensive analysis with a variety of sophisticated visualization tools. • Software agents will search electronic supplier databases to make optimum purchase decisions for farmer. • Electronic market feeds keep farmer aware of changes in commodity prices and global crop sales. • Productivity of farmland is precisely measured through the use of global positioning satellites that create digital maps of the land. The results of cultivation, fertilization, seeding, watering and harvesting are all automatically recorded against the digital farm maps. Analysis and visualization tools are used to understand and optimize farmland crop production. Imaging satellites take periodic pictures of the farmland during the growth season which permits contour maps to be automatically produced that highlight low growth sections requiring attention.
Police	• Automated database searching using key words, images, voice prints, finger prints, DNA markers, etc. • Automated traffic control systems will adjust traffic lights to maximize traffic flow, automatically recognize transgressions, and electronically issue tickets. • Officers will have wrist- or chest-mounted personal communicators. • Officer location will be traceable through global positioning systems allowing efficient dispatch. • Electronic monitoring will permit increased use of house arrest as a cost-effective and safe alternative to expensive prison incarceration.

(continued)

Table 1.2
Continued

Information Age Profession	Enabling Information Technologies
Police	• Pictures of crime scenes taken with digital cameras and dispersed electronically. • Police artists' sketches of perpetrators on pen-based tablets dispersed electronically.
Sales People	• Mobile electronic offices in their vehicles with voice-activated cellular phone, fax, notebook computer, e-mail, color printer, and videoconferencing. • Orders transmitted through wireless communication at point of sale. • Price sheets, template contracts, and new sales programs are all communicated by e-mail and wireless communication. • 3-D display software is used to provide multimedia and interactive presentations to clients. • Artificial intelligence software is used to configure solutions for customers at customer sight.
Doctors	• Expert systems will assist in the diagnosis of illness and selection of treatment regimens. • Pen-based computers will record medical notes and automatically update patient records. • Global consults will be possible as communication technologies permit x-rays, medical charts, patient histories, and other medical test results to be shared with remote colleagues. • Mobile videoconferencing technologies will permit remote physicians to participate in rounds at distant hospitals. • Communication-driven virtual reality robotics will permit a physician to perform surgery remotely. • Groupware will permit separated physicians to share the same information on their computer screens. • Patient records are stored securely on the internet permitting 24-hour global emergency access.
Insurance Claims Adjuster	• Mobile worker with voice-activated cellular phone, wireless e-mail and fax, pager, and personal computer. • Global positioning system used to locate adjuster.

**Table 1.2
Continued**

Information Age Profession	Enabling Information Technologies
Insurance Claims Adjuster	• Client records downloaded to adjuster. • Digital camera and pen tablet used to record damage and send to home office through wireless connection. • On the spot claim settlement through electronic funds transfer.
Teachers	• High-speed, interactive, and multimedia communications will permit remote students. • Artificial intelligence programs will adjust to the learning needs of each student. • Global databases will be available through interactive systems to enable student research and learning. • Learning will become a byproduct of a fun interaction or hobby of the student as the software will require the use of mathematics, English, etc. to accomplish the student's natural interest. • Students' progress will be automatically collected and monitored. Exception notifications will direct teachers to students requiring personalized help. • Artificial intelligent software will diagnose learning disorders and direct teachers and parents to the need for specialized help. • Videoconferencing and virtual reality technologies will permit students to take school trips without leaving the classroom.

**Table 1.3
Disintermediation**

Professions Subject to Disintermediation	Nature of Disintermediation
Utility Meter Readers	• A relic occupation like blacksmiths. Utility meters automatically transmit utilization data to billing collection system over home phone or cable lines. Atypical consumption of utility product is automatically sent to utility system to permit automated generation adjustment.

(continued)

Table 1.3
Continued

Professions Subject to Disintermediation	Nature of Disintermediation
Stock Brokers	• Consumer directly buys and sells stocks, bonds, and other financial instruments. • Investment portfolio and relevant market data is made available to individuals on home PC to permit them to analyze their investments. • Research literature from the brokerage firm is directly chosen by the consumer.
Travel Agent	• Consumer directly connects to reservation system of hotel, car rental, airline, and so on.
Ticket Brokers	• Consumer directly orders tickets interacting with theater or stadium database. • Consumer is able to see layout of theater and view from seats before buying. • Consumer is able to review clips of events before making purchase decision. • Ticket database tracks consumer buying habits and automatically notifies them of availability of events based on previous interests.
Retail Stores of Media Materials (books, videos, recordings)	• Consumers buy product directly from publisher or even bypass publisher and buy from author. • Product is provided to consumer in electronic form. • Consumer customizes purchase at point of sale, electronically buys mix of recordings and leaves on seller's database negating the need for local storage.
Pharmacists	• Doctor and then patient directly order prescriptions for patients from drug manufacturer.
Newspaper/Magazine Stand	• Consumer buys newspaper or magazine electronically. • Newspaper is customized to consumer's personal choice, i.e., world news from one source, national news from another, etc.

Table 1.3
Continued

Professions Subject to Disintermediation	Nature of Disintermediation
Toll Collector	• Intelligent vehicle highway system automatically identifies vehicle and electronically debits preestablished account. • Perfect knowledge of demographics of facility usage permit less intrusive scheduling of repair activities.
Retailing	• Consumers buy products electronically from electronic retailers or bypass retailers and buy directly from manufacturer. • Consumers buy retail products from global marketspace. • Destruction of brick and mortar and location barriers to entry permit anyone to become a retailer. • Consumers become participatory front step of manufacturing process, i.e., customized clothes, color selection, cuts, etc., making the distributor obsolete.
Real Estate Broker	• Consumers advertise and search for homes in electronic databases. • Software agents search for house meeting consumer needs. • Software agents select best available mortgage terms.

In the information age, the economy shifts from an industrially dominated economy to an information-centric economy. An information economy occurs when information work (the creation, analysis, synthesis, movement, processing, interpretation, and dissemination of information in all its forms) exceeds work related to the traditional economic sectors of industry, agriculture, and services. Society becomes dependent on knowledge as the critical variable in wealth creation. People are no longer hunters, farmers, sailors, or laborers; they become, first and foremost, knowledge workers. Figure 1.6 illustrates this movement to knowledge work from the traditional economic sectors of manufacturing, agriculture, and services.

In 1995, 45 percent of the US gross national product was based on information product and services. For both Europe and Japan, the 1995 gross national product that was information based was 40

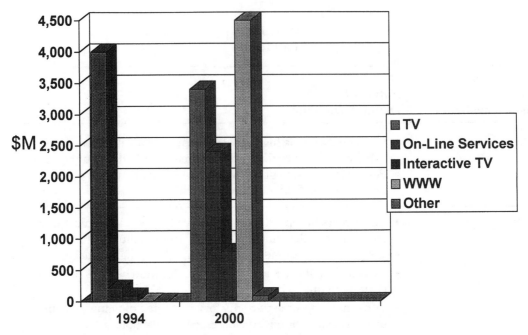

Figure 1.5   Home shopping revenue. It is anticipated that home shopping sales will increase by a factor of 2.5.

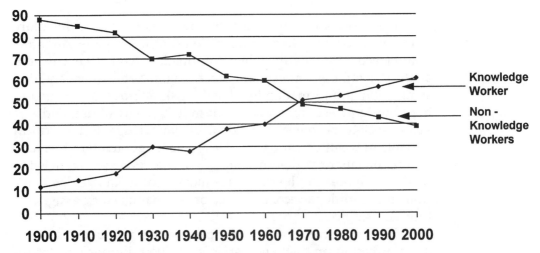

Figure 1.6   Job migration. Knowledge work has become the dominant form of employment.

percent. As illustrated in Figure 1.7, telecommunications, software, and media (all primary information age businesses) have employment that exceeds that of the auto industry. The movie industry also employs more people than the auto industry.

This shift in wealth is reflected in the comparative stock market value of different economic sectors. There are three popular Dow Jones averages: the Dow Jones Industrial Average, the Dow Jones Transportation Average, and the Dow Jones Utilities Average. They all represent industrial age companies. Figure 1.8 compares some representative companies from each of those indexes with two information age companies. Figure 1.9 illustrates the shift in industry wealth that occurred in 1995. Four of the top ten groups were information age companies with Computer Software and Services being number one. The obvious conclusion from that comparison

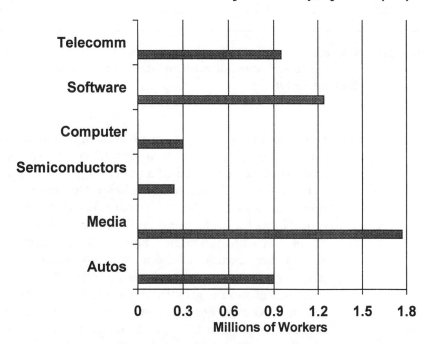

Figure 1.7   US 1996 projected employment. The information age
              industries of telecommunications, software, and media
              all have employment in excess of the auto industry, which
              is the symbol of the industrial age.

Dow Jones Industrial Average

Stock	Market Value (1/19/96)
DuPont	$39.7B
GM	$35.4B

Dow Jones Transportation Average

Stock	Market Value (1/19/96)
Delta	$3.7B
Conrail	$5.7B

Dow Jones Utilities Average

Stock	Market Value (1/19/96)
Con-Edison	$7.9B
AEP	$7.9B

Information Age Companies

Stock	Market Value (1/19/96)
Microsoft	$53.8B
Intel	$42.6B

Figure 1.8   Comparative value of economic sectors. Wealth has shifted from the industrial age sectors of manufacturing, transportation, and utilities to information age sectors.

is that wealth is migrating from cars, railroads, manufacturing, airlines and electric power to information technology. It is migrating from asset rich companies to knowledge-rich companies.

Professor Paul Romer of Berkeley University promotes an economic theory called New Growth Economics that provides a theoretical basis for understanding the primacy of knowledge and ideas as the basis of information age wealth creation. Professor Romer argues that traditional theories of economic growth missed the major factor. He argues that it is not capital, labor, or raw materials that spur economic growth; it is ideas that are the engine of wealth creation. Knowledge and new ideas is what drives economies to higher levels. So in the industrial age, the wealth of nations was a function of land, labor, and capital. Going forward, the wealth of nations will be a function of knowledge and ideas.

It is customary in business media to publish measures of leading economic activity. Consistent with an industrial age view, Table 1.4

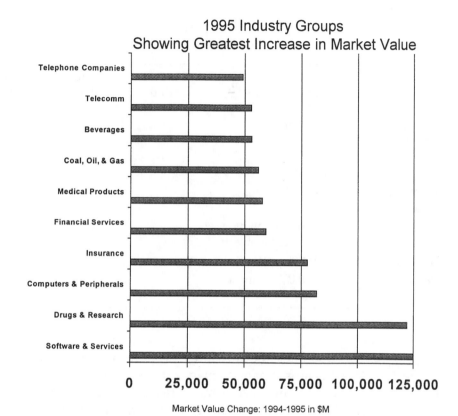

Figure 1.9   Business Week 1000. The Business Week 1000 illustrates
the shift in wealth to information age companies.

Table 1.4
Industrial Age Measures

Industrial Item	Unit of Measurement	Current Period	Prior Period	One year Ago
Steel	1,000 tons			
Autos	1,000 cars			
Coal	1,000 tons			
Lumber	1,000,000 feet			
Rail Freight	billion ton miles			
Crude Oil	1,000 barrels			

Table 1.5
Information Age Measures

Information Age Item	Unit of Measurement	Current Period	Prior Period	One year Ago
information appliances	number			
e-mail	1,000,000 messages			
microprocessor/ memory chips	1,000,000 chips			
media	1,000,000 downloaded multimedia objects			
software	10,000 applets			
internet access	1,000,000 connect hours			

illustrates the measures that one would typically find in many business/financial magazines and related media. Table 1.5 illustrates a new set of measures that will soon need to be published. While the industrial age measures will remain relevant and important, they will be surpassed by the new information age metrics of economic activity. Table 1.6 illustrates a precursor of this new type of activity measurement extracted from an IT industry magazine. It attempts to quantify the shift to on-line Internet services. It will be

Table 1.6
Internet Measurement

Internet Service	Current Quarter Hours	Percent Change From Year Prior	Prior Quarter Hours	Percent Change From Year Prior
All Internet Services				
E-mail Only				
World Wide Web Only				
All Other Services				

more important to understand the velocity of things that move bits than the velocity of things that move atoms.

In summary, the information age can be understood from five primary perspectives:

1. *Technology:* Continued innovation in information technologies results in information technology permeating all aspects of life. As the internal combustion engine permitted the automating of labor, the computer permits the informating of society.
2. *Economics:* The economy becomes information-centric. Wealth creation is closely tied to the ability to create new information-based products and amend existing products with information. Information technology permits entirely new ways of collaboration to create products and services with closer ties to all value chain participants.
3. *Employment:* The density of employment shifts to knowledge workers. Most people make their living creating, moving, analyzing, interpreting, or disseminating information.
4. *Spatial:* The networking of computers throughout the world results in a collapse of the traditional market constraints of time and space. The world becomes one global marketspace. It is as easy to engage in transactions with a business in Brazil or Hungary as it is with a store around the corner.
5. *Cultural:* Society become media-laden. Information is readily available in multimedia formats, customizable and interactive. We expect information in forms that are readily accessible and convenient to our needs. The social capabilities of computers and communications permit new social structures to emerge.

The information age will be a period of contradictions for the typical person. On one hand, as a consumer, you will have new products and services with unparalleled convenience and ease of use. On the other hand, as workers, the marketplace and marketspace will become incredibly competitive. As is to be expected during the transition between any pair of eras, change will radically alter the rules of the game and prosperity will gravitate only toward those who proactively and creatively adapt.

The skeptic, who is inundated with endless media hype and has grown suspicious of each new announcement of another monumental event, listens to these arguments cynically and asks the obvious questions: Why now? Why didn't we have an information age before? What has happened that permits this new age to spring forth and with such incredible capabilities? The answer is embodied in one word: *convergence.*

CONVERGENCE

Before one can understand convergence and its imposing implications, it is necessary to have a clear understanding of what information technology means. As was the case in the prior section when we formulated a precise definition for the phrase information age, if we don't agree on a definition for information technology, we will engage in meaningless cross talk. The definition of information technology that I volunteer is the following:

> Information technology (IT) comprises those technologies engaged in the operation, collection, transport, retrieval, storage, access presentation, and transformation of information in all its forms (voice, graphics, text, video, and image). Movement of information can take place between humans, between humans and information processing machines, or just between multiple information processing machines. Management of IT insures the proper selection, deployment, administration, operation, maintenance and evolution of the IT assets consistent with organization goals and objectives.

Figure 1.10 illustrates this definition.

There are forms of information such as smell and taste that are not included in Figure 1.10. This is because we do not as yet have a smell or taste technology. When and if such technologies come into existence, the horizontal entries of Figure 1.10 would need to be extended to include them. For now, information technology consists of performing the four primary functions of preparation, processing, storage, and transmission (we collectively refer to these functions as a function chain) against information in the forms of data, graphics, image, video, and sound. When such information forms are combined, the resulting information form is called multimedia. When the multimedia can be dynamically manipulated in real time by the user, it is called interactive multimedia. Multimedia may be static, such as text, data, and graphics, or it may be highly time-sensitive and active, such as audio, video, animation, and virtual reality. When goggles, gloves, sensors or other touch

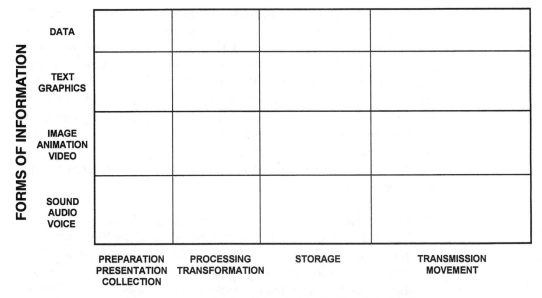

Figure 1.10 Form versus function. Information technology can be understood as the application of function on form. (Source: *The Art of Strategic Planning for Information Technology*, Bernard H. Boar, John Wiley & Sons, 1994.)

devices are used to engage the tactile sense, it is said that the multi-media has been extended to include kinesthetic feedback technology. Multimedia is also sometimes referred to as infomedia.

Two terms related to multimedia are hypertext and hypermedia. Hypertext refers to static media that has embedded links that, when selected, will move the user to another static page of text and graphics. Hypermedia is the same idea, but with all forms of media involved in the linking. Both hypertext and hypermedia used in an interactive manner provide exciting ways to communicate with customers or other value chain participants in a sensory-filled, participatory, and engaging way.

Convergence means that formerly independent industries are become one mega-industry (converging) because of three simultaneous events:

1. The digitalization of information regardless of form.
2. The rapidly declining cost of computing.
3. The availability of broadband communications.

Table 1.7 categories the formerly independent industries into the three broad classifications of communications, computers, and information content groups. Figure 1.11 illustrates the consequences of convergence. All these formerly related but independent industries become highly intertwined. Figures 1.12 and 1.13 attempt to illustrate the unified size of these industries. As you would anticipate, the chaos of this type of massive restructuring not only causes an earthquake within these industries but shakes the foundations of supplier and customer industries as well.

We will now analyze the three collaborating factors that are driving convergence:

1. *The Digitalization of Information Regardless of Form*
   Figure 1.14 provides a simple way to visualize life before convergence. As illustrated in Figure 1.14, the data function chain consisted of electronic data processing (EDP) technologies and the voice function chain consisted of telephony equipment. Each form of information had a distinct set of functional technologies. Figure 1.15 even more vividly demonstrates how each form of information had its own historical and private function

Table 1.7
Convergent Industries

Representative Convergent Industries		
Communications Group	**Computer Group**	**Information Content Group**
• Communications Equipment	• Computers	• Newspapers
• Carriers	• Peripherals	• Periodicals
• Paging	• Software	• Books
• Wireless Services	• Accessories	• Advertising
• Radio Broadcast	• Services	• Commercial Art
• TV Broadcast	• Semiconductors	• Motion Pictures
• Household A/V	• Electrical Equipment	• Video Rentals
• Cable	• Search/Navigation	• Music
• On-Line Service Providers	• Consumer Electronics	• Games
	• Sensors/Signaling	• Information Services
	• Video Games	• Photography

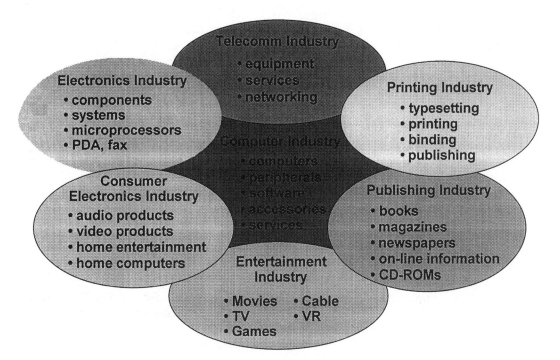

Figure 1.11   Convergence. Previously independent businesses in the communications, computer, and information content sectors become one huge overlapping industry.

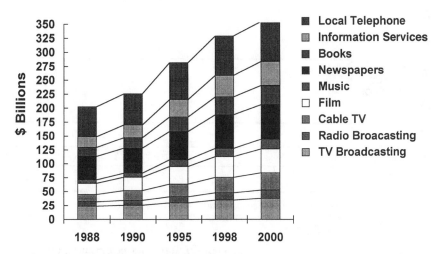

Figure 1.12   Communicating and media spending. By the year 2000, the combined revenue of these convergent industrials will be $350 billion.

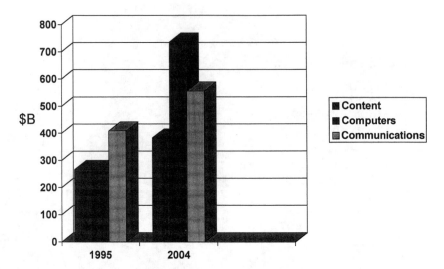

Figure 1.13   Growth of convergent industries. By the year 2000, the combined revenue of the three convergent groves will be about $1.5 trillion.

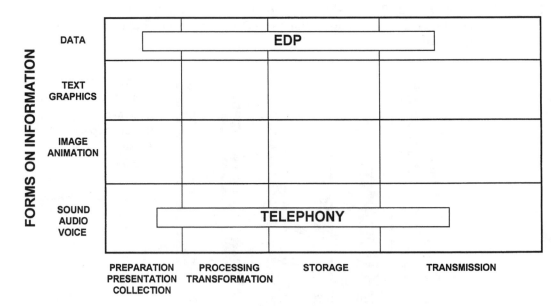

FUNCTIONS ON INFORMATION

Figure 1.14   Preconvergence. Prior to convergence, different sets of technologies managed voice and data.

	CREATION	TRANSMISSION	PROCESSING	STORAGE/ RANDOM ACCESS	DISPLAY	MANIPULATE/ ALTER
TEXT	Author	Teleprinter	Typewriter	Paper/ None	Printed Page	Unavailable
	Author with Hypertext	E-Mail/Fax	Computer	Disk	Color Monitor	Yes
GRAPHICS	Artist	Mail	Blueprint	Chart Rack	Drawings	Unavailable
	Artist with CAD	E-Mail/Fax	Computer Graphics	Disk	Color Printer/ Monitor	Yes
DATA	Researchers	Mail	Calculators	Punch Cards	Paper	Unavailable
	Researchers/Data Collection Devices	File Transfer	Computers	Mag Tape	Color Printer/ Monitor	Yes
AUDIO	Musicians	Telephone	Amplifiers	Vinyl Records	Gramophone	Unavailable
	Musicians with Synthesizers	Digital Radio	Computerized Recording Studio	CD	Digital Music System	Yes
VIDEO	Scriptwriters	TV	TV Studio	Celluloid Film	B/W TV	Unavailable
	Scriptwriters with Special Effects	Cable TV	Multimedia Studio	Disks	HDTV	Yes

Information Business:
Circa 1950

Information Business:
Circa 1996

Figure 1.15   1950 versus 1996. In 1950, each form of information had a distinct set of technologies that operated on it; by 1996, the functional information technologies had converged.

chain. It shows, as well, how those function chains have evolved
from 1950 until today.

After one reflects on the 1996 function chains (Figure 1.15)
for each individual form of information, it becomes clear that
each function chain is simply a different instance of the same
function chain. This is illustrated in Figure 1.16. Since all forms
of information now have the same DNA, a series of digitized 1s
and 0s, the function chains converge into one continuous set of
digital information processing technologies. An information
appliance simply consists of a set of viewers and players that
can present/collect information from an unlimited number of
unimedia or multimedia broadcasting channels. From a function chain perspective, there is no longer any difference
between a TV broadcast, a radio broadcast, or a video broadcast. The information function chain melds at each functional

	Input	Storage	Manipulative Alter	Transmit	Random Access	Output
Text Data Image Audio Video	Digital Information Appliances	Digital Storage	Yes, Intermix	Digital Signals— Wired and Wireless	Yes	Digital Information Appliances

Figure 1.16   **The same DNA. Since all information regardless of form is digitized, it can be managed using the same technology function.**

level. Now all forms of information can not only be intermixed, but they can also be randomly accessed and dynamically manipulated. Figure 1.16 should be thought of as a common schema for the 1996 view in Figure 1.15.

An interesting and instructive example of all information having the same DNA and being able to share the same function chain is richly illustrated by digital video disk (DVD) technology. DVD is a digital storage medium that can store from 4.7 to 17 gigabits (GB) of information. It is expected that it will replace CDs, videotape, and audiotape. It is appropriate for applications that are storage-intensive, such as multimedia. DVD technology is being previewed, discussed, and analyzed concurrently in consumer electronics, computer, video, audio, games, and entertainment magazines. All these formerly independent industries are interested in understanding how the exact same storage medium will impact their business.

This is the devilish joke that explains a great part of the industry disruption that we are witnessing. Competition and value creation, prior to convergence, was horizontal as illustrated in Figure 1.15 (1950—horizontal rows). With convergence, (1996—

vertical columns), competition and value creation become vertical, taking a 90-degree shift. What could be more unsettling?

To summarize, with the digitalization of all forms of information, the function chains converge and all information becomes interoperable, transportable, and subject to interactive manipulation by the consumer. This has the net effect of radically changing business value chains, dramatically altering products and services, and completely revising consumer expectations. Everyone suddenly has to cope with and readjust to a 90-degree shift in information creation, processing, storage, and transport.

2. *The Rapidly Declining Cost of Computing*
The physics of computing has caused a dramatic decline in its price/performance for the past 30 years, and the exact same impact is anticipated for the foreseeable future. This point is broadly accepted, is nonargumentative, and requires little elaboration. Figures 1.17 through 1.19 provides different perspectives on the continued plunging price/performance of computing.

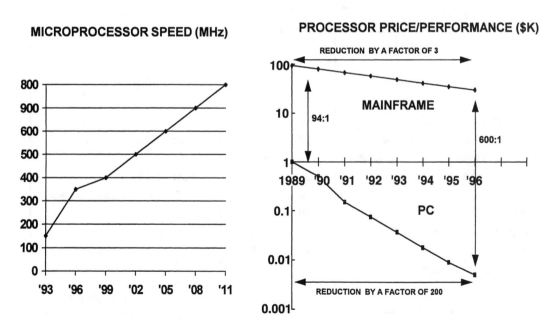

Figure 1.17 Microprocessor performance trends. Microprocessor performance trends show a continued favorable direction.

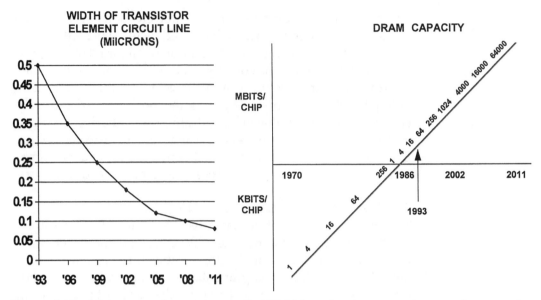

Figure 1.18   Memory performance trends. DRAM performance continues to improve by a factor of four.

TECHNOLOGY	FROM	TO	TREND
Microprocessor Transistor Density/Chip	78	96	29K to 5M
Microprocessor Transistor Density/Chip	78	2001	29K to 100M
Microprocessor MIPs	78	2001	.5 to 800 MIPS
Microprocessor Clock Speeds	78	2001	10 - 250 MHz
PC/Mainframe Price/Performance	78	2001	700:1
DAT Storage	89	2000	Factor of 12 Increase
DRAM Density	70	95	1KB/DRAM to 4096MB/DRAM
$/MB DRAM	70	2000	$500 - $5
PC Disk Form Factor	91	98	2.5" to .5"
MB/PC Disk Platter	91	95	Factor of 12 Increase
Video Compression	78	93	Bandwidth to Carry Video Conference Reduced from 6MBPS to 80KBPS

Figure 1.19   Computing performance trends. The price/performance direction of all computing technologies demonstrate a continuing favorable trend.

This cost efficiency is critical to convergence because it enables computing to become ubiquitous and available with sufficient power at an enabling and attractive price point.

3. *The Availability of Broadband Communications*
The emergence of broadband communications is critical to convergence because multimedia is both storage-intensive and time-sensitive. Figure 1.20 illustrates how the feasibility of applications is a function of both the interactive session length and session data volume. Since key to the notion of the information age is the idea that anyone anywhere can reach any information in any form, this will only be true if communications speeds in the 100s of megabit (MB)/second become available.

Multimedia is extraordinarily storage- and resource-intensive. Consider the following:

- One second of sound equates to 15 kibbit (KB) to 150 KB of digitized storage.
- Ten seconds of sound equates to approximately one MB of digitized storage.

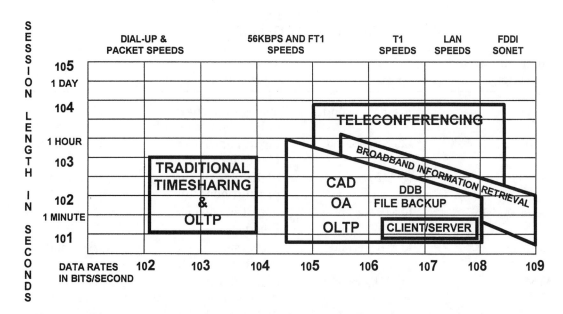

Figure 1.20   Application needs. Media-intensive applications have longer sessions and require larger volumes of information to be moved to the user.

- 75 seconds of fidelity sound equates to 600 MB of digitized storage.
- One pixel of video animation requires three bytes of storage.
- One frame of video equates to 1.5 MB of digitized storage.
- An 8" by 11" image would consume the following storage:
  - Black and white: 50 KB to 100 KB
  - 16 bit color: 200 KB to 400 KB
  - 24 bit color: 1.2 MB to 2.4 MB

This tremendous demand of interactive multimedia for resources is illustrated in Tables 1.8. through 1.10, which show respectively the time to move a one MB file at different speeds, the storage requirements of various media, and the minimum necessary bandwidths for effective communications of different media. Information age applications such as multimedia mail, interactive television, videos on demand, videoconferencing, and remote education only become practical with the wide availability of broadband communications. Laboratory demonstrations have already been made of broadband connections at 400 billion bits per second (BPS) in 1995

Table 1.8
Time to Send a One MB File

Communications Technology	Speed	Transport Mechanism	Time
Modem	28.8 KB/second	analog signal over public phone network	5.7 minutes
ISDN	128 KB/second	digital signal over phone line	62.5 seconds
T1	1.5 MB/second	digital signal over private phone line	16 seconds
Cable Modem	10 MB/second	digital signal over Ethernet	.8 seconds
T3	45 MB/second	digital signal over private phone line	.53 seconds
ATM	155 MB/second	digital signal over ATM switched network	.05 seconds
ATM	1 GB/second	digital signal over ATM switched network	.008 seconds

Table 1.9
Multimedia Storage Requirements

Multimedia	Storage Requirements (Uncompressed Storage)
500 pages of text	1 MB
5 minutes of audio	2.4 MB
1 photo	7.7 MB
1 minute of animation	600 MB
1 minute digital video	1.65 GB

and 1 trillion BPS in 1996. It is therefore not surprising, as shown in Table 1.11, that many of the most prominent IT trends of today are communications-centric.

These trends will enable information age companies to improve both the efficiency and effectiveness of work as follows:

- Individual personal productivity will be enhanced through wireless communications, fax, and personal digital assistants.
- Rather than people moving to work, work will move to people through telecommuting and videoconferencing.
- Business organization structures can become more adaptive to include virtual structures, remote employees, and part-time employees.

Table 1.10
Multimedia Bandwidths

Communications Technology	Bandwidth Speed	Suitable for Broadcasting
Modem	14.4 KB/second	AM radio sound
Modem	28.8 KB/second	FM radio mono sound, still pictures
ISDN	144 KB/second	FM radio stereo sound, begin videoconferencing
ISDN or T1	1544 KB/second	CD quality sound, acceptable quality video
ATM	622 MB/second	CD quality sound, broadcast quality video, virtual reality

Table 1.11
Communications Turbulence

Information Technology Trend	From ————> to	Is Trend Communications-Centric?
Architecture	Private Application Architectures to Global Reach, Range and Maneuverability Architecture	Yes
Broadband	Voice Speeds to GB/second speeds	Yes
Client/Server Computing	Host Centered Computing to Network Computing	Yes
Collaboration	Smoke Pipe Systems to Cross Value Chain Systems	Yes
Customization	One Size Fits All to Cut and Paste	No
Digitalization	Analog to Digital	Yes
Diminution	Mainframe to Minicomputer to PC	No
Electronic Commerce	Paper to EDI	Yes
Globalization	Local to National to Global	Yes
Instanization	Batch to Real-Time	Yes
Mobility	Fixed Place to Untethered	Yes
Multimedia	Distinct Information Function Chains to Single Information Function Chain	No
Parallelism	Sequential Processing to Massively Parallel Processors	No
Price/Performance	Expensive Unit Costs to Zero Unit Costs	No
Software Engineering	Artisan to Engineer	No
Standards	Closed to Open	Yes

- Information can be made widely available to all employees through intranets.
- Electronic commerce can be used to interoperate with all value chain partners (suppliers, distributors, customers, regulators, etc.).
- Work processes can be enabled by bringing appropriate interactive multimedia, hypertext, or hypermedia to each task. The daily generic work activities of problem solving,

decision making, creativity, process management, information exchange, relating, and influencing can all be enriched by informating them.

- Lifelong professional learning can be brought, just in time, to each employee at the point of need using multimedia educational materials. It is one thing to learn by reading a passive book with graphics. It is quite a different thing to learn by participating in hypermedia-based training that includes audio, video, animation, and interactive solicitation and feedback.

In this way, the company benefits by reducing dead time, improving the quality of work, improving customer service, enabling faster response times, and enabling massive collaboration across its value chains towards its shared set of objectives.

Figure 1.21 illustrates the evolution of Figure 1.14 and attempts to visualize the grand effect of convergence. With the unification of information function on all forms of information, ubiquitous and inexpensive computing, and widely available broadband commu-

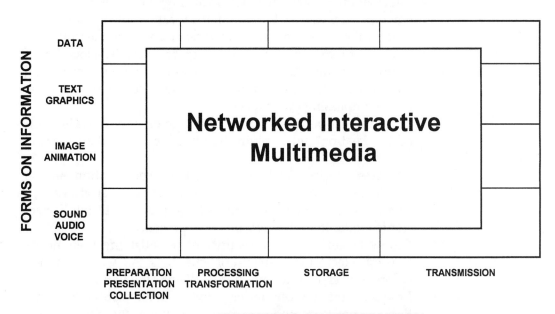

Figure 1.21 Convergence. With convergence, the same technology can operate on all forms of information, and results in networked and interactive media.

nications, an integrated world of digitized, networked, and interactive multimedia is born. It is a world with numerous implications and impact for both the business manager and the IT strategist.

IMPLICATIONS AND IMPACT

From what we have learned, it is obvious that the information age is indeed BIG change and BIG change brings implications and impacts that first need to be understood and then creatively responded to. The key implications of the information age are as follows:

- All information becomes digitized and is subject to interactive manipulation. The interface to the user becomes multimedia rich and is as much entertainment as it is instructive or transactional.
- The economy becomes digital. More and more, products and services take on electronic personas. Employment is dominated by knowledge work.
- Information becomes available to all anywhere, anytime, and in any form. It is as easy to find out the weather forecast for Tokyo as it is to find out the weather forecast for your home town.
- Information exchange occurs on a global basis. The location of information and the people with whom you interact is virtual to you and their location makes no difference. There is just one all encompassing cyperspace.
- The economy becomes very knowledge-centric. Value is created by creating and applying knowledge rather than making things.
- Business, shopping, leisure time, games, socialization, and so on all take on an electronic character. It is easier, more efficient, and convenient to conduct daily affairs through electronic media than through physical presence.
- People become more self-sufficient in satisfying their needs through electronic distribution channels. As we mentioned before, this is the phenomenon of disintermediation.
- Products and services undergo mass customization. Information age products undergo final assembly at the point of purchase in response to the exact desires of the consumer. Consider the following six examples of information-based mass customization:

1. *Music sales:* A consumer buys musical selections from an interactive multimedia database. The consumer can listen to the music and create a mix of any combinations of songs and videos as desired. The resulting product is stored in the network multimedia database and downloaded as desired. The consumer does not have to store the purchase nor is it subject to wear and tear. The provider maintains a record of all purchases and notifies consumer of special offers or new releases of interest. Billing is done electronically.

2. *Lawn care products:* The ground sensors on your home lawn management system automatically send information to the lawn care company, which customizes fertilizer, weed killer, bug killer, and so on, exactly to the current specifications of your lawn. The lawn care company electronically sends reminders to you that it is the appropriate time to perform maintenance activities on your lawn.

3. *Daily newspaper:* You view a newspaper as a collection of modular sections, such as international news, national news, local news, sports, entertainment, book reviews, and so on. You define your own newspaper by selecting sections from different news sources. Your morning paper is automatically assembled to your specification and electronically delivered to you at the time you requested. The assembly is intelligent enough to dynamically alter the assembly based on your interests. For example, at your request, sports articles on your favorite teams are included not only from your preferred hometown paper but other selected city papers when your team is on the road. An interesting example of a personalized electronic newspaper is the Wall Street Journal Interactive Edition. It provides 24 hours a day and 7 days per week continuous updated news. The reader controls a profile that identifies the news that is desired. The personalized profile also will track and value a personalized portfolio of stocks and mutual funds. The mass market paper Wall Street Journal is converted into an information age electronic and personalized Wall Street Journal.

4. *Interactive television:* Using your hand controller, you can dynamically select the camera view of the sporting event that you prefer to watch. You are able to bring up statis-

tics on teams, players, coaches, and so on. During intermission, you can select videos of highlights by team, type of play, position, or player.

5. *Electronic baseball cards:* Baseball and other collector sports cards are now full multimedia objects. Baseball cards consist of:
   - video clips of the player
   - voice interviews with the player
   - complete career offensive and defensive statistics in a user manipulative form for statistical analysis
   - hypermedia links to famous teams and events that the player participated in
   - electronic security keys to provide authenticity of ownership
   - subscriber services that can provide new articles about the player

   Cards are traded on electronic card exchanges, electronic auctions, and through electronic card flipping.

6. *Rehearsals:* The creative process of musical composition, theater rehearsals, and other practice performances and development activities for the creative arts are all electronically recorded. Fans of performers and students of the arts can observe all or part of the entire creative process.

- Computing is ubiquitous. Everything that can benefit from being made smart is made smart. Once made smart, it is necessary that it be connected to be able to relate its knowledge to others. Like the availability of electricity today, the universal presence of computers will be taken for granted.

- Information becomes democratized. The first 30-year tyranny of text data comes to an end as image, video, audio, animation, and so on are all equally accessible and, often, much more valuable.

- Speed is of the essence. A digital society is a society where things happen quickly. A business must have the ability to respond ever more quickly to rapidly changing consumer tastes. In the industrial age, the large companies ate the small companies. In the information age, the fast and agile companies eat the slow and ponderous companies.

- Human agents are replaced by software agents that search, negotiate, and buy for you. Imagine the following extreme scenario. Your software agent becomes a digital persona of yourself. As it does more and more transactions for you, it grows in its ability to represent you and matures, in essence, into a digital self; a digital reflection of you that mirrors your personality. At the same time, psychiatric software agents are developed that intermingle with consumer software agents to search for the *digitally insane.* Impossible—why not? An outer possibility but, nevertheless, a perfectly reasonable implication of information age possibilities.

- Business becomes hyper-competitive. Traditional barriers to market entry as well as historical market constraints of time and space collapse. It becomes a war of all against all as customers become free to choose from a global marketplace. Market power shifts to consumers as information access creates a perfect marketplace where consumers have unlimited ability to comparison shop.

- Commerce becomes continuous. Business is conducted around the world around the clock without respite. Neither your personal software agents nor the databases that they operate on ever need a vacation or time off.

- Pricing becomes a dynamic reverse auction for both perishable products and services. Consumers register bids for perishable products such as airline seats, hotel rooms and entertainment tickets. The supplier revises the price of the item as the time of perishability arrives and bidders are electronically notified of the acceptance of their bid. Perishable pricing permits sellers to discover the optimum balance between price and volume and permits buyers to obtain services at a *willingness to pay* price.

For most businesses, what is particularly challenging about these implications is the competitive fervor that they foreshadow. Figure 1.22 illustrates the Five Forces strategic model. Among other things, what this model teaches is the importance of barriers to entry as a means to protect one's market position. Barriers to entry are being eradicated by the information age. Consider the following two examples:

- *Newspapers/books/magazines:* The cost of printing presses and distribution systems constrained entry. With information age

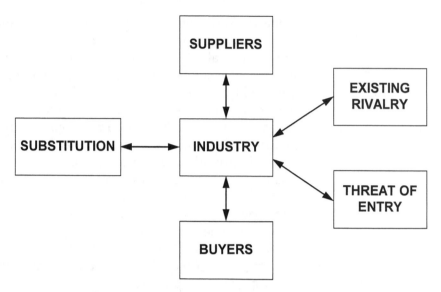

Figure 1.22   Hyper-competition. Many of the traditional Five Forces barriers to entry collapse in the information age and make competition more virulent than ever before.

electronic newspapers, magazines, and books, anyone can become a publisher. The huge costs of printing, shipping, storing, and distributing are eliminated.

- *Radio stations:* The cost of station equipment, staff, and licensing constrained entry. Net.radio is an Internet only radio station with international reach that went into business in Minneapolis for $250,000 as opposed to the $22.5 million license fee charged to the last FM station to get an FCC license in Minneapolis. Net.radio has the advantage of an international audience and a tremendous cost advantage in charging less for advertising. In the information age, anyone will be able to become a disc jockey and broadcast their choice of music over the Internet, which has unlimited channels.

The following industrial age barriers to entry are compromised by the information age:

- Economies of scale: Scale is not required to be cost competitive.
- Differentiated products: It is difficult to maintain sustainable competitive advantages.

- Capital requirements: Markets can be entered with a minimum investment.
- Switching costs: It is easy to experiment with alternative suppliers.
- Distribution channels: The primary distribution channel, the information highway, is open to all.
- Location: Everyone has the same location; everyone is everywhere in cyberspace.
- Regulation: Government regulation that restricts entry becomes obsolete (i.e., limiting the number of radio stations due to radio spectrum bandwidth).
- Specialized skills/knowledge: The Internet, recursively, provides access to needed knowledge and skills to compete on the Internet.

This collapse of barriers to entry is exaggerated by the collapse of time and space constraints on markets. The practical problems related to physical distances have historically controlled the definition of markets. As shown in Figure 1.23, the world has been shrinking for centuries but electronic markets result in the creation of one megamarket. Not only are local barriers to entry collapsing but competitors are free to electronically attack each other's markets creating a competitive bonanza for consumers. Table 1.12 shows the global alliances that have been formed in the previously discussed communication industry to cope with rampant global competition.

Information Age Impact

The impact of these implications transcends all enterprises, not just the obvious convergent industries (Table 1.7). Table 1.13 segments industries into three distinct groups as follows:

- *Convergent industries:* This group consists of the industries previously itemized in Table 1.7 whose products and services are primarily information-based and are directly impacted by information age technologies that change how they fundamentally do business.
- *Secondary industries:* This group consists of industries whose products and services can, in their entirety or to a large measure, be redefined by information age technologies. The product or service in these cases is essentially information-based.

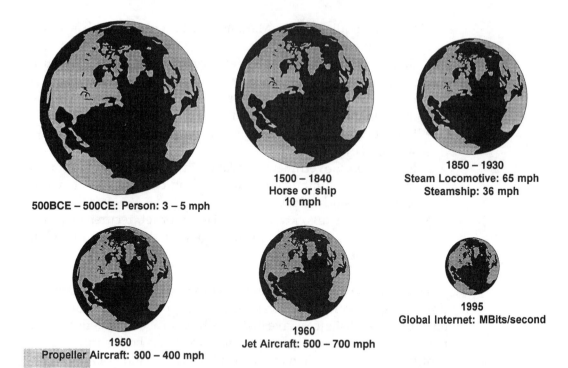

500BCE – 500CE: Person: 3 – 5 mph

1500 – 1840
Horse or ship
10 mph

1850 – 1930
Steam Locomotive: 65 mph
Steamship: 36 mph

1950
Propeller Aircraft: 300 – 400 mph

1960
Jet Aircraft: 500 – 700 mph

1995
Global Internet: MBits/second

Figure 1.23   Destruction of time and space constraints. The information age destroys
time and space constraints on markets and increases competition.

Table 1.12
Global Telecommunications Alliances

Concert Alliance	World Partners Alliance	Phoenix Alliance
British Telecomm	• AT&T	• Germany
MCI	• Sweden	• France
Norway	• Switzerland	• Sprint
Finland	• Netherlands	
Denmark	• Spain	
Japan	• Japan	
	• Australia	
	• Hong Kong	
	• New Zealand	
	• Singapore	

Table 1.13
Information Age Impact

Convergent Industries (see Table 1.7)	Secondary Industries	Other Industries
• Computer • Communications • Information Content	• Banking • Insurance • Brokerage • Government • Library/Research • Legal	• Health • Manufacturing • Travel • Shipping • Retailing • Energy

- *Other industries:* This group consists of industries whose products and services are inherently physical in nature and cannot be replaced by information age substitutes but for whom marketing, logistics, sales and internal business process can all be made more efficient and effective through exploiting information age technologies.

Some examples will facilitate illustrating the impact on secondary and other industries:

- *Airline industry:* Convergence offers new opportunities to reduce costs through electronic ticketing, self-reservations, smart cards, and electronic direct billing. Convergence also threatens airline travel due to reduced need to travel because of groupware, videoconferencing, and virtual reality meeting.
- *Financial services (banks, insurance, brokerage, mutual funds):* Most of the services that these industries provide can be done wholly electronically. This is because they are paper-based and manage the movement of money, both of which can be substituted for electronically. Insurance polices can be offered, processed, authorized, issued, and vaulted electronically. There already exist virtual banks such as the First Direct Bank of Leeds, England, that has no branches and does all its transactions electronically or by phone. Physical money is dispensed through ATMs. Banks in the US are offering certificates of deposit and other bank products such as deferred annuities in Internet/Web-only versions with superior terms because of cost savings to the

banks. Digital signature, digital signature guarantees, digital notaries, digital cash, and digital documents vaulting are all becoming available, making electronic banking a complete replacement for the aging paper-based equivalents.

- *Retailing:* The Electronic marketplace creates entirely new channels to directly reach consumers. Physical stores will move to emphasizing entertainment to draw customers. All value chain processes involving logistics of products and store management are enabled through information age technologies. The need to customize products to each customer's needs creates need for massive data warehousing applications.

- *Government:* Government processes and services are made more efficient and effective though networked interactive multimedia. Information about taxes, social security, veteran affairs, educational grants, and so on are all made available electronically. Human welfare services such as food stamps are revised by giving recipients identity cards that identify them at point of service and automatically debit their electronic benefit accounts. Government-held records about you as well as government reports, records (Federal Register, Congressional Register, IRS forms and regulations, Social Security information, and so on) and studies are available to you for interactive perusal.

- *Health care:* Patient record keeping is vastly improved as all test results, doctor notes, x-rays, and so on are collected and stored electronically. Specialists do consultations by looking at MRI scans remotely. Medial databases provide consumers with information on symptoms, treatments, alternative providers and self-care. Sharing of research information, patient case studies, and new procedures is enabled through subscriber Internet services.

Since every business, at its core, may be viewed as a massively parallel information processing factory, it is not surprising that networked interactive multimedia will have such a significant impact on all businesses.

The Marketspace

The most important impact of all of the momentous shocks of the information age is the shift to the *marketspace* from the marketplace.

Figure 1.24 provides a highlighted view of the previously presented Figure 1.4 that focuses in on the final attribute: the marketplace. In the nomadic society, the marketplace was conducted in a one-to-one manner as people engaged in personal barter with other members of their tribe. In the agrarian society, the marketplace moved to the village square and was born in the morning when farmers brought in their food and died in the evening when they returned to their huts. In the mercantile society, permanent stores were established in the towns for trade. In the industrial society, the shopping center or mall took on the role of the marketplace. But in the information society, the marketplace shifts to cyberspace and become the marketspace.

A marketspace is a marketplace that is created, defined, nurtured, and exploited through information technology. It is a virtual realm where products and services exist in digital form and are delivered through information-based distribution channels. For convergent and secondary industries (Table 1.13), virtual products

Age Attribute	Nomadic Society	Agrarian Society	Mercantile Society	Industrial Society	Knowledge Society
Defining Work	Hunter	Farmer	Sailor	Laborer	Knowledge Worker
What Are You Doing?	Surviving	Eating	Trading	Automating Labor	Informing
Organization Form	Tribe	Feudalism	Trading House	Hierarchical Bureaucracy	Networks
Logistics	People	Animals	Ship	Trains, Ships, Trucks, Air	Communication Network
__The Market Place__	*__Person to Person__*	*__Village Square__*	*__Town Stores__*	*__Shopping Malls__*	*__The Market-space__*

Figure 1.24 The marketspace. The most significant impact of the information age is the shift to the marketspace from the marketplace.

and services replace and supplement physical products. For other industries, the marketspace provides a rich distribution channel.

The reason that the notion of the marketspace is so important is that the primacy of economics as the moving force of history. Engels said:

> The economic structure of society always furnishes the real basis from which we can alone work out the ultimate explanation of the whole superstructure of judicial and political institutions as well as the religious, philosophical and other ideas of a given historical period. The final causes of all social changes and political revolutions are not to be sought in men's minds, not in men's insights into eternal truth and justice but changes in the methods of production and exchange.

As shown in Figure 1.25, the shift to virtual markets from physical markets meets Engel's definition and will cause unstoppable profound change. The notion of the marketspace identifies the core impact of the information age from which all other effects are

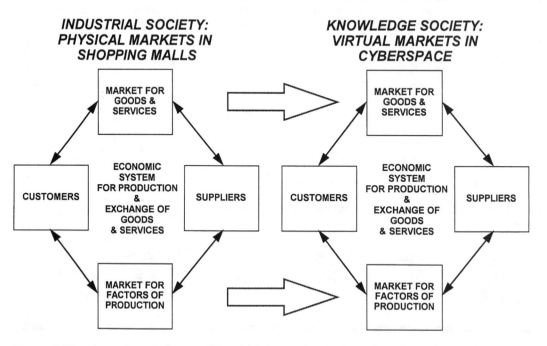

Figure 1.25   A profound change. The shift from physical markets in malls to virtual markets in cyberspace changes everything.

explainable. The massive change that we will undergo in the forth-coming years is due to the fundamental changes in the methods of production and exchange that convergence creates and the market-space personifies. As shown in Figure 1.26, as the information age progresses on its S curve, it will eventually cause a reorganization of society and industry as it fundamentally and irrevocably changes the system for the production and exchange of goods and services. The impact on all of us from both a personal and business perspective will have its roots in economics, and it is the market-space perspective that must ultimately guide our understanding of the information age and how we must respond to it to be success-ful. This is the reason that I said before that I believe that calling this era the digital economy or virtual economy (Table 1.1) is most appropriate even though I persist in using the most commonly accepted information age label.

Figures 1.27 and 1.28 illustrate the frantic rush to the market-space as both consumers and suppliers go on-line. This is very important beyond the obvious benefits because it illustrates the network externality of the information age. In economic theory, an externality occurs when two parties engage in a transaction and that transaction has an unintended impact on a nonparticipatory third party. This impact can be positive or negative for the third

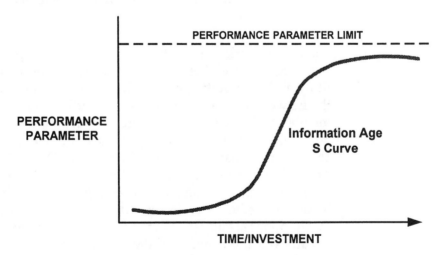

Figure 1.26 **Technology-induced change. As the information age pro-gresses, it will cause the reorganization of industry and society.**

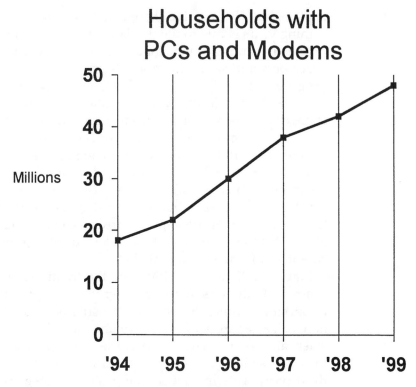

Figure 1.27   The marketspace buyers. Households with PCs and modems are increasing in number dramatically.

party. A network externality is a special case of a positive externality wherein all members of a community, a network of users, benefit by each additional person who joins the network. The value of the network increases for all by the addition of the new network member. This is what is occurring as both suppliers and consumers go on-line with the World Wide Web and other forms of electronic commerce (e-mail, EDI, EFT, interactive TV, etc.). The network externality nature of the information age results in everybody benefiting as each additional person or organization joins the network because it further extends the network's reach. This is why it is said that as nodes are added to a network, the cost of the network grows linearly but the benefits of the network grow exponentially. It is therefore not surprising that most of the attempts at substitute private networks to the internet such AT&T's Interchange On-line, eWorld, The Microsoft Network, Genie, and others have failed.

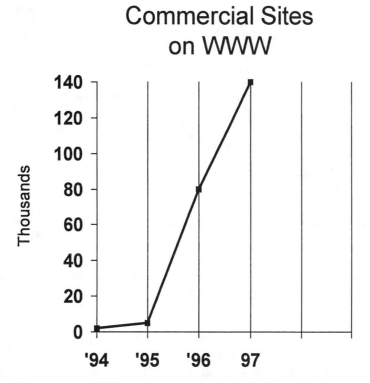

Commercial Sites on WWW

Figure 1.28   The marketspace sellers. Commercial sites on the World Wide Web are increasing dramatically.

They have failed because nobody is big enough and strong enough to control the marketspace.

IT RESPONSE

The information age has also been referred to by many in jest as the advice age. As shown in Figure 1.29, as we move between eras or rapidly try to ride an era, there is great uncertainty and chaos, and decision makers aggressively seek wisdom from advice givers. Since the duration of ages is shrinking from millennia to centuries to decades, the urgency for skillful advice grows. Nowhere are there more gurus, pundits, oracles, seers, market researchers, academics, consultants, prophets, diviners and soothsayers prepared to offer sagacious advice then in the information technology industry.

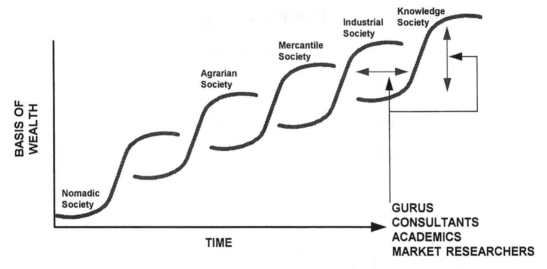

Figure 1.29　The advice age. Periods of rapid change always result in the emergence of a large market for advice givers.

On one issue, everyone seems to agree. In the information age, information technology is of strategic importance. While one might think that this is tautologically obvious, given the long history of disappointment with IT by senior business managers, some persuasion is often needed to convince them that they are not being duped again. Figure 1.30 can be used to make the strategic case. That which is strategic must have direct impact on business success and the business must be dependent on it for its success. In the industrial age, IT had only a support or factory/production role. In the information age, for all the reasons we have discussed, every business becomes dependent on IT. IT becomes the business because it defines the way goods and services are produced and exchanged in the marketspace.

After agreeing that IT is strategic, the advice gets scattered and things get pretty ugly pretty quickly. Among a seemingly endless list, the IT decision maker is advised to implement teams, implement total quality management, reengineer her processes, implement an enterprise IT architecture, move developers from the central IT organization to the business units, recentralize the developers, outsource, focus on customer satisfaction, focus on alignment, run the IT organization as a profit center, implement technologies x and y but absolutely not z, and so on and so forth.

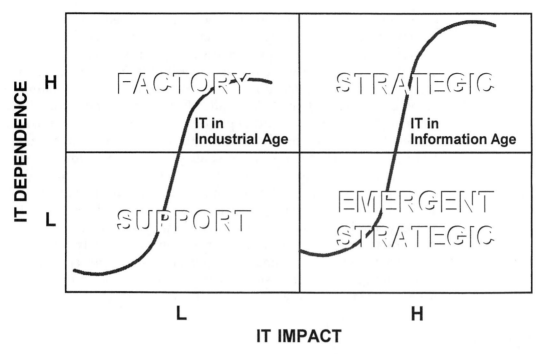

Figure 1.30 Strategic importance. The strategic importance of any corporate asset, competency, technology, process, or other resource can be evaluated from the perspective of business dependence and impact.

The list is not only infinite, it is often contradictory. Who should the decision maker listen to and what should the decision maker do?

It is my response that the first action that must be taken to respond to the ongoing turbulence of the information age is to become strategically competent. The information age will be characterized by continuing upheaval; it is doubtful that things will ever settle down again. The nature of an interactive multimedia society lends itself to change, speed, nimbleness, and entrepreneurship. A set of actions conceived at a moment of time, however wise, will not be sufficient. What is first and foremost required is the ability to assess, develop, and implement strategy in a manner consistent with ever-changing times and circumstances. So the first response and the response from which all other responses germinate is to develop strategic acumen. The best person to bet on is, as always, yourself. If you don't have confidence in yourself, why will your customers have confidence in your products?

The remainder of this book will address this need. We will first review strategy and strategic thinking in the next two chapters and then propose a strategy of potentiality as the mandated response. A strategy of potentiality means that one builds fundamental and highly flexible infrastructure capabilities from which dynamic responses to change may be made; friction is eliminated. The strategic IT response is to put in place a maneuverable IT organization that can enable the business to attack anywhere and defend everywhere. Only then is your strategy complete. Without the preparation, however, of understanding strategy and strategic thinking, the proposed strategy of potentiality would not make sense. It is our intent to help you understand how to develop an IT strategy that is deep and far-reaching so that you can navigate not only the information age, convergence, and the marketspace, but can also respond to any and all opportunities that present themselves to you and your business. The people to whom it is best to listen to for strategic advice is yourself and your staff.

CONCLUSION

This chapter has painted a succinct by powerful picture of the information age. The information age will change everything about society and commerce and it is vital to be primed to respond creatively. The key notions that have been presented in this chapter are multimedia, convergence, the marketspace, and strategic acumen. In the information age, companies will engage in IT fighting. IT fighting means the use of convergent IT as the master means to build new advantages, sustain and compound existing advantages, and depreciate the advantages of competitors. Actions must be developed to leverage information age technologies to create a cyber-corporation that is prepared to engage in global IT fighting to win global markets.

Some people are understandably skeptical of all the information age hype, and view the media coverage as just the next exaggerated element of the consultant-full employment act that started with TQM and business processing reengineering. I believe that they are wrong and that the information age is not just another Hagen Daaz flavor of the month. They are wrong because the history of free Western market economies is that businesses ultimately gravitate to technologies that offer superior products and services at favorable costs while consumers inevitably gravitate to products and services that offer them superior value at competitive prices. The marketspace has been created at the intersection of these two economically driven needs and, as Engels said: *The final causes of all social changes and political revolutions are not to be sought in men's minds, not in men's insights into eternal truth and justice but changes in the methods of production and exchange.* The information age is not this week's consultant's scam because it fundamentally changes the methods of production and exchange.

Companies that wish to continue to prosper into the next millennia will have no choice but to engage in IT fighting to enable a generic business model that includes the following five basic components:

1. Interactive multimedia distribution channels will be used to reach customers in a personalized, one-to-one, manner.
2. All products that can be digitized will be. Other products will be immersed in information to increase their value.
3. All value chain partners will be electronically bonded to expedite the sharing of information and to dramatically improve the efficiency and effectiveness of all value chain processes.
4. An information chain will support the physical value chain to provide knowledge in the appropriate format to each employee at the point of need.
5. Massive data warehousing and analysis will be deployed to understand what happened, what is happening, and anticipate what will happen.

Do you believe that more of the same will successfully compete against this?

Success will go to those who have the ability to develop and implement strategy in a superior manner. Strategic competence is the ultimate core competency that no one can ever take from you and from which advantage can be continually reborn. Your strategic wits will need to be applied for the first time to the problem of how does one compete when products and services are bits (virtual things) rather than atoms (physical things); how does one win at IT fighting? Not only is every business in the information age in the information movement and management business, for many businesses, increasingly, there is just the customer, the business, and the marketspace. The future of interest to the aware individual is a future defined by bits.

2

Strategy

Before we can propose what actions an IT organization should take to position itself for IT fighting, it is necessary to fully understand strategy and its derivative concepts of strategic thinking, strategic frameworks, strategic paradox, and strategic planning. Strategy and all its associated terminology are part of the everyday vernacular and what is meant is often erroneously assumed. Strategy is a discipline just like mathematics, logic, computer science, or politics. It is first necessary to understand the definition of each concept and its implications before developing a strategic response. It is one of the most puzzling and persistent contradictions of our times that while strategy compounds in importance as one climbs the corporate ladder and the times grow more chaotic, there is routinely little to no formal training in strategy conducted and, amazingly, people are routinely told to develop a strategy without any formal preparation whatsoever. To engage in superior information age IT fighting, we will need to do significantly better than that.

STRATEGY

From an academic perspective, the purpose of strategy is to provide direction, concentration of effort (focus), constancy of purpose (perseverance), and flexibility (adaptability) as a business relentlessly strives to improve its position in all strategic areas. Strategy is mathematics and is equal to direction plus focus plus perseverance plus adaptability. At a very pragmatic level, strategy can be viewed simply as finding a way short (the shorter the better) of *brute force* to accomplish one's ends. Strategy should be comprehended as the movement from a current position to a more desirable future position but with economies of time, effort, cost, or resource utilization. There is neither elegance nor insight in brute force, but there must be both in strategy.

My view is that the eternal struggle of business is the struggle for advantage. The one with more advantages wins, the one with fewer advantages loses. The purpose of strategy is the building, compounding, and sustaining of advantage. Sun Tzu said that when rocks rolled down a mountain, *it is because of the mountain, not the rocks.* As shown in Figure 2.1, the idea is to use strategy to elevate the entire business so that your employees roll at the marketplace with the inherited force of your strategic advantages.

Business strategy must, therefore, focus on:

- Building new advantages that increase customer satisfaction and create distance from competitors.
- Elongating existing advantages that increase customer satisfaction and create distance from competitors.

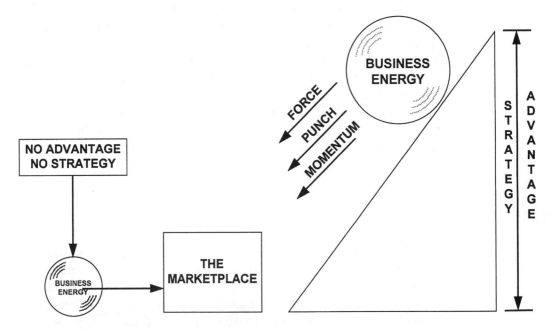

Figure 2.1   **Advantage. The idea of advantage is to take broad actions that elevate the market power of all employees.**

- Compressing or eliminating the advantages of competitors.

The lone purpose of business strategy is the nurturing of advantage. Advantage can be realized through infinite combinations of strategic moves. While there are many ways to build advantage, all advantages can be classified into five generic categories:

- Cost advantage: The advantage results in being able to provide products/services more cheaply.
- Value-added advantage: The advantage creates a product/service that offers some highly desirable feature/functionality.
- Focus advantage: The advantage more tightly meets the explicit needs of a particular customer.
- Speed advantage: The advantage permits you to create products, deliver products, and service customer needs quicker than others.
- Maneuverability advantage: The advantage permits you to adapt to changing requirements more quickly than others. Being maneuverable permits you to constantly refresh the other types of advantage. It is the only advantage that your competitors can never take from you.

So you win by being cheaper, more unique, more focused, faster, or more adaptable than your competitors in serving your customers. At a minimum, your advantages must satisfy your customers and, at best, delight them to the point of excitement.

Sun Tzu said:

> The one with many strategic factors on his side wins. . . . The one with few strategic factors on his side loses. In this way, I can tell who will win and who will lose.[1]

If an action does not lead to the development of an advantage, it is of no strategic interest. The struggle always has been and remains the perpetual struggle for competitive advantage.

The culmination of advantage is the building of a set of sustainable competitive advantages (SCA) for the business. An SCA is a resource, capability, asset, or process that provides the enterprise with a distinct attraction to its customers and a unique advantage over its competitors. An SCA has seven attributes that are itemized in Table 2.1. Without a well-designed set of sustainable competitive advantages, a business engages in a frantic life-and-death struggle for marketplace survival; after all there is no compelling reason for consumers to choose that company's products or services. Figure 2.2 provides a way to deduce whether an advantage is sustainable by analyzing in terms of the cost and time it would take a competitor to imitate it. Whether a competitor will attempt to imitate a contestable advantage depends on:

- Degree of relative advantage: Does the competitor feel that it is worth the effort?
- Compatibility: How harmonious is the advantage with the rest of the competitor's product plan?
- Simplicity: Does the competitor have immediate access to the skills necessary to imitate the advantage?
- Trailability: Can prototyping or other expediting techniques be used to quickly trial their version of the advantage?
- Observability: How hard is it for the competitor to understand the internals of the advantage?

Table 2.1
Sustainable Competitive Advantage (SCA)

SCA Attribute	Definition
customer perception	The customer perceives a consistent difference in one or more key buying factors.
SCA linkage	The difference in customer perception is directly attributable to the SCA.
durability	Both the customer's perception and the SCA linkage are durable over an extended time period.
transparency	The mechanics/details of the SCA are difficult to understand by competitors.
accessibility	The competitor has unequal access to the required resources to mimic the SCA.
replication	The competitor would have extreme difficulty reproducing the SCA.
coordination	The SCA requires difficult and subtle coordination of multiple resources.

It is an interesting insight from Figure 2.2 that, with reflection, it would seem that time is strategically a stronger deterrent than cost in inhibiting imitation. This is because it is much easier to acquire money than to acquire more time.

The complement to sustainable competitive advantage is temporary competitive advantage. A temporary competitive advantage (TCA) provides an attraction to a customer but the advantage can be contested and imitated in a relatively short time by competitors. Temporary advantages, by their inherent nature, have to be continually refreshed. Figure 2.3 compares the two types of advantages. We will later argue that the IT response to the information age must take into account a dramatic shift to temporary advantages from sustainable advantages and must therefore enable speed and nimbleness by the business.

To summarize, the kernel ideas of strategy are:

- The purpose of strategy is to build advantage.
- Advantage can be built in many ways.

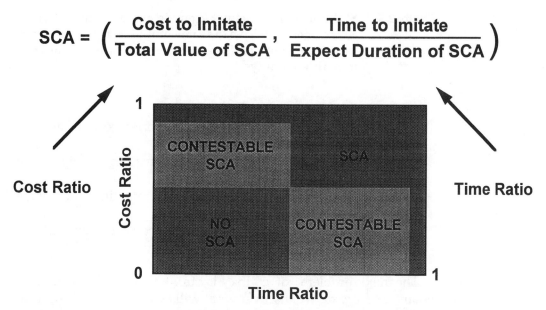

$$SCA = \left(\frac{\text{Cost to Imitate}}{\text{Total Value of SCA}} , \frac{\text{Time to Imitate}}{\text{Expect Duration of SCA}} \right)$$

Figure 2.2 Sustainability of advantage. The sustainability of an advantage may be deduced by examining the time and cost it would take a competitor to replicate it.

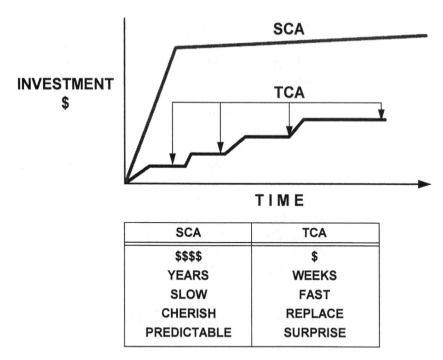

SCA	TCA
$$$$	$
YEARS	WEEKS
SLOW	FAST
CHERISH	REPLACE
PREDICTABLE	SURPRISE

Figure 2.3   SCA and TCA. Sustainable and temporary competitive advantages both have the same objective, that is, to create a compelling reason for a customer to choose you, but do it in different ways.

- Advantage is classifiable into five categories: cost, differentiation, speed, focus, and maneuverability.
- The culmination of advantage is the creation of sustainable competitive advantage (SCA).
- The complement to SCA is temporary competitive advantage (TCA).
- Those with more advantages win; those with fewer advantages lose.

The next problem, of course, is, from where do advantages emanate? How do we discover what will be elegant and insightful so that we may win without exhausting ourselves by using mindless brute force? The answer is that we postulate, analyze, and select strategic actions through *strategic thinking*.

STRATEGIC THINKING

Strategic thinking is the method that strategists use to think about things. It is quite different from the daily thinking that governs our routine and daily lives. Figure 2.4 illustrates the three dimensions of strategic thinking:

- *Time:* Strategists think across time. They think about a problem from the perspectives of the past, the present, and the future.
- *Substance:* Strategists think about problems in turns of both their concrete and abstract natures.
- *Cardinality:* Strategists think about multiple issues concurrently. Synthesis, not analytical decomposition, lies at the heart of strategic thinking.

Most of the time, most of us, as illustrated in Figure 2.5, engage in *mundane thinking* to solve our daily problems. All we need to do, to meet our needs, is to think about one issue at a time, in the present, and in the concrete. Anything more sophisticated would be overkill.

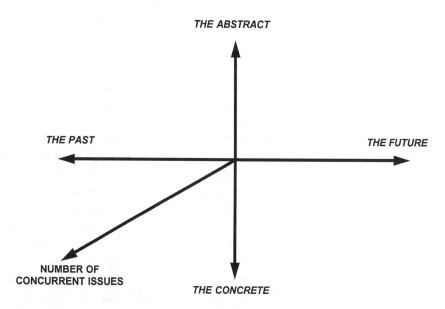

Figure 2.4   Strategic thinking. Strategists think about strategic problems in terms of the three dimensions of time, substance, and cardinality.

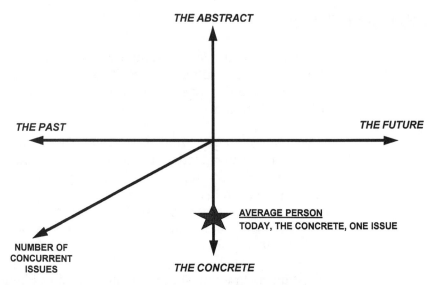

Figure 2.5   Mundane thinking. Daily problems do not require strategic thinking for their successful resolution.

This thinking pattern that we use to solve our daily problems is also referred to as *point thinking* because all our problem solving efforts converge on one point.

Figure 2.6 illustrates the strategic thinking bubble. A strategist uses the same dimensions as the mundane thinker but thinks dynamically within the thought bubble defined by those three dimensions. A strategist concurrently thinks about many issues in multiple dimensions at many levels of abstraction and detail over time (past, present, and future). Strategic thinking is a creative and dynamic synthesis which is the exact opposite of point thinking.

Synthesis as opposed to analytical decomposition is a particularly critical part of strategic thinking. When you examine things in artificial isolation from their natural linkages, you lose the dynamics of the big picture. You simplify and hide from the complexity of the real world relationships. Having lost the linkages by virtue of your analytical decomposition, it is often impossible to reintegrate them until implementation problems surface. Synthesis permits you to discover the whole that is greater then the sum of the parts.

When a strategist looks at a problem, she thinks about it in terms of certain established and proven strategic ideas or themes. While new perspectives can always be developed, time and experience

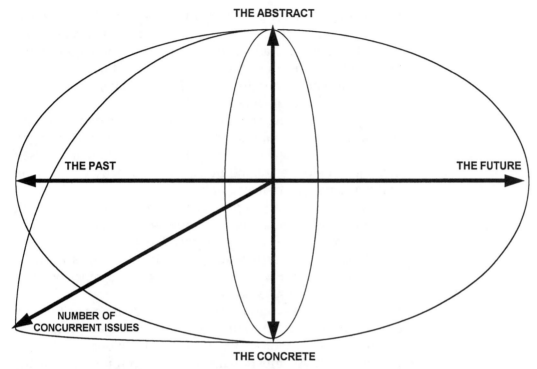

Figure 2.6   **Strategic thinking bubble. A strategist not only thinks within three dimensions, she thinks dynamically within a thought bubble created by the three dimensions.**

have demonstrated the power of looking at problems through certain enduring and tested strategic lenses. The following are a partial and representative list of powerful strategic ideas:

- Assessment: It is the responsibility of the leadership to fully assess the situation before committing its forces to conflict. Based on the assessment, an overarching strategy is adopted. Tactical maneuver and adaptation take place within this strategy.
- Alliances: It is necessary to develop a community of allies. The strength of the alliance is stronger than the simple additive strength of the individual members.
- Structure: Structure depends on strategy. Forces are to be structured in a manner to enable the realization of the strategy.

- Indirection: Opponents should not be confronted directly. The maximum gain at the minimum expense is achieved by deception, surprise, and chipping away at the edges of the opponent. Exhaust them before you confront them.
- Speed: All matters require speed. Speed, alone, can compensate for numerous other shortcomings.
- Strategic conflict: The opponent is to be contested strategically. Attack and ruin their strategy; do not engage their advantages.
- Self-invincibility: The first order of business is to make oneself invincible. Before engaging in expansionist activities, be sure that you cannot be defeated at home.
- Prescience: The leadership must have deep and far-reaching foresight. Leaders must see and know what others do not. The height of prescience is to see the formless and act on it.
- Formlessness: The architecture of your advantages must be inscrutable. In this way, they do not know against what to attack and against what to defend.
- Positioning: Forces must be preplaced in winning positions by design. In this way, the actual confrontation is anticlimatic as you have already won by your superior positions.
- Commitment: All must share the same commitment to the objectives. Forces that do not share the same aims will lack the will and resolve to overcome the endless barriers to victory.
- Maneuver: Maneuver means finding the best way to go. Forces must be able to maneuver to exploit gaps.
- Leadership: The leadership is responsible for the well-being of the community. Leaders must lay deep plans for what others do not foresee.
- Efficiency: Extended confrontations drain the community of its wealth. The best victories are swift and at the absolute minimum cost.
- Coordination: The problem of coordination is the problem of managing the many as though they were one. The few can defeat the many if they act with one purpose. When perfect coordination is achieved, one cannot distinguish the will of the individual from the will of the many, nor the will of the many from the will of the individual.
- Discipline: There must be an impartial system of reward and punishment. Good leadership rewards the worthy.
- Psychological conflict: Victory and defeat first occur in the mind. Defeat your opponent psychologically so that even if

they are intact, they lack the will to contest you. Musashi said, *You first beat your enemy with your spirit.*

- Foreknowledge: All matters require competitive intelligence. Nothing is more important then understanding the plans of your opponents and the needs of your customers.
- Love of the people: True leadership is not a function of title but a function of the love of the people. Leaders must share the struggle of their forces. One must win the affection of one's employees so that they will extend themselves for you.
- Learning: One must continually learn and adapt based on that learning. All progress includes making mistakes, but the same mistake should not be made twice.

All these themes, not surprisingly, converge on one grand strategic idea—the building, sustaining, and extending of advantage.

So what a strategic thinker does is:

- Choose a problem (or set of problems).
- Sample strategic ideas (singularly and simultaneously).
- Think about solving the problem(s) by applying the strategic ideas within the Figure 2.7 bubble. This demands intuitive, holistic, dynamic, and abstract thinking. It demands being able to synthesize as opposed to unidimensional analytical decomposition.

Since the combinations of strategic ideas are inexhaustible, strategic thinking is a very powerful way to develop insight about problems and solve them in novel, unanticipated, and creative ways. It is from this kind of thinking that advantage is born and nourished.

To summarize:

- Strategists think differently than people solving mundane problems.
- Strategists think about problems in terms of a three-dimensional thought bubble of time, substance, and cardinality.
- The use of strategic ideas guides the thought process across the three dimensions.

Strategic thinking is particularly challenging because it is a holistic, dynamic, and must cope with paradox.

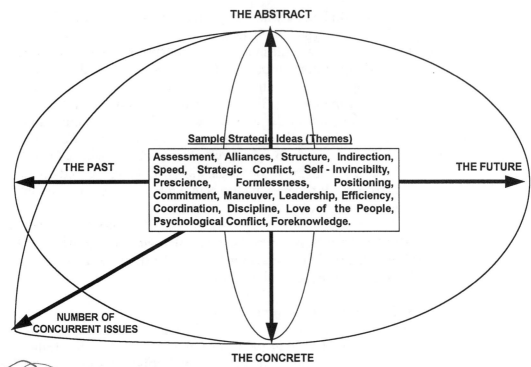

THE ABSTRACT

THE PAST

THE FUTURE

Sample Strategic Ideas (Themes)

Assessment, Alliances, Structure, Indirection,
Speed, Strategic Conflict, Self - Invincibilty,
Prescience, Formlessness, Positioning,
Commitment, Maneuver, Leadership, Efficiency,
Coordination, Discipline, Love of the People,
Psychological Conflict, Foreknowledge.

NUMBER OF
CONCURRENT ISSUES

THE CONCRETE

Figure 2.7   Strategic ideas. A strategist thinks about problems within the thought bubble in terms of established and novel strategic ideas.

STRATEGIC PARADOX

In conducting our daily lives, purposeful opposition to our routine efforts does not exist. No one has the goal of deliberately and continually thwarting our actions. We use what is called *linear logic* to solve our problems. Linear logic consists of using common sense, deductive/inductive reasoning, and concern for economies of time, cost, and overall effort to solve problems. One is commonly criticized for taking a circuitous route when a more direct one is available. Daily life applauds the logical, the economic, and the abundant use of common sense.

Business strategy, to the contrary, is executed against a background of hyper-conflict and intelligent counter-measures. Able and motivated competitors purposefully and energetically attempt to foil your ambition. Because of this excessive state of conflict, many strategic actions demonstrate a surprising paradoxical logic.

There are two types of strategic paradox:

- *Coming together of opposites:* A linear logic action or state evolves into a reversal of itself (A becomes not-A); as they say, "You can have too much of a good thing." An example of this is that an advantage, unrefreshed, becomes a disadvantage. This paradox occurs because conflict causes an inevitable reversal due to the complacency of the winner and the hunger of the loser. While the current winners gloat in their success, this same success lulls them into a false sense of permanent security while it paradoxically stimulates the current losers to tax their ingenuity to overcome it.
- *Reversal of opposites:* To accomplish your objectives, do the reverse of what linear logic would dictate. So, "If you wish peace, prepare for war," or to accomplish A, do the set of actions to accomplish not-A, or your primary competitor should be yourself. This occurs because the nature of conflict reverses normal linear logic. While taking a long and dangerous circuitous route is bad logic under daily circumstances, in a state of conflict (i.e., war), this bad logic is good logic exactly because it is bad logic (it is less likely to be defended). The logic of conflict is often in total opposition to the logic of daily life.

Conflict causes strategic paradox to occur, bad logic becomes good logic exactly because it is bad logic, and the able strategist must learn to think and act paradoxically. Figure 2.8 updates our illustration of strategic thinking to extend the thought bubble to a fourth dimension of linear logic and paradoxical thinking. Paradoxically, strategists often have to recommend, to an unbelieving and astonished audience, that they should take actions which are directly contrary to routine business sense.

An example of reversal of opposites thinking is illustrated by the *Kano Methodology:* The Kano Methodology is a analytical method used to stimulate strategic thinking. As illustrated in Figure 2.9, the logic of Kano suggests that candidate strategic actions be divided into three types:

- Threshold actions: For every dollar invested in this type of action, customer satisfaction increases but gradually reaches a point where less than a dollar of satisfaction is achieved for

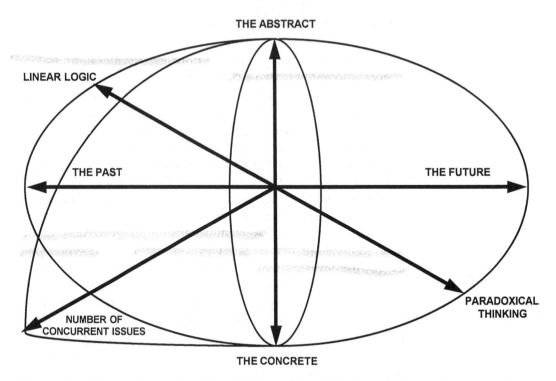

Figure 2.8   Strategic paradox. The addition of the idea of strategic paradox necessitates that the strategic thinking bubble be extended to a fourth dimension.

each dollar of investment. It therefore doesn't make sense to invest beyond the break-even point.

- Performance actions: For every dollar invested in this type of action, there is a constant positive increase in customer satisfaction in excess of your investment. It pays to continually to invest in these actions.
- Excitement actions: For every additional dollar invested in this type of actions, there is an exponential increase in customer satisfaction. These are prized actions and are the best actions to invest in.

While this is solid linear thinking, the true brilliance of the methodology occurs next through using paradoxical thinking. What is suggested is that after one has developed the excitement capability, that it be presented to the customer as a threshold

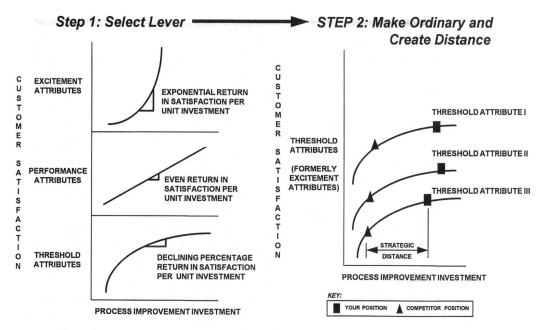

Figure 2.9   **Kano Methodology. The Kano Methodology provides an example of how to apply strategic paradox.**

attribute, that is, paradoxically; the truly extraordinary is most extraordinary when it is presented as the ordinary. What this does is position your capability as the minimum ante to play the game. A customer may be willing to forgo the exceptional but will minimally expect and demand the ordinary. Since you can do it and your competitors can't, you create strategic distance between yourself and your competitors. While they struggle to do the exceptional as the norm, you raise the tempo of the game and work on converting another excitement attribute to a threshold attribute, and so on, ad infinitum. So the great insight of the Kano Methodology is not the linear thinking of excitement attributes, where most people would have stopped, but the recognition that maximum value and market disruption occurs when excitement capabilities are presented, paradoxically, as the ordinary (reversal of opposites).

The information age is a period of extraordinary competition. As we have previously argued, the collapse of traditional industrial age barriers to entry, such as economies of scale, access to distribution systems, mass advertising, location, and competency access, all conspire to make the information age hyper-competitive. The nature of digital products enables mass customization, while the ability to perform comparative shopping electronically drives prices to commodity levels. Suddenly, everything becomes a generic product.

Consumers, for the first time in history, can have almost perfect knowledge of what is being offered, at what price, and with what value proposition. The result is the creation of a highly competitive and swift marketspace that prizes speed, nimbleness, aggressiveness, entrepreneurship, and creating niches; a marketspace that rewards maneuver—as opposed to attrition—fighters. It is, therefore, not surprising that companies that compete in the marketspace will be subject to strategic paradox (due to the hyper-competition). Information age companies will have to clearly understand the paradoxes of the information age, deduce their implications, and adapt to them appropriately. The business logic of the more staid industrial age will not suffice in the extremely cutthroat information age.

The information age demonstrates a startling reverse relativity. In Einstein's famous Theory of Relativity, as a spaceship relative to you on earth approaches the speed of light, time would dilate and indeed go slower. Though to the people on the spaceship everything would seem perfectly normal, to you, the earth observer, time would actually slow down.

The information age creates a converse relativity where time on the information age ship accelerates rather than slows. While time proceeds normally for the industrial age company, the information age business experiences the ability to do everything more quickly. So, for example, while an industrial age company will perform a year's worth of work, the information age company will be able to perform three years' worth by virtue of the heightened speed capabilities delivered through convergent technologies and life in the fast lane of the marketspace. Obviously, the industrial age company will not be able to compete in this war of speed.

This chaotic information age environment will result in a shift to the nurturing of temporary competitive advantages at the expense and decline of sustainable competitive advantages. Rather than making huge investments, with the associated risk of imitation, and expecting to create an advantage that provides extended benefits, companies will covet styles and systems that enable the rapid creation of sequential and overlapping temporary advantages. Companies will prize speed, surprise, opportunism, niches, prototyping, and modularity to enable dynamic reusability. The tempo of competition will accelerate as there are no longer any safe fortresses and the marketspace becomes an ever more frenzied war of movement.

There is a Chinese saying: *The marketplace is a battlefield.* We would update this wisdom to say: *The marketspace is a furious battlefield.* It is a battlefield with neither certainty nor predictability because the balance of advantage is constantly changing and shifting in a state of upheaval as the temporary advantages rise and fall. As shown in Figure 2.10, using military metaphors, the successful marketspace battle plan will favor flanking maneuvers, bypass maneuvers, and guerrilla warfare over industrial age frontal attacks and encirclements.

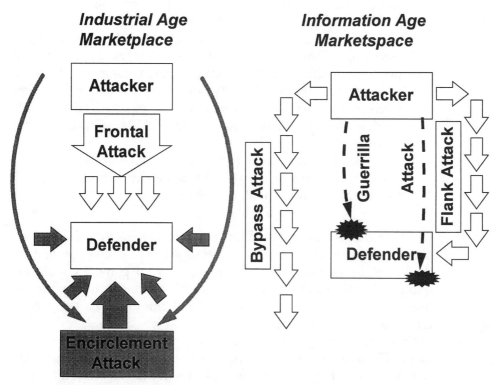

Figure 2.10 Methods of attack. Frontal and encirclement attacks, the art of marketplace warfare for the industrial age, will be replaced by guerilla flanking and bypass marketspace attacks in the information age.

The competitive fervor of the information age results in the information age eating its own young. Consider the following action in a six-month period:

- The World Wide Web (WWW) is recognized as a tremendous innovation that permits previously unimagined information exchange in a personalized manner but on a mass scale.
- Hyper-text mark-up language (HTML), the mark-up language of the WWW, is criticized as being static and dull; the text and graphics just sit there.
- Java, a procedural object-oriented programming language is made available that permits applications to be distributed on demand and permits the WWW pages to become fully animated with programmable movement and logic.
- Java, an interpretive language, is criticized as being too slow.
- Developers rush to provide just-in-time compilers, caching, and Java chips to accelerate its speed.
- Critics complain that the future is not two-dimensional HTML web pages but three-dimensional interfaces such as those developed with the virtual reality modeling language (VRML).
- Java is made compatible with three-dimensional presentation interfaces. It is also extended to permit easy invocation of network services through a standard set of APIs (application program interface).
- Inferno, a Lucent competitor to Java, is announced.
- The Java run-time Java Virtual Machine environment is ported to server, as well as client, machines.

In a period of no more than a few months, the absolutely astounding accomplishment of broadly accessible but passive hypertext on the Internet is devalued and the ante to play the game becomes on-demand Java-controlled hypermedia. All of this occurs before no more then a handful of the development community even gets to use Java for the first time.

Given this unruly, competitive, and combative environment, the aware IT strategist must be sensitive to the following six information age strategic paradoxes and take them into account in formulating how she will engage in IT fighting. The first four paradoxes occur at the information age level. The last two are paradoxes specific to IT.

Information Age Strategic Paradox I

As the world get smaller, small companies get bigger and big companies get smaller.

Explanation. The basis of this paradox was illustrated in Figure 1.23. As products and services become digitized and the primary distribution channels shift to electronic commerce, the world shrinks and many industrial age advantages of large companies erode. Small companies have access to the same consumer reach technologies and value-chain enhancement technologies as large companies but, in addition, often have the advantage of being non-bureaucratic, nimble, fast, specific customer (market fragment) focused, and entrepreneurial. Everyone, large or small, shares the same storefront location in cyberspace. The competitive playing field is leveled by broad availability of convergent technologies and the ability to precisely choose whom to serve and how to serve them. So as the traditional time and space constraints on markets are dislodged by global electronic markets, large companies find themselves confronting thousands of small companies fighting for every niche and exploiting one-to-one marketing and customized services to overcome large company mass advertising and scale advantages. Of course, a little niching here and a little niching there and before you know it, there is nothing left.

Implications for IT Fighting. In all things digital, you must have flexibility and speed. It is flexibility with speed that makes you maneuverable. If you are efficient but frozen, they will break you by your inability to change. What good is it to be efficient when they move the value proposition so that what you are very efficient at is no longer desired by the consumer? Companies that compete purely on efficiency will be engaged in diving prices to commodity levels. It is more likely that companies will want to engage in a game of temporary advantage leap-frog. IT, therefore, will have to permit rapid zigs and abrupt zags. The only way to get above commodity prices will be to create an inexhaustible stream of IT-based temporary advantages.

Information Age Strategic Paradox II

To create advantage, you must quickly destroy your advantages.

Explanation. The strategic paradox of *opposites coming together* is at work here. In a world of hyper-competition, it is better to eat your young then have others do it. The pace of information age change will rapidly convert advantages into disadvantages. It will be necessary to ride learning curves and continually roll out new temporary advantages even though they destroy your own incumbent temporary advantages. So what you may expect to see, paradoxically, is companies announcing new releases and features of products that appear to make obsolete their own products prematurely for no apparent reason. Quite the opposite, however, is what is really happening. What they are doing is not permitting the coming together of opposites to occur. An advantage terminated before its time is much better than an advantage held onto beyond its utility. Since no one can control the marketplace or have intimate knowledge of competitor plans and announcements, the result is to err, of necessity, on the side of rapid self-obsolescence.

Implications For IT Fighting. It will be more necessary than ever to get your priorities straight. In the industrial age, the dominant logic of IT was first, second, and third to minimize cost. IT strategy was driven by the perfect industrial age linear logic of economies of scale. In the information age, the dominant logic will be first maneuverability and second cost. In a world of uncertainty and swift change, what is most prized is a coping mechanism for the unknowable. So, again, in all things, you must be flexible, fast, and maneuverable, and then efficient. If your first strategic IT vector is cost, how you will ever be able to abruptly change when abrupt change is the normal state of the environment? The economies of scale but highly rigid traditional monolithic mainframe computing environment was exactly right for the industrial age but exactly wrong for those who will have to engage in fluid IT fighting.

So a new arrangement of priorities will have to take place. The scales that have historically been extremely tilted on the side of cost efficiency will have to be recalibrated to lean more favorably towards maneuverability. As always, cost efficiency will remain vitally important but the quest for economies will, however, have to be conducted with sensitivity to the consequences of those decisions on the even more important, or at least equally important, pursuit of maneuverability. If you cannot quickly bend, they will break you by continuously changing the rules of the game.

Of course, the artful strategist will realize that there need not be any tension between adaptive maneuver as a strategic thrust and cost sensitivity. Those who can adapt can not only alter their value-added focus, or speed, they can more easily integrate new modes of efficiency. So while often presented as a dilemma, a maneuver strategy can yield both improved economics and flexibility.

Information Age Strategic Paradox III

To make money, you don't need money.

Explanation. The greatest barrier to entry of all industrial age barriers to entry was the scarcity and cost of capital. This resulted in the common maxim: *To make money, you need money.* The basis of wealth in the industrial age was capital (land and labor). In the information age, the basis of wealth is ideas. The wide availability of convergent technologies with global electronic markets makes it relatively inexpensive to start a business and gradually scale it as it grows. So smarts, not capital, will drive who makes money. More than in any other era in time, the information age will reward entrepreneurship, risk taking, and foresight.

Implications for IT Fighting. Prototyping, trial and error, experimentation, "start small, gain acceptance, and evolve," and leapfrog will characterize the ways that small startups will compete and grow. To compete, large companies will also need to be able to perform the same types of learning experiments. Few of us get anything of any complexity right the first time. The battle is a battle of who can ride the leaning curves quickest. The business will, therefore, demand that the IT assets permits rapid prototyping, exploration, and the conversion of those experiments into production scale products and services.

Information Age Strategic Paradox IV

To remain innovative, don't listen to your customers too carefully.

Explanation. Established customers have huge financial, skill-related, and emotional investments in existing technologies. They most often state new requirements only in terms of the evolutionary development of those technologies. Current customers tend to want to sustain investments in existing technologies rather than underwrite research and experimentation in innovative but disruptive technologies that date their own skills and investments. As a consequence, if you listen and follow your customers requirements too closely, you will meet their stated needs through incremental improvements to what is while starving research and development in innovative technologies that will eventually substitute for them. Paradoxically, when entrepreneurial companies, unbounded by these customers, do innovate, your conservative customers, who limited your fields of investment, will abandon you for the superior and now demonstrable substitute.

Implications for IT Fighting. IT organizations have historically been excellent examples of customers who wished to sustain technological investments rather than experiment with disruptive but innovative technologies. Evolution is easier but disruption creates opportunities. The reward and recognition systems need to promote experimentation and curiosity for novel ways of solving customer problems.

As a supplier to your own customers, you need not let them keep you in a strait jacket of incrementalism. When you discover new technologies, use them to solve different market applications that are not solvable with existing technologies. As the technologies mature, they can then be promoted as substitutes for existing technologies. The information age will result in shorter product cycles and more innovation than ever before in our industry. It is crucial not to be blind to radical new ways of solving problems. If you listen to your customers too closely and only think and act incrementally, you will eventually lose your customers to suppliers who didn't listen to them at all.

Information Age Strategic Paradox V

To concentrate your IT power, you must disperse it.

Explanation. Concentrated computing power, as personified by mainframe computing, is positioning you for a mindless war of attrition. With one-size-fits-all computing, everybody knows, more or less, what the other party can do and can match each other MIP for MIP. The configurations of computing power are limited by intent. IT fighting needs to:

- Be able to concentrate computing power at the point of need with the amount and type of resource required.
- Bring applications dynamically to the point of need.
- Share resources, as required, with other points of need.
- Configure IT resources in a configuration consistent with the exact needs of the application.

This is accomplishable with distributed computing models, such as client/server computing, not traditional host-centered computing. Concentration of power is mathematically equal to your power at the point of need less your opponent's concentration of power at the point of need. It is not your absolute power but your relative power that gives your advantage. So you force differences in power by dispersing power while concurrently creating the ability to link dispersed power when and as needed. In this way, you concentrate your power by dispersing it.

Implications For IT Fighting. The future of interest to the aware strategist is not only bits; it is dispersed bits. Technologies of extreme importance for IT fighting are technologies that support distributed models of computing. These technologies include client/server computing, distributed objects, broadband communications, software agents, groupware, e-mail, videoconferencing, EDI, and distributed databases. The pressing need to collaborate electronically across the value chain with customers, suppliers, regulators, financiers, and so on will drive the need for distributed computing.

Information Age Strategic Paradox VI

To use IT efficiently, you must use it in excess.

Explanation. The most striking strategic paradox of IT in the information age is that the cost-concerned strategist does not seek to use just enough means but an excess of means to accomplish her ends. Excess means more than analytically justified by circumstances; it does not mean, however, wasteful or prodigious. Convergent IT achieves, paradoxically, its greatest value for the business when it is used in excess.

It is typical to observe customer teams engage in extensive and exhaustive cost justifications exercises (net present value, return on investment, cost/benefit justification, pay back period, etc.) to convince cost-conscious decision makers to approve each IT expenditure. Their actions are understandable by linear logic but are inappropriate because of *reversal of opposites.* When the battle shifts to IT fighting, IT becomes subject to strategic paradox and must be managed as such to achieve optimum results.

Consider a military commander who needs to engage his enemy. If he uses linear logic and deploys *just enough* resources, he will win but it will be an expensive (Pyrhicc) victory. If he applies a force far in excess of his opponent, he will achieve his ends with minor causalities. All the downstream costs of battle will be avoided (damaged weapons, confusion, wounded/killed soldiers, etc.) So at the point of conflict, the efficient commander does not seek to use *just enough,* but applies means far in excess of her opponent. She does not use accounting logic, which holds in nonconflict situations but applies paradoxical logic, which rules at the point of battle.

Unquestionably, it is easier to accept this paradox with regard to the military situation than IT. This is because of the differences in the two situations between cause and effect. In the military situation, the cause and effect are tightly coupled in time and space. One can immediately see the results of the excess and correlate the success to that excess. In IT fighting, the cause and effect are often dispersed across wide gaps of time and space. The use of excess IT will have the desired effect but it may occur, perhaps, months later at a remote branch office.

The strategist must take solace in that she is engaged in deep and far-reaching strategy, not tactical short-term decisions. Things that are readily cost-justifiable are things that are obvious and known to all. Strategic thinking is involved in seeing victory before it exists. How can anyone cost-justify the formless? Sun Tzu said, "Vision is seeing victory before it exists. This is the strategist's path to strategic triumph." While cost-conscious accounting methods are appropriate for sustaining wealth, strategic vision has always been the required ingredient to create it.

So while it stretches and strains your business common sense, I believe that strategic paradox is an important dimension of the spirit of exploiting convergent IT. Ultimately, experience will prove that those who use it in excess will achieve greater benefits than those who attempt to rigorously cost-justify, exactly parcel it out, or horde its deployment. They will learn that their approach is mathematically correct but strategically sterile.

Implications for IT Fighting. Businesses need to aggressively expand their core competencies in IT. The purpose of a business is to make money, not to save it. It is interesting that while downsizing, ruthless cost-cutting, cost-motivated outsourcing, and other such activities are highly popular, they are, by definition, poor strategies. They are poor strategies because they are self-limiting. The more successful you are, the less marginal benefit there is to achieve. Growth, on the other hand, is an infinite strategy. With global markets, the only constraints on you are your vision and execution. So while it remains fashionable to treat IT as an expense to be cut at all costs, the aware strategist should work to educate management on the pressing need to expand, not contract, the depth and breadth of IT expertise. In this way, the necessary technologies will be available to the firm to engage in expansionist IT fighting.

Conclusion

In the hyper-competitive information age, our actions are curved by the laws of strategic paradox. To engage in IT fighting, you must accept that linear-thinking, bad logic becomes information age good logic, and linear-thinking, good logic becomes information age bad logic; you must often think and act paradoxically. The future is not only a future dominated by bits; it is a future of bits frequently implemented in contradiction to everyday common sense. In strategy the long way home is often the shortest.

Strategic paradox, like all strategic thinking tools, has to be practiced with proper respect for contemporary business etiquette. Having its origins in fierce military conflict, it sometimes offers correct strategic advice that must be moderated or not executed. Consider the information age problem of customer retention in a world where substitution and choice is a click away. Reversal of opposites thinking would suggest, "To retain your customers, have them experience your competitors." The action indicated would be to encourage/motivate your customers in mass to use your competitor over a very compressed time period. Wouldn't this be the paradoxically correct action by the champions of traditional PCs who believe that the new Web information appliances are useless? Such a flood of customers would overwhelm the Web information appliance's feature and service capabilities and result in a poor experience for the consumers. Nevertheless, this would certainly be inconsistent with acceptable modern business behavior. So while it does generate insight, strategic paradox needs to be always tempered by modern business ethics.

It is common to be initially uncomfortable with strategic paradox. Technical people, quite understandably, prize their rational nature. I would suggest that you take the notion of the learning person to heart and, with an open and thoughtful mind, consider the ideas; do not, a priori, sit in judgment on them. Strategic paradox is not an aberrance to ignore or discount; it is a normality of hyper-competitive environments, that is, the furiously antagonistic information age.

Strategic paradox even explains the fundamental rationale for engaging in strategy and strategic planning. The paradox of strategy is: *To accomplish the absolute most, you must do the absolute least.* Recall the definition of strategy; the purpose of strategy is to find a way short, the shorter the better, of brute force to accomplish your ends. The shorter way is the better way because you accomplish your ends by doing less.

STRATEGIC FRAMEWORKS

It is a recurring experience that when I teach strategic planning, a number of students will inevitably tell me that strategic thinking is particularly difficult and that they believe most of their colleagues will not be able to do it very well. They are absolutely correct. Thinking dynamically across four dimensions (which is beyond our ability to conceptualize) in the abstract and about multiple issues concurrently is certainly not easy. Most of us, as is the case in performing any skillful act, achieve at best a proficiency level of average. Of course, since we know that strategy is the struggle for advantage, if deep and far-reaching strategic thinking was simple and could be done with excellence by all effortlessly, it would be of little competitive value.

So, as illustrated in Figure 2.11, to improve the efficacy of our strategic planning and rise above a level of mediocrity, rather than trying to go directly from strategic thinking to strategic actions, we

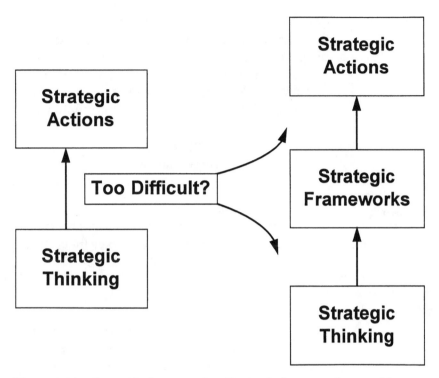

Figure 2.11 Strategic frameworks. Strategic frameworks provide insightful help in performing strategic thinking.

cheat and use strategic frameworks as strategy aids. Strategic frameworks are methods developed and offered by academics, consultants, and practitioners that capture some important strategic insights and package them in away that makes them usable by many. The more substantive the framework, the easier it is to use, but the shorter it will be applicable because of changing times and circumstances. The more abstract or generic the framework, the harder it will be to use, but the longer it will be current as it provides abstract ideas that have to be interpreted according to time and circumstance. The teachings of the greatest strategists such as Sun Tzu and Miyamoto Musashi are aphoristic in nature and maintain their eternal relevance by presenting abstract ideas that need to be reinterpreted for each time and circumstance. Most of the popular strategy books that are published each year are substantive and quickly surrender their value. Whether substantive or abstract strategic frameworks are selected, they can be a tremendous help to the beleaguered strategist as long as they are used as thought stimulators to provoke debate and insight but not for the purpose of mindlessly filling in the blanks.

Table 2.2 summarizes some of the most popular strategic planning frameworks. We will now review five frameworks that are particularly helpful to understanding the information age and IT fighting.

Table 2.2
Strategy Frameworks

Strategic Planning Framework	Definition
Critical Success Factors	The identification of the key things that absolutely must be done well to compete.
Strength, Weakness, Opportunity & Threat, (SWOT) Analysis	A thorough analysis of your environment from the perspectives of: • What are your strengths to be nurtured. • What are your weaknesses to be addressed. • What opportunities are being presented to you. • What threats to your success are emerging that need to be parried.
Value Chain Analysis	An analysis and decomposition of a value chain to determine opportunities to increase speed, reduce cost, or increase value.
Five Force Analysis (Figure 1.22)	A methodology to determine the relative importance of five key forces and their associated factors on your competitive position.
Bottleneck Analysis	The investigation of a process to discover and eliminate process bottlenecks.
Benchmarking	The comparison of yourself to best in class to determine your relative performance standing and to stimulate ideas about how to improve your performance.
Distribution Chain Analysis	A methodology to analyze the status and direction of your distribution channels.
Kano Methodology (Figure 2.9)	A methodology that stimulates thinking about what will excite your customers and then shows how to use strategic paradox to optimize your implementation.
Gap Analysis	A methodology that calls for comparing a current and desired future state to determine the gap between them and to stimulate thinking about how to close the gap.

Strategy Framework 1. Technological Substitution and Diffusion

The dynamic of change that fuels our industry is best understood as the recurring phenomenon of *technological substitution and diffusion*. Technological substitution is the process by which one technology displaces another technology in performing a function or set of functions for a market. The substitute technology offers the customer an inducement to switch by virtue of an improved value proposition. Diffusion is the process by which a marketplace learns about a substitute technology. Diffusion provides an understanding of the logic and speed of switching by customers. So substitution is the process by which one technology challenges and replaces another, and diffusion is the process through which the substitute is accepted/rejected by the marketplace. Market diffusion is the dynamics of market acceptance of the substitution of a new product for an existing product.

Technological substitution and diffusion theory teaches that the life cycle of a technology can routinely be illustrated through the use of S curves (Figure 2.12). The basic logic of an S curve is as follows:

- All technologies should/must be understood in terms of performance limits. As investments are made in a technology, its price/performance improvement will follow an S curve shape but eventually flatten out as it reaches its limit. For example, the performance limits of current microprocessor technology will be limited by fabrication costs, lithography tools, and shrinking micron widths.
- At first, Stage 1, the product will be incomplete and expensive and only appealing to a niche market with very specific objectives for using the product. All technologies are born deformed.
- In Stages 2 and 3, dramatic improvements are made in the product. For every dollar invested in improving the product, there is a significant greater return in its value proposition. There is an intense rush of innovation to improve the product. The movement of a technology up the S curve with the associated periodic release announcements is formally called *successive generations*.
- In Stage 4, the limits of the technology are reached. It is increasingly difficult to squeeze out improvements. For every dollar invested in R/D, less than a dollar in added value is generated.

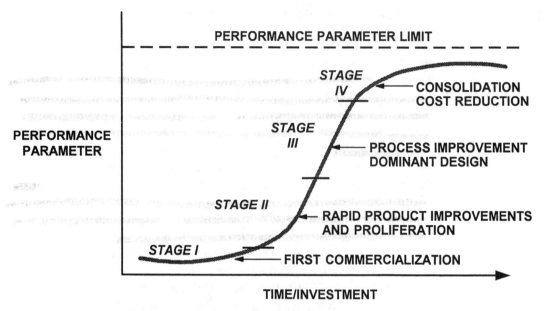

Figure 2.12   Technological substitution and diffusion. The evolution of many technologies follows an S-curve pattern.

In technological diffusion and substitution jargon, the incumbent product is referred to as the *defender* and the substitute product is referred to as the *attacker*. As shown in Figure 2.13, there is a marketplace battle of dueling S curves as the defender struggles to defend its incumbency and the attacker strives to displace it.

The speed of diffusion is a function of:

• Value proposition: How superior is the value proposition of the attacker to the defender?
• Infrastructure: How much infrastructure support must be put in place to support the new product?
• Learning: What communication channels are used to reach, persuade, and influence the market?
• Ease of substitution: How much effort (time, cost, training, etc.) is required to adopt the attacker?
• Defense: How does the defender defend itself and, in doing so, alter the comparative value propositions?

Diffusion and substitution are usually expressed in terms of market share.

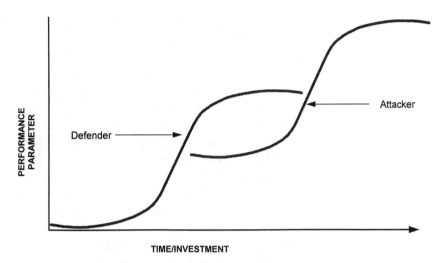

Figure 2.13 **Attacker and defender. The history of economic progress is the history of an established technology on an S curve being attacked by a more innovative technology on a superior S curve.**

The IT community is often unreasonably impatient when it comes to diffusion. It is common to see articles lamenting the disappointing penetration and growth of this or that hyped technology. In practice, diffusion often takes much longer than we would like or imagine. For example, consider the diffusion time periods within the US for the following no-brainer technologies:

- Electric lights took approximately 50 years to achieve a 95% diffusion level.
- The radio took approximately 35 years to achieve a 95% diffusion rate.
- The telephone took approximately 80 years to achieve a 90% diffusion rate.
- Television took approximately 30 years to achieve a 90% diffusion rate.

By their very nature, IT technologies that are capital-, infrastructure-, and skill-intensive require time to diffuse. Success should be measured by steady S curve growth in market share, not by market scenarios that have no relationship to the governing realities of S curve theory.

Understanding S curves and interpreting events in terms of them is a crucial skill for all IT strategists. Much of the technological change that dominates our industry is best explained, interpreted, and reacted to through the lens of S curves. If you do not think in S curves, change becomes an emotionally laden event as opposed to the pragmatic decision-making process of deciding when and if to jump S curves. For example, S-curve "when and if analysis" can be of great assistance in analyzing the current attack of the Web PC on traditional PCs, Web groupware on Lotus Notes, and the substitution of the Internet for private wide area networks.

We can illustrate how an S curve perspective of the world can provide welcomed relief to the IT strategist as follows:

- *Know-How Curves:* Figure 2.14 illustrates that each S curve has a corresponding and shadow-like know-how curve that mirrors its life cycle. The know-how curve reflects the accumulated knowledge that has been gathered on how to exploit the technology. When you move between S curves, it is often the case that rather than jumping curves, you take a giant step where for some period of time you have one foot on the new S curve but the other foot on the old know-how curve. It is therefore not surprising that the initial experiences with new technologies almost always prove disappointing; you need time to develop the missing but much needed know-how. The implications for IT fighting are as follows:
  - Understand the existence and implications of the shadow know-how curve for each S curve.
  - Anticipate the paucity of know-how when you switch curves and plan appropriately. You must either plan to throw one away (prototyping), or buy assistance from those who already have the know-how.
  - Your know-how can be a source of competitive advantage. You should carefully consider whether it is truly advisable to share your know-how, and by doing so enhance the ability of others, including your competitors, to climb know-how curves quickly and erase your hard-won knowledge.
- *Thrashing:* The reason to jump S curves is to achieve a new feature/performance benefits with a finite time period. If there are simultaneous S curve attacks occurring (the attacker herself is being attacked while attacking), if you jump curves too often, within a finite time period, you may experience the

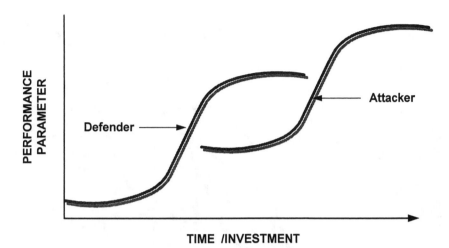

Figure 2.14 Know-how curves. Each S curve has a shadow know-how curve that reflects the cumulative knowledge of how to exploit the technology.

anomaly of thrashing. Thrashing occurs when, because of too many jumps (even though you have the potential for better price/performance) within your time window, you are actually worse off than had you not jumped or, at least, not jumped as often. Figure 2.15 illustrates thrashing. In the example shown, the user would have been best off to make only one jump. By making the second jump, she is actually worse off then had she stayed with the original technology. Since the information age demands exceptional use of the most advantageous IT to engage in IT fighting, IT strategists should carefully consider the time effect of their S curve jumps. By jumping too infrequently, you leave yourself in a position of technological inferiority. By jumping too often, you thrash. Managing IT in an environment of simultaneous S curve attacks requires:

- A deep understanding of S curve theory.
- An understanding of business needs to guide your choice of new technologies.
- Seasoned judgment.

Thrashing is an excellent example of the strategic paradox of the coming together of opposites, or that you can have too much of a good thing.

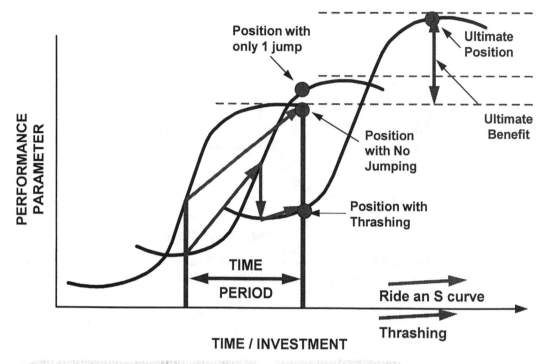

Figure 2.15   Thrashing. If you jump S curves too often within a finite time period, you
                may be worse off than if you did not jump curves at all.

The very act alone of thinking about your technological choices
in terms of S curves will radically improve your ability to choose
both what new technologies to invest in and when to invest in
them. Though exaggerated, but only slightly so, with apologies to
the Beach Boys who wanted you to catch a wave, if you catch an S
curve at the right time, you can be sitting on top of the world.

Strategy Framework 2. Scenarios

Scenarios provide a structured way to define possible futures,
understand the causation chains that lead to those futures, and
develop options and strategies to deal with the uncertainties. A
causation chain is a time-ordered set of events that moves you from
a start state, the world today, to a plausible end state. Figure 2.16
illustrates scenario thinking.

Figure 2.16 **Scenarios. Scenarios provide a way to speculate about alternative futures and how those futures may emerge.**

Scenarios provide a structured context to stretch your thinking about what may happen and prepare for the eventualities. For desired futures, you can develop actions to help make them happen. For undesirable futures, you can develop actions to block them from unfolding. Where multiple futures share a common pivotal event, you can position yourself on that event so that you are prepared to spring in multiple directions.

Scenario exercises offer the following benefits:

- They force an external focus. Rather then maintaining a provincial view of the world, you are motivated to take a fresh and open view.
- They stimulate deep, creative, and insightful thinking. It takes the complete resources of a team to imagine the future.

- They broaden your understanding of what drives the IT industry. What you take as conventional wisdom today may or may not still hold tomorrow.
- They challenge and provoke community learning. They are a shared experience that forces everyone to think out of the comfortable box.
- They prepare you to recognize futures as they emerge; you can face the future in a state of informed alertness.

Scenarios and S curve theory strongly complement each other, and it is highly advantageous to mix the new techniques in your strategic thinking.

When you think about the future in terms of scenarios, you open your planning to the following options:

- You can hedge your bets and prepare for multiple futures.
- You can emphasize making reversible decisions.
- You can stagger your initiatives and commitments.
- You can keep resources in reserve.
- You can choose actions that permit meeting multiple futures.
- You can maintain a state of hyper-vigilance, watch for the emergence of a winning scenario, and react quickly to it.

The ability to position yourself in any or all of these ways is highly compatible with mediating the necessity to take deliberate actions while coping with the heightened uncertainties and risks of our times.

Strategy Framework 3. Core Competencies

Core competencies represent the collective learning of an organizational community. They emphasize especially hard-to-coordinate, diverse skills that integrate multiple streams of technologies. They provide the *roots* of competitive advantage because they can be leveraged to develop and support multiple products for varied markets.

Core competencies have the following defining attributes:

- They provide access to a wide variety of markets.
- They make a significant contribution to customer's perceived benefits of the product.

- They are difficult to imitate; they are sustainable.
- They often represent the complex coordination of multiple heterogeneous technologies and applied skills.

Core competency provides a highly leveraged environment by substituting competence for capital. Core competency-driven organizational units maintain a portfolio of competencies that enable them to create/evolve a portfolio of products for a collection of markets. Figure 2.17 illustrates a core competency diagram and, most importantly, demonstrates their leverage quality.

The obvious impact on IT fighting of core competencies is that you need to carefully reflect on what those core competencies are to be and how they should be defined. Speculating on what your set of competencies should be is expedited by coordinating such an activity with the other strategic frameworks of scenarios and S curves. For each scenario future, what competencies would I need to master it? If attacking technology S curves win, what competencies will I need to master? Conversely, if I believe this is a set of

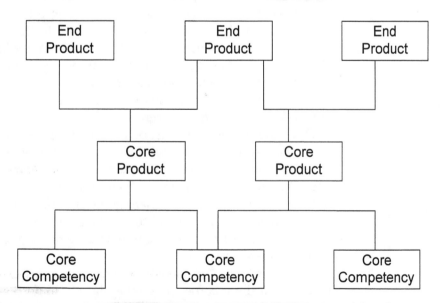

Figure 2.17   Core competencies. Core competencies provide a framework to relate competencies to end products and services in a high-leverage manner.

winning competencies, what scenarios must win and what S curves must prevail?

The more interesting implication of core competencies is the impact on staffing and competency definition. Many IT employees have historically associated their professional identifies very strongly with specific technologies. So, you can imagine people wearing ID cards that say "I am DB2" or "I am C language" or "I am Powerbuilder." This is totally incompatible with the needs of a fluid IT organization.

Staffing and career policies need to promote the notion that the value of staff members is a function of their generic specialty as opposed to the temporary instance of that specialty that they happen to be working on at the time. An individual who does database design for Oracle is of value because she is a database design expert who happens to be applying those valuable skills to an Oracle problem, as opposed to an Oracle database expert whose mission in life is to preserve her skills investment in Oracle against any and all enroachments by substitute technologies.

It is very important to define competencies in terms of their generic skills, and to promote a strong distinction between what a person's competency is and the short-term application of that competency. If employees associate their value to the organization in terms of generic competencies, they will be more likely to accept change. If my ID card reads "I am a database performance maven," I have much less to fear and resist from a decision to bring in Oracle when I have been working on DB2 then if my ID cards reads "I am a DB2 performance maven."

Of all the things that must be designed for flexibility and speed, the human resources are the most crucial. Musashi said: "It is dangerous for a warrior to know only one thing." People invest a great deal of themselves in their work and will fight bitterly to preserve that investment. How you manage your staff perceptions of their competencies will be critical to creating a fluid infrastructure that will allow you to zig and zag in harmony through changing times and circumstances.

Sun Tzu taught: "Those who are good at taking care of problems, take care of them before they take place." Of all the problems that you can take preemptive actions to deter, the most important are people issues. Remember, technology either works or it doesn't, and with time and money, you generally can make it work. Technology doesn't push back; people do.

Strategy Framework 4. Dominant Logic

A dominant logic is a pervasive and universally accepted logic of how an industry works and how you compete in that industry. A dominant logic does not usually have to be defended, and actions contrary to the dominant logic are automatically held suspect. It could also be referred to as the conventional wisdom of the times.

Table 2.3 provides a structure to document historical, contemporary, and a projected dominant logic for your industry and the associated logic of IT assets needed to support that logic. The reasoning of the framework is:

- How is it generally agreed that you win in this industry today and how do you deploy IT assets to make that happen?
- How is it generally agreed that you won in this industry five years ago and how did we deploy IT assets to make that happen?
- How will you win in this industry five years from now and how will IT have to be deployed to make that happen?

While this framework is built on conventional wisdom and progress is made by breaking conventional wisdom, conventional wisdom is often not only conventional, it is often right and, as a

Table 2.3
Dominant Logic

D o m i n a n t L o g i c					
5 years Ago		**Today**		**5 Years into the Future**	
How do you win?	How do you deploy IT assets to win?	How do you win?	How do you deploy IT assets to win?	How do you win?	How do you deploy IT assets to win?

component of your strategic thinking, can provide interesting insights. The common and ordinary often have much to teach and can always be a good starting point for learning. You can also do the technique of substituting *Best in Class* for conventional wisdom, as well as vary the time frames to get other thought-provoking results. As was the case with core competencies, it should be obvious how nicely this technique integrates with S curves and scenarios in projecting futures.

IT strategy both impacts business strategy and enables it. As John McGraw said, "The idea of the game is to win." The problem for the IT strategist is understanding how the business wants to win so that IT assets can be selected and deployed to both influence how they will win and enable that winning to occur. Dominant logic provides a remarkably simple but highly enlightening framework to conceptualize this information, achieve a consensus on how IT can be used to win, and develop a shared agenda of what needs to be done to make it happen.

Strategy Framework 5. Reach, Range, and Maneuverability

Reach, Range , and Maneuverability (Figure 2.18) is an IT-specific framework that suggests that IT strategic decisions should be deliberated in terms of three fundamental and overarching vectors:

- *IT Architecture Reach:* IT architecture investment should focus on continually increasing the reach of the architecture. Reach defines who can access information, from where, with what security, with what interfaces, and in what mode (wireless or wired). The domain of reach includes both within and outside the company and enables creating virtual organizational structures and bonding with value chain partners.
- *IT Architecture Range:* IT architecture investment should focus on continually increasing the range of the architecture. Range defines what forms and structures of information (simple files, text databases, multimedia databases, messages, distributed databases, etc.) can be accessed. Like reach, the domain of range is both within and outside the company and enables creating virtual organizational structures and bonding with value chain partners.
- *IT Architecture Maneuverability:* IT architecture investment should focus on continually increasing the maneuverability of

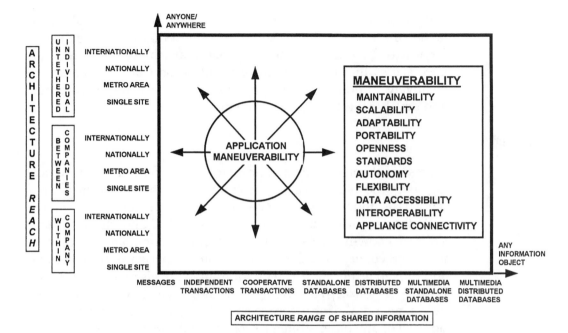

Figure 2.18   Reach, range, and maneuverability. New technologies may be evaluated strategically in terms of how they extend reach and range, and improve maneuverability.

the architecture. Maneuverability defines the options available to alter the configurations of hardware and software. Typical maneuverability issues are portability, scalability, adherence to standards, reconfigurability, and modularity.

One way to understand Figure 2.18 is to view it as a ouija board. Using reach and range as the borders of the game board, you would like to be able to maneuver your applications at maximum speed and minimum cost anywhere on the board. Reach, range, and maneuverability define the battlefield of IT fighting.

Reach, range and maneuverability provide a very powerful framework from which to think strategically about IT. It suggests that the strategic decision making is actually straightforward though not simple. Given a finite budget and a set of user demands, what combination of moves that increase reach, range, maneuverability will yield the maximum utility to the business. The permanent quest of IT strategy is to achieve the unobtainable state of perfect reach, perfect range and perfect maneuverability. It is the differences in the pursuit of that quest that will make the difference to IT fighting. Those companies that achieve the correct balance across the three dimensions will be best able to maneuver creatively to build new advantages, sustain existing advantages, and devalue the advantages of competitors.

Conclusion

Professional consultants and academics have a sustainable advantage over the average corporate IT strategist; they do strategy on a daily basis under a variety of stimulating circumstances. They have both the cognitive knowledge of know-what and the execution skills of know-how. As a consequence, they are able to trial their ideas and convert their hands-on learning experiences into reusable and proven techniques. The use of frameworks is mandatory for all IT strategists, except the truly gifted, and, as you have seen, can provide a great deal of structure to assist in the analysis of the information age or any other strategic problem that confronts you.

STRATEGIC PLANNING

Strategic planning provides a context with an associated structured process in which to develop a plan to build advantage. As illustrated in Figure 2.19, strategic planning consists of three mega-steps:

- *Assessment:* A thorough analysis, from both an internal and external perspective, of what is happening and its potential impact on the business. Assessment ends with the development of a set of succinct conclusions that demand management attention and action.
- *Strategy:* The development of a desired future state and the actions necessary to obtain that future. Strategy ends with the modeling of the desired future, a set of initiatives to realize that future, and change and commitment plans to sustain organizational perseverance to that future.
- *Execution:* The execution and tuning of the actions to achieve the desired future. Execution consists of the strategic monitoring and control of the strategic actions to assure their success.

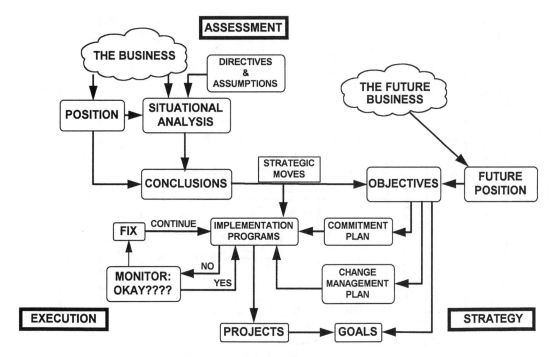

Figure 2.19 Strategic planning. Strategic planning provides a formal methodology to apply strategic thinking to develop a business or IT strategy.

The overarching intent is to move the business from its current state to the desired future state (Figure 2.20).

The success of strategic planing is closely associated with many issues but, most importantly, it is a function of the depth and breadth of the strategic thinking that guides the process. Sun Tzu said:

> When your strategy is deep and far-reaching, then what you gain by your calculations is much, so you can win before you even fight. When your strategic thinking is shallow and near-sighted, what you gain by your calculations is little; so you lose before you do battle. Much strategy prevails over little strategy, so those with no strategy can not but be defeated. Therefore it is said that victorious warriors win first and then go to war, while defeated warriors go to war first and then seek to win.

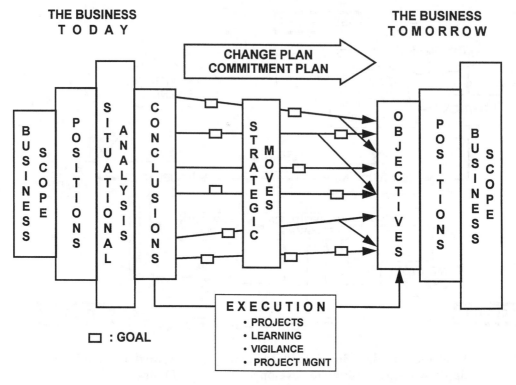

Figure 2.20   Movement. Strategic planning yields a plan to move an organization from its current state to a desired future state.

Strategic frameworks are used throughout the process to stimulate strategic thinking and focus the discovery of issues and their resolution. Table 2.4 summarizes the sub-steps of the strategic planning process. The key to performing all of them is the excellence of your strategic thinking. Those truly gifted in strategic thinking achieve a deep, often unexplainable, and intuitive understanding of the intricate web of cause and effect that actions will yield. Always remember, victory occurs first in your mind.

Formal strategic planning has come into disfavor in recent years and has been subjected to a wide variety of disapproval. Some of the most pressing criticisms are:

- It is too slow and bureaucratic; more dynamic processes are required.
- It is impossible to predict the future; we are better off letting strategy emerge.

Table 2.4
Strategic Planning Sub-Steps

Mega-Step	Sub-Step	Sub-Step Function
Assessment	Business Scope	Defines the current business model in terms of: vision, mission, values, strategic intent, markets, products, geography, competitive advantages, & market style.
	Assumptions and Directions	Documents assumptions, constraints, and directions provided to you by other business entities that will bound your action space.
	Positions	Documents the current state of key strategic areas along one or more strategic dimensions.
	Situational Analysis	Analyzes the state of the business from internal and external perspectives in terms of competition, environmental changes, competencies, technological changes, market changes, etc.
	Conclusions	Generates list of strategic issues that demand management attention and actions with the accompanying rationale.
Strategy	Future Business Scope	Defines a future business model in terms of: vision, mission, values, strategic intent, markets, products, geography, competitive advantages, & market style.
	Objectives and Goals	Defines a specific set of measurable objectives and interim goals to be achieved with associated dates and completion measurements.
	Strategic Actions	Defines specific initiatives to be taken to achieve the objectives.
	Change Plan	Defines specific objectives and actions to enable change while minimizing resistance.
	Commitment Plan	Defines specific objective and actions to be taken to sustain organizational commitment to the strategic plan.
Execution	Programs	Grand projects to realize the strategic actions.
	Projects	Targeted sub-programs.
	Monitoring, Review, and Control	Management control, tuning, and review of strategic progress.

- There is always a lack of commitment to the resulting plan; why bother?
- What we need is action, not more strategy; there is no time to plan.
- The process often degenerates into a financial planning exercise and filling in the blanks.
- Strategic thinking is ignored and replaced by rote extrapolation of the status quo.

My reaction to these criticisms is that *only a poor workman blames [her] tools*. Musashi said: "The weapon in itself is meaningless without the proper application of its virtue by the warrior." Most of these complaints say a lot more about those who are doing the planning then the process itself. My experience is that there is often inadequate training and commitment to the process; not surprisingly, strategic planning suffers as would any process. Companies will invest weeks in training and mentoring before they permit a person to design a database, but strategy work is routinely assigned without any consideration of the required training or preparation.

Regardless of how you go about it, you really have little choice but to follow the Figure 2.19 process. If you don't do assessment, how do you know what you need to focus on? If you don't do strategy, how do you know what to execute? So while the form of the alternative processes varies widely, even the most informal *Ready, Fire, and Aim* approach still has to have those steps performed.

If you are going to engage in IT fighting, you are going to have to be competent in strategic planning. Initiatives need to be holistic. You will need to model where you are, consider the horizontal impacts, model a desired future and create initiatives to move you to the future. Either you create and execute a plan or you execute endless muddling through. If you don't move forward within the backdrop of a deep and far-reaching plan, you will inevitably create a mess even worse than the original one from which you had hoped to escape.

KNOWLEDGE

Strategy is inspired by visionary strategic thinking and implemented through strategic planning built on a solid foundation of knowledge. Vision is a clear and compelling winning image of the future that attracts employee respect, enthusiasm, and commitment. It is normally quite different from a simple linear extrapolation of the present and requires massive changes in how a business operates.

Vision is the highest attainment of knowledge because it means that you have become an *aware* individual. An aware individual is someone who sees what others do not see, knows what others do not know, senses what others do not sense, lays deep plans for what others do not plan, proceeds with assurance when others vacillate, and takes actions based on that which has barely taken shape. Sun Tzu said: "Vision is seeing victory before it exists. This is the strategist's path to strategic triumph." An individual with such exceptional foresight has more than a point of view about the future; she has a plan of how she will impress her attitude on the marketplace, mobilize her resources, overcome all obstacles, and be triumphant in that future.

Knowledge, in its more conventional forms, provides the basis for rational planning. All planning is based on knowledge. Sun Tzu was completely unambiguous on this point:

> Compare the strengths of the enemy with your own and you will *know* whether there is sufficiency or lacking. After that, you can see the advisory of attack or defense. . . . If you *know* others and know yourself, you will not be imperiled in a hundred battles; if you do not *know* others but *know* yourself, you will win one and lose one; if you do not *know* others and do not *know* yourself, you will be imperiled in every single battle. . . . What the aware individual *knows* has not yet taken shape. What everyone *knows* is not called wisdom. A leader of wisdom and ability lays deep plans for what others do not *know*. . . . What enables an intelligent leader to overcome others and achieve extraordinary accomplishments is *foreknowledge*. All matters require *foreknowledge*. . . . It is easy to take over from those who do not plan ahead [emphasis added].

An entire chapter in *The Art of War* is devoted to espionage. In modern terms we would translate espionage to mean market/consumer research, competitive intelligence, and technological/social/economic forecasting. A business that builds its strategy on a foundation of knowledge can engage in a maneuver market strategy. Businesses must always be prepared to respond creatively to marketplace dynamics. As we have suggested, the marketspace will be a marketplace in a state of constant upheaval. It is clear that those companies that can navigate with greater alacrity, speed, and dexterity will have a distinct advantage. In fact, with speed, dexterity, and alacrity as your allies, you can further exaggerate your advantage by deliberately promoting marketplace mayhem to the benefit of your customers and the detriment of your competitors.

Companies take two basic approaches to engaging the marketplace:

1. Attrition Fighter: Marketplace supremacy is achieved by taking a strong but fixed position and "slugging it out" for marketplace dominance. Through confrontational marketplace battles, by concentrating superior assets against inferior foes, you win by exhausting the opponent's will and ability to compete. The optimum situation is to win in a few decisive battles and, by virtue of your proven superior power, deter prospective competitors from stepping into your marketplace and challenging you. An attrition fighter, like a classic heavyweight boxer, wins by brute superiority of assets and the ability to deliver a crushing and decisive knockout blow.

2. Maneuver Fighter: Marketplace superiority is achieved by staying in a state of perpetual motion. A maneuver fighter continually looks for opportunistic gaps in the marketplace and swiftly moves her assets to maximize the opportunity. The maneuver fighter attempts to continually disrupt the marketplace by changing the rules of competition. It is through the actions of movement that advantage is gained. Advantage is best understood as a succession of overlapping temporary advantages rather than a set of sustainable competitive advantages. The maneuver fighter expects that the maneuver process will cause friction and disruption in the ability of her opponents to respond. At best, this will eventually lead to a collapse in her opponents' business systems. A maneuver fighter uses speed, flexibility, opportunism, and dexterity to chip away at the edges of the marketplace until the entire marketplace has been taken. In doing so, unlike the attrition fighter, a deliberate attempt is made to avoid expensive, time-consuming and exhausting confrontations with competitors. You win by artfulness, guile, and indirection; not by brute force.

The information age marks a fundamental marketplace transition from national wars of attrition to global wars of maneuver, and successful companies must internalize this shift.

Sun Tzu described the eternal character of maneuver warfare when he said: "Go forth where they do not expect it; attack where they are unprepared." As advantageous as this is, it is not easy to do. It demands intelligence. Intelligence is both the sense of being smart and having knowledge about your competitors and customers. A maneuver fighter must continually zig and zag. Where and when to zig and zag are crucial decision-making problems. Done well, the maneuver fighter will delight her customers and drive her competitors bonkers. Done poorly, the maneuver fighter will inadvertently zig or zag directly into the attrition fighter who will crush her.

Knowledge is the mandatory prerequisite for a maneuver strategy. An infrastructure of knowledge must be available to engage in maneuver fighting. With a solid infrastructure of accessible information that can be manipulated on demand, the maneuver fighter can make calculated judgments as to where and when to move. Without such knowledge, a maneuver fighter will make one guess too many and be cornered by the behemoth attrition competitor.

An instructive example of such maneuver is happening in the retail industry. Historically, retailers engaged in *push* marketing whereby they purchased large volumes of an item from a supplier and then attempted to convince their customers to buy it. Retailers are now moving to *pull* marketing wherein they attempt to exactly understand what customers want to buy and provide a desired product assortment at ideal value points. The former doesn't require much knowledge about one's customers, while the latter requires a great deal. The push retailer stands still and doesn't need much information while the pull retailer needs precise information to support continuous zigging and zagging to stay slightly ahead of her customers and out of the way of the attrition fighters.

So a crucial way to understand knowledge as a building block of strategy is to understand it as the necessary foundation for changing your business from being a slow and ponderous industrial age attrition fighter to an agile and quick information age maneuver fighter. Attrition fighters stand still across time. If you're going to stand still, of what value is knowledge to you? To the contrary and as illustrated in Figure 2.21, a maneuver fighter is a business in constant motion, an information age IT fighter whose actions are founded on knowledge.

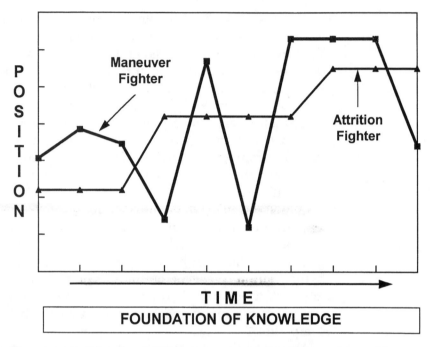

Figure 2.21   Maneuver fighter versus attrition fighter. An attrition fighter stands, moves, and stands, while a maneuver fighter moves, stands, and moves.

Figure 2.22 illustrates the relationship of knowledge to the other aspects of strategy that we have discussed. If you are going to engage in IT fighting, the implication of this is not subject to debate; you must put in place intelligence-gathering processes that enable you to have foreknowledge. IT fighters win through intelligence, not brute force. In this way, by virtue of knowledge-enabled strategic thinking, you act sooner rather than later, you learn rather than repeat, you anticipate rather than react, you know rather than guess, you change rather than atrophy, you exceed rather than satisfy, you avoid rather than being cornered, and, ultimately through the accumulation of *rathers*, you win rather than lose. Who knows, with extraordinary effort, study, tenacity, will, and experience, you may even become one of the few truly aware individuals.

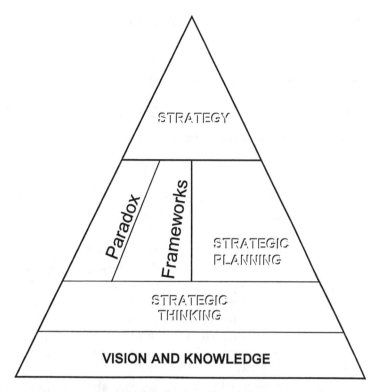

Figure 2.22 Strategic relationships. All aspects of this strategy are built on a foundation of knowledge.

ACTUALITY AND POTENTIALITY

In Miyamoto Musashi's classical book on strategy, *The Five Rings,* he teaches that all weapons have a distinctive spirit. It is the challenge of a warrior to understand that spirit, master it, and become in harmony with it. In that way, there is perfect integration between the warrior and his weapon.

When I think strategically about the information age's distinctive spirit, I think about *time.* More than any other strategic notion, I believe that what competing in the information age means is competing across (not against) time (Figure 2.23).

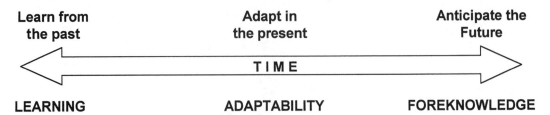

Figure 2.23   Time. In the information age, you compete across time.

The importance of time to strategic thinking has been demonstrated repeatedly in this chapter:

- Sustainable competitive advantage: Time was one of the two key dimensions of sustainability (Figure 2.2).
- Kano Methodology: You create strategic distance between yourself and your competitors that takes them time to bridge and provides you with time to convert another excitement attribute to a threshold attribute (Figure 2.9).
- S curves: Competing technologies duel across time (Figure 2.13).
- Scenarios: We conjecture about future time (Figure 2.16).
- Dominant logic: We analyze winning across time (Table 2.3).
- Reach, range, and maneuverability: We design so that we can endlessly reconfigure our IT assets across time.

Time sits at the heart of all strategic thinking.

One competes across time as follows:

- From the past: One must learn from the past so that the best lessons can be learned and deployed and mistakes not repeated.
- In the present: One must be able to quickly analyze current events so that one can maneuver in real-time to adapt to them.
- From the future: One must have prescience about the future so that opportunistic investments and actions can be taken now to position for an even better tomorrow.

So the strategic ideas that resonate to me from the information age are the time-oriented ones of learning, maneuverability, prescience, and foreknowledge.

These four strategic ideas are not just any set of strategic ideas; they are uniquely important. They are uniquely important because they overlay the time dimension of strategic thinking (Figures 2.4 through 2.8, horizontal axis). What this means is that time is one of the four fundamental dimensions of strategic thought and IT fighting must enable one to directly compete across that dimension. To engage in IT fighting means many things but, most importantly, it means to compete across the primary strategic dimension of time.

This leads one to play an instructive mind game. While unquestionably it would be best of all to be excellent in learning from the past and excellent in maneuvering in the present and excellent in anticipating the future, which one would you choose if you could only be excellent at one? Yes, you of course aspire to be peerless in all, but in the rules of this mental game, you may choose to be superior only in one and will be reduced to mediocrity in the other two. Which do you choose?

While skillful arguments can be made in favor of each choice, with reflection, I believe that you must choose one and only one; the one that must be chosen is the ability to maneuver in the present. The reason for this is that of the three, it is the only one that can compensate for the shortcomings of the others. If you choose superiority in learning from the past, how do you respond effectively when the present turns out to be not subject to the same logic as the past and you are middling in adapting? If you choose superiority in anticipation, how do you respond satisfactorily when the future becomes the present but it varies from your educated guess? If, however, you are superior in adaptability in the present, you can accommodate both failures of learning and failures of anticipation.

Table 2.5 presents this argument in the form of a payoff table. Being maneuverable is what game theorists call the minimax choice; it minimizes your maximum loss. Therefore, at the core of an IT response to the information age must be the ability of the IT organization to enable maneuverability to permit one to compete across time.

How does one put in place a strategy to compete across time? In *The Five Rings*, Musashi provided an answer: "An attack must be executed with quickness, not speed. Attack with power; not strength. There is a great difference between speed and quickness, power and strength. It is the essence of strategy." This aphorism is most confusing. Most would think, contrary to what Musashi states, that those pairs are the same thing. What does he mean?

Table 2.5
Minimax

Time Variable of Excellence	Results if You Do Well	Results if Only Time Variable You Do Well In
Learning from the Past	Excellent Results	Failure
Adaptable in the Present	Good Results	Good Results
Anticipating the Future	Outstanding Results	Failure

I interpret this to mean there is a difference between a strategy of potentiality and a strategy of actuality but that they flow by intent into each other. A strategy of actuality is a specific set of actions taken to achieve a specific set of objectives. You know exactly what it is that you wish to achieve. A strategy of potentiality is a nonspecific set of actions that position you to strike. Since you don't know exactly what will have to be done, or events are in a state of constant flux, you position yourself like a tight spring that is ready and able to uncoil in any direction with tremendous force and quickness when it is decided to release it.

Speed and strength are attributes of potentiality. They represent generic capabilities in a state of readiness. Quickness and force are attributes of actuality. They are speed and strength focused and concentrated for a specific purpose. Potential speed, focused and concentrated, becomes actual quickness. Potential strength, focused and concentrated, becomes actual force. Potentiality flows into actuality. So the essence of strategy, according to Musashi, is to create an infrastructure of potentiality that can swiftly transform itself into actuality at the moment and place of opportunity.

Musashi goes on to to say: "Falling on the enemy is attacking without preconceived ideas as to how to conclude the battle." Musashi's advice, for an environment of extreme conflict, is to enter conflict with a strategy of potentiality and, as events unfold and opportunity emerges, switch with power and quickness to a strategy of actuality.

This is the core of IT fighting. An IT organization must position itself in a state of potentiality that can switch on demand to a state of actuality. This means putting in place a nimble infrastructure that stands, coiled like a tight spring, ready to strike where, when, and how needed. Information age IT fighting is built on the ability to maneuver. You compete across time through a strategy of potentiality.

We discussed earlier how S curves could be of assistance in evaluating the technology attacks of the Web PCs against contemporary PCs, the Internet as a groupware replacement for Lotus Notes, and the Internet as a replacement for the corporate wide area network. If one sets the performance limit against which you analyze the dueling S curves (Figure 2.13) as potentiality, you can see how strategically both the Web PC and the Internet are extremely attractive. They both support a much more dynamic environment than their predecessors. They position you for applications on demand and reach on demand. These would seem to be ideal examples of how an information age IT strategist would like to position herself to be able to maneuver. By using these technologies, as opposed to the defenders, you are always poised to execute any application provided by any service provider and connect to any new value chain partner. So I predict that these attacks will gradually succeed as they progress on their S curves because the attackers offer improved performance against the newly prized performance limit of competing across time. They offer superior potentiality.

CONCLUSION

In this chapter we have intermingled two paths. We have reviewed the concepts of strategy and the application of those concepts to the information age. Strategy is a discipline that requires study and preparation, a discipline that enables one to develop deep and far-reaching conclusions about the information age and IT fighting.

An IT organization that executes a rich strategy of potentiality is an IT organization that will always be in alignment with the business. Alignment has often been thought of as a point-in-time idea. We know that that is hopelessly wrong. The business is in a state of motion and must compete across time. For IT to align with the business, it must also be in a state of motion that mirrors the business motion. So an IT organization that seeks to enable movement will achieve a continuous state of alignment, while an IT organization that executes a strategy of actuality will align but for a moment. Such an organization is called *outsourced*.

Our conclusions are as follows:

- The information age is a period of unprecedented change and the disruption of established norms as we move from a world where atoms are the source of value to a world where bits are the source of value.
- The information age incites competitive fervor.
- The information age changes the rules of advantage. We move from prizing sustainable competitive advantage to prizing throwaway temporary advantages.
- The information age makes IT the means to create temporary competitive advantages. Information age companies engage in IT fighting.
- Strategic paradox becomes common in the information age and makes the illogical logical and the logical illogical. In a world of extreme conflict, bad logic becomes good logic because it is bad logic.
- Strategic thinking leads us to the inference that to compete in the information age means to compete across time.
- To compete across time means to be able to maneuver across time.
- To be able to maneuver means to execute a strategy of potentiality that can dynamically transition to a strategy of actuality.

This is the logic of information age IT strategy. You do not compete in the information age through data centers driven by economy of scale, by casually dispersing computing to the point of anarchy, reengineering individual processes on empty slogans, or empowering aimless and wandering teams. You compete by carefully crafting a state of IT potentiality that is in perfect harmony with the most delicate and barely perceptible cause and effect relationships of the information age. We will demonstrate in later chapters that you implement a strategy of potentiality by creating *strategic configurations of power.*

3
Strategic Ideas

INTRODUCTION

In Chapter 1, we concluded that the first response, and the response from which all other responses come forth, is strategic acumen. Conflict, the petulant child of competition, promotes the need for strategic competence. The hyper-competitive nature of the information age makes elevating your strategic acumen to a peerless level a nondiscretionary act. How else will you be able to respond to the swirling changes about you in an insightful, timely, and favorable manner?

In Chapter 2, we introduced the notion of strategic ideas (Figure 2.7). A strategic idea is a strategic theme that, over time, has proven itself as a beneficial way to think about strategic problems. Strategic themes provide time-proven guidance in navigating and managing the limitless strategic thought bubble.

Suppose the strategic issue of concern was IT architecture. One might wish to think about what strategic actions are necessitated in terms of the strategic ideas of commitment, change, formlessness, speed, flexibility, friction, and alliances. For example, for the issue of architecture, what might I do to optimize alliances with vendors, promote organizational commitment to adherence, and increase its flexibility? Strategic ideas provide a starting point for productive thinking about the problem.

In the remainder of this chapter, we are going to focus on strategic ideas. We will divide strategic ideas into two groups: business strategic ideas and classical strategic ideas. Table 3.1 is a representative list of business strategic ideas. As these are quite

Table 3.1
Business Strategic Ideas

Strategic Business Idea	Description
Barriers to Entry	Hurdles that dissuade competitors from entering a market.
Cost	Drive all non-value-creating costs out of a process.
Economies of Learning	The efficiency of a process is a function of the learning curve.
Economies of Scale	The efficiency of creating a product is a function of the volume of the product produced.
Economies of Scope	The efficiency of a production process is a function of the number of products that the process can support.
Economies of Substitution	The efficiency of a product is a function of evolving its modularity as each component rides its own S curve.
Exit Barriers	Barriers that dissuade competitors from leaving a market.
Key Buying Factors	The variables that determine the ultimate reasons that a customer buys a product.
Location	Advantage by virtue of a physical site.
Market Ambition	The intent (defend, grow, challenge, harvest, retreat, etc.) of your market actions.
Parallelism	Efficiency is a function of the ability to do process steps in an overlapping matter.
Pricing	The price at which a market is created.
Retention	It is less expensive to retain a customer than acquire a new one.
Stakeholder Satisfaction	The interests of all stakeholders, employees, owners, and management must be served.
Strategic Intent	The long-term ambition of your efforts.
Synergy	Overall efficiency is a function of the ability of different products to stimulate demand for each other.
Value Proposition	The total value of all features of a product that a customer buys.

familiar to most people, we will not give emphasis to them. For the selected classical ideas, we will provide an analysis in the following format:

- Strategic Idea: the name of the idea.
- Quotation: a quotation from Sun Tzu (ST), Miyamoto Musashi (MM), B. H. Liddell-Hart (LH), or Machiavelli (NM) that provides insight into the idea.
- Description: a short description of the idea.
- IT Fighting: what the idea suggests about the business intent, conduct and nature of IT fighting.

In this way, we engage in leverage by learning about strategic ideas and applying them to our immediate problem at the same time.

While they are abstractions, strategic ideas also have a eminently practical character. Some ideas are combinations of other ideas. Some ideas overlap with other ideas. Some ideas are variant of each other that accentuate different nuances. Some ideas exist in logical relationships to others. They do not, as a collection, present the elementary rigor of a scientific taxonomy of primary constructs.

Not surprisingly, strategic ideas converge on the notion of advantage through movement. In strategic conflict, the way to win is through opportunistic adaptability. You must be like lightning at the point and moment of opportunity. Such quickness is not an accident; it is the consequence of prepositioning yourself with the generic capabilities of speed and flexibility. This message resonates throughout the strategic themes and is why we have, again, recommended a strategy of potentiality for the IT organization as the only carefully deliberated response to the wildly competitive information age.

THE IDEAS

The following are 50 powerful strategic ideas with an associated interpretation of their implications for IT fighting. The ideas are presented in alphabetical order; there is no notion of a priority ordering. The relative priority of a strategic idea is not a function of the strategic idea but a function of the strategic issue, your insights, and the times and circumstances.

Strategic Idea: Action (Execution)

Quotation. Some rulers are fond of words but do not transfer them into deeds. (ST)

Description. Strategy has always consisted of the intertwined trinity of assessment, the strategic plan, and execution. While all three steps are vitally important, consistent with the times and circumstances, different ones rise to prominence. While the business leadership has always been frustrated by the time and cost of acting on their information-based initiatives, the information age elevates their sense of urgency to a near-panic level because the information age is an era of action. If you wait, you miss the fleeting window of opportunity. Time is the critical variable in a war of movement based on temporary competitive advantages. Many are fond of words and do not act because the frozen and glacial nature of their IT infrastructure obstructs them from doing.

IT Fighting. Speed and agility replace the mantra of cost as the first vector of IT decision making. You are no longer building an application; you are building a living organism that has to continuously evolve. The optimum solution is not a point-of-time solution, it is an across-time solution. Your information systems are inherently strategic because they must enable you to compete across time (Figure 2.23). The tactical problem presented to you by your clients is a business system that they want now. The strategic problem is a living business system subject to continuous revision. If the information systems cannot maneuver with limitless adaptability, how will they act, react, act, react, and so on. The only solution to this is a strategy of potentiality that focuses on building strategic configurations of IT power.

Strategic Idea: Advantage

Quotation. Struggle means struggle for advantage; those who get the advantage are victorious. (ST)

Description. Advantage is the margin between your ability and your competitor's ability to satisfy customer key buying factors. Over time, customers gravitate to those suppliers who fulfill their key buying factors in a superior manner. Without advantage, products and services are reduced to a commodity state and prices fall towards cost.

IT Fighting. In the information age, the character of advantage changes from the prior industrial age and becomes IT-centric. Table 3.2 summarizes some of the changes in the nature of advantage and how IT is instrumental in enabling them. The dominant advantage that IT can provide in the information age is the ability to maneuver, without friction or hesitation, in harmony with the continually shifting requirements of the marketplace. The historical emphasis

Table 3.2
Information Age Advantage

Industrial Age Advantage	Information Age Advantage	IT Advantage Role
Mass production	Mass customization	Create customized information-based products at moment of sale.
Mass marketing	One-one marketing	Marketing customized to the personalized needs of each customer.
Function chains optimized for each information form	One information function chain	Single networked interactive multimedia interaction with customer.
Customer is basis for research into product	Customer participates in designing product	IT enables customer to be first step in value chain.
Physical value chain efficiency	Information value chain efficiency	IT enables completely electronic value chains for information-based products and services.
Physical collaboration with suppliers	Information-based collaboration with suppliers	IT enables electronic joining of value chains.
Excellence in customer service	Self-service	IT enables disintermediation.
Physical location	Virtual globalization	IT enables reaching global marketplace.
Physical products delivered to door	Virtual products delivered to information appliance	IT provides infrastructure for delivery of virtual products.
Knowledgeable sales help	Software agents	Software agents search for and negotiate optimum purchase arrangements in cyberspace.

on building sustainable competitive advantage is replaced with an emphasis on constructing a continuous and overlapping flood of information-based temporary competitive advantages.

Strategic Idea: Alliances

Quotation. When there are many more then one against you, you must even the sides as quickly as possible. (MM)

Description. Customers buy products based on the total value proposition that is offered at a given price. Alliances with other members of your value chain—suppliers, distributors, and so on—permit you to enrich the value proposition and create advantage. The intricate integration of the value chain permits the creation of a value proposition that cannot be achieved when you work at arm's length from your collaborators. This is due to the holistic nature of the value-creating process.

IT Fighting. Use IT to integrate the value chain and drive out all inefficiencies and friction in the product creation process. While you and your suppliers are legally distinct companies, IT-based collaboration can enable you to be one continuous virtual company. Groupware, e-mail, EDI, videoconferencing, database access, and so on can all be used to create processes, collaborative efficiency, and effectiveness that elevates the value proposition for the customer.

Strategic Idea: Assessment

Quotation. Compare the strength of the enemy with your own and you will know whether there is sufficiency or lacking. After that, you can assess the advisory of attack or defense. (ST)

Description. To compare requires information. To have access to information means to be able to apply your intellect to create knowledge. One can engage in assessment based on wishful thinking, self-aggrandizement, or on factual information. As the information age consequence of assessment will be strategic initiatives that demand action, the richer the information base, the higher the likelihood of favorable movement and outcomes. The eternal decision-making problem of what to do has become even more conspicuous because one cannot stand still when the marketplace changes at ever-increasing velocity. One must take action but which?

IT Fighting. IT will be used extensively to provide information on the environment to be assessed. Data warehousing with information being sourced both from internal operational databases and external information providers will be critical to enable prudent assessment of the situation as it is in truth. A fundamental principle of strategy is that one must proceed based on an understanding of the situation as it is in fact. Otherwise, one proceeds from a state of fantasy with the predictable results. IT structures that permit timely assessment of situations will be a major avenue for IT investment.

Strategic Idea: Boldness

Quotation. It is better to be bold than cautious. (MM)

Description. A bold act is an act for which success is uncertain but from which you can accept a setback. This is opposed to a gamble where you bet everything on a high-risk action. The information age will lend itself to bold acts. While decision making is historically risk-adverse, the marketspace will reward the bold. It will reward the bold because the information age ushers in a purer form of capitalism where success is highly correlated to risk. So in a marketplace where imitation will, as always, be flattering but will often be too little too late, boldness will be the means to delight customers. Table 3.3 summarizes the relationship of boldness to other ideas.

IT Fighting. Boldness is a special form of acting. It is a form of extreme acting where speed and accommodation are even more crucial. IT, to be of value to bold leadership, will be IT that is expected to deliver in months, not years, and in weeks, not months.

Table 3.3
Boldness

	Act is Successful	Act is Unsuccessful
Common Conservative Risk Adverse Actions	Incremental Improvement in Competitive Position	Incremental Worsening of Competitive Position
Boldness	Large Improvement in Competitive Position	Recoverable Loss
Gamble	Rescue of Competitive Situation	All Is Lost

You must design your strategic configurations of power to permit speed, speed, and even more speed. Speed is mandatory to execute the bold move, to reinforce and exploit success, and to recover promptly if unsuccessful. If they are bold and you cannot be bold, then you will always be a follower. Being a follower in a world of temporary competitive advantages means that you concentrate your forces at the point of opportunity after the time of opportunity has waned. This is not the way of winning.

Strategic Idea: Chance (Fortune)

Quotation. Some princes flourish one day and come to grief the next without appearing to have changed in character or in any way. This I believe arises because those princes who are utterly dependent on fortune come to grief when their fortune changes. I also believe that those who adapt their policies to the times prosper, and those whose policies clash with the times do not. This explains why prosperity is ephemeral. If times and circumstances change, he will be ruined if he does not change his policy. If he changed his character to the times and circumstances, then his fortune would not change. (NM)

Description. Fortune is the eternal wild card. To cope with chance, as Machiavelli said, one must adapt one's policies to the times and circumstances. Information age use of IT, as was illustrated in Figure 1.30, is quite different than industrial age use. In the industrial age, the dependence of the business on IT was high but the impact was low. IT was therefore optimized to run the information processing factory. In the information age, the dependence of the business on IT is high and the impact of IT on the business is high. It is therefore necessary to optimize IT for its strategic value to create growth. If you do not make this change, your IT policies will clash with the times and you will be ruined.

IT Fighting. Downsizing and other forms of corporate anorexic behavior are inherently self-limiting and doomed strategies. They are self-limiting strategies because the more they are applied, the less one can use them again. Good strategy is open-ended. Sooner or later, to remain a viable enterprise, you must grow. In the information age, IT must be used as an engine for growth. Deploy IT to optimize the value chain and the customer touch experience. Use

IT to collect information about customers as you sell to them so that your next sale can be even more personalized.

Strategic Idea: Change

Quotation. As new weapons are developed, they should also be studied with the proper intent. (MM)

Description. As we discussed in Chapter 2, Figures 2.12 through 2.15, the engine of economic progress is dueling S curves. If there was not an endless progression of challengers, eventually we would hit the performance limit and productivity improvement would cease. The IT discipline, perhaps more than any predecessor technology area, is subject to rapid technological substitution but suffers from all the normal human friction that resists diffusion.

In my prior book, *Cost-Effective Strategies for Client/Server Systems*, I focused on the example of The Mainframe Preservation Society, a fraternal organization for those who have chosen to be left behind. They seem to believe that one understands and masters the universe by studying only one planet within it. Unwilling to jump S curves, they engage in the friction activity of slowing and delaying the inevitable assent of distributed computing. The lesson of this experience is that emotive ties to a specific technology can prevent organizations from undergoing orderly and inevitable S curve migrations.

IT Fighting. If we date the modern era of IT starting in 1964 with the announcement and introduction of the IBM 360 architecture, then we would suggest, contrary to what most would suggest, that the first 32 years of the modern era has been the Stage 1 (Figure 2.12) part of the IT S curve. With convergence, the S curve wars will accelerate in frequency and ferocity. S curve cycles will shrink and attacks will quicken.

The only reason to jump S curves is to gain advantage. Resistance to change built on emotional attachments to databases, operating systems, compilers, development tools, transaction monitors, and other temporary technologies defines organizational friction. IT management must focus on shifting staff allegiance to their generic skills rather than specific manifestations of those skills so that resistance to change is eliminated. IT technologies are the weaponry of IT fighting. If your competitors study and adapt them with the proper intent and you do not, you concede advantage to them. Frictionless absorption of new weaponry is of vital importance. Since you understand holistic thinking, you understand that you cannot be technologically current and competent if you can't get people to change. The human element of change management is a critical IT competency.

Strategic Idea: Command and Control

Quotation. Those skilled in military operations achieve cooperation in a group so that directing the group is like directing a single individual with no other choice. (ST)

Description. In another part of *The Art of War,* Sun Tzu said: "Strategy is a problem of coordination not masses." This idea is applicable to IT fighting in two ways: one is the issue of technological coordination, and the other the issue of human collaboration. One must put in place infrastructure processes and practices that structurally promote community success by motivating all to work as one, knowingly and unknowingly, towards a shared winning agenda.

IT Fighting. The strategic configurations of power of architecture and the economy are intended to achieve these ends. Architecture is the means to technological coordination. It provides the rules for orderly information exchange so that the information systems of those who do not even know of each other, work together. Led by the invisible hand of the architecture, system developers build systems that inherit the architecture's attributes of interoperability, portability, scalability, reach, range, and reconfigurability. Through no intent of their own, by adhering to the architecture they build systems ready to work with each other.

The design of the business economy promotes collaboration inside of the corporation just as marketplace mechanisms promote collaboration in the public marketplaces. Economic rewards work to voluntarily align self-interests across those who do not even know each other. Through this configuration of power you achieve cooperation of the efforts of many as though one. You achieve this cooperation, not through stifling and bureaucratic-demanding command and control procedures, but through mechanisms that structurally achieve your desired ends.

Strategic Idea: Cohesion (Morale, Espirit de Corp)

Quotation. This way means inducing the people to have the same aim as the leadership, so that they will share death and share life, without fear of danger. (ST)

Description. The logic of cohesion is as follows: Cohesion yields trust, trust yields commitment, commitment yields belief, and belief yields effort. Herculean effort is what is demanded to compete in a frantic marketplace. You, however cannot create effort. Effort is an outcome. You must create a cohesive environment from which effort spurts due to the concern of each for everyone, and everyone for each.

IT Fighting. We are again confronted by the holistic nature of strategic thinking. IT strategy cannot be limited to just focusing on information technologies, as many technologists would advocate. Average technologies implemented with effort and zeal to win will yield much better results than better technologies implemented with a mediocre effort. Effort is not a technology but it is critical to technological success.

Your technological success is very closely associated with the morale of your staff. They can go through the motions and implement something, or due to their mutual respect and concern for each other they can stretch for success. You do not want or need servile compliance; what you want and need is extended and passionate effort.

This is a function of how they are treated and their affection for each other. You should carefully reflect on whether the modern fad of treating employees as throwaways creates the necessary cohesive workforce that you need to win. The beneficial consequences of cohesion are a product of the whole. Cohesion takes time and demonstrated concern to create. Turnstile employment does not create a cohesive environment and will not result in generating the effort demanded to win. It is refreshing to see the reemergence of books such as *The Loyalty Effect* by Frederick Reichheld, which emphasizes the high correlation of loyalty to success. While most IT executives are consumed with harnessing MIPS and bytes, they will be better served being more attentive to harnessing staff loyalty and the resulting passion to act.

Strategic Idea: Commitment

Quotation. Your attack must be filled with concentration and purpose. A small man can defeat a much larger man and one man can beat many men. Do not permit yourself to be intimidated by their size of the enemy. You can not attack half-heartedly. (MM)

Description. There are two classical stories of commitment; one had it right and one had it wrong. When the Spanish invaded Mexico, they burnt their ships after the conquistadors landed. Seeing the ships in flames and thousands of miles from home, the soldiers understood that they were committed to conquering Mexico. The Trojans, in the *Iliad,* had it backwards. In a great battle scene, they attack the Greek boats with the intent of torching them. If they succeeded, how could the attacking Greeks then leave? Rather than burn the boats, they should have tried to make them shipshape and ready to go.

The point of both these stories is that great results demand great efforts. Blasé efforts are readily abandoned when the doomsayers start bellowing as soon as the inevitable obstacles and barriers present themselves. If you are going to accomplish great things with IT, just as is true with anything else, you will have to commit yourself to the effort. You will have to commit yourself because commitment is what is required to overcome that which will attempt to deny you your prize.

IT Fighting. Commitment transforms staff skepticism and cynicism into effort. Most employees view management initiatives as temporary diversions from their true focus—political shenanigans. They believe, based on hard-won experience, that this too shall pass. Staffs that believe that today's IT initiatives are a temporary diversion that will be long forgotten tomorrow, as management's attention deficit disorder turns itself to something else, will devote themselves half-heartedly to the effort. IT fighting is too important for such games. To earn the effort required, you must demonstrate to your staff the sincerity of your commitment so that they also will commit themselves fully to the effort.

Strategic Idea: Communication

Quotation. Cymbals, drums, banners and flags are used to focus and unify people's ears and eyes. Signals are used to indicate

direction and prevent individuals from going off by themselves.
(ST)

Description. The purpose of communication technologies has not
changed since the times of Sun Tzu. As it was then and remains
today, the purpose is to unify effort. Communications can permit
those who are physically dispersed to be virtually concentrated.
Communications is a technology of alignment.

IT Fighting. Use communication technologies to:

- Destroy time and space barriers to markets (Figure 1.23).
- Exploit networked interactive multimedia.
- Reach mobile employees.
- Bond with value chain partners.
- Communicate change.

As the reach and speed of your communications technology
increases, you can better stay in harmony with or deliberately disrupt the tempo and rhythm of the marketplace to your advantage.

Strategic Idea: Comparative Advantage (Benchmarking)

Quotation. Therefore, use these assessments for comparison, to
find out what the conditions are. That is to say, which political
leadership has the way? Which general has ability? Whose discipline is effective? Whose troops are stronger? Whose officers and
soldiers are better trained? Whose systems of reward and punishment clear? This is how you can know who will win. (ST)

Description. Advantage is only meaningful as a relative concept.
One does not have absolute advantage; one has marginal advan-
tage. It is therefore necessary to know the difference in advantage.
This is known as strategic distance.

IT Fighting. Industrial age IT shops commonly tell you, excitedly,
how big they are. They tell you how many MIPS they manage, how
many terabytes are in their disk farms, and how many transactions
they process per day. An information age IT shop is not interested
in how big they are, they are interested in their relative supremacy
over their competitors. They are, therefore, interested in the differ-

ence in revenue per transaction, the difference in cost per transaction, and the difference in time to create new transactions. They are interested in comparative superiority, which can only be known through benchmarking as a systemic practice.

Strategic Idea: Competitors

Quotation. What motivates competitors is profit. What restrains competitors is harm. Wear enemies out by keeping them busy and not letting them rest. Make them rush about trying to cover themselves and they will not have time to formulate plans. (ST)

Description. The paradox, of course, is that it is your very success that causes competitors to enter your market. It is the bounty of your profits that attracts them.

IT Fighting. The way to handle competitors is not to naively expect them not to come, but to have superior ways to deal with them. The best way to deal with them is to make it too costly for them to compete in your market. Competitors enter markets to make profits, not to engage in exhaustive market battles. Use IT fighting to exhaust their commitment. If you use IT to continuously change the value proposition, excite customer expectations, and to do the unexpected as the routine, they will grow weary of the chase. The way to defeat information age competitors is to use IT to place them on an accelerating treadmill, which dissipates their will to compete. Use maneuver to turn their advantages into disadvantages. Even if they are more efficient than you, what does it matter if what they sell is yesterday's product.

Strategic Idea: Concentration of Force

Quotation. Concentration is the product of dispersion. To maximize your concentration, your opponent must be dispersed. (LH)

Description. Concentration means to concentrate your resources and effort in time and space. Concentration is a relative concept. Though smaller than a competitor in absolute terms, through maneuver, you can be larger at the point and time of marketplace engagement. Since concentration is a relative concept, maximum concentration occurs when you are concentrated and your opponent is dispersed. To maximize your concentration, you must take actions to force your opponent to disperse her resources.

IT Fighting. Concentrating your resources and deconcentrating your opponent's resources is a large part of the underlying strategic logic behind distributed computing. Mainframe against mainframe is a mindless war of attrition. Both you and your opponent are concentrated and the best you can hope for is some marginal advantage. Distributed computing forces a dispersal of computing resources. If you take the initiative, you use communications to reconcentrate your distributed resources at the time and place of opportunity. Your competitor, not knowing your plans, remains dispersed. Rather than the mathematics of advantage being your concentrated computing power less her concentrated computing power, the mathematics of advantage is your concentrated distributed computing less her dispersed distributed computing. So IT fighting must concentrate on making the network the computer so that you can dynamically concentrate computing resources at the point of need with alacrity while your opponent remains dispersed and weak.

Strategic Idea: Contingency

Quotation. Make plans for contingency, even when it appears that they are improvising. (MM)

Description. Contingency deals with low probability events that would have a severe impact on your success should they occur. The purpose of developing a contingency plan is to avoid surprise and paralysis. While most people think of a contingency plan as a prepared reaction to a negative event, it can just as well be an anticipated reaction to an extremely unlikely but favorable event.

IT Fighting. The notion of contingency is an alternative way to think about the recommended strategy of potentiality. A contingency plan prepositions you to react to a scenario that may or may not occur. If it occurs, you are able to respond and prevent a setback or exploit a favorable breakthrough. A contingency plan is a state of potentiality that, on trigger, converts to a state of actuality.

A strategy of potentiality may be understood as a grand contingency plan. It functions at the limits of contingency planning as it prepositions you to react, but with a nonspecific reaction capability; no exact event is being prepared for. If unfolding events were just slow-motion linear extrapolations of the present, there would be no need for a contingency plan. In the information age, a strategy of potentiality sits at the frontier of contingency planning. It defines a new outpost for contingency planning because more is unpredictable than predictable.

Strategic Idea: Deception

Quotation. A military operation involves deception. Even though competent, appear to be incompetent. Though effective, appear to be ineffective. (ST)

Description. The purpose of deception, in classical strategy, is to gain advantage through deliberately misleading an adversary. If your adversary believes that you will do actions A and B, while in truth you are doing action C, they disperse their resources to respond to A and B while your resources are concentrated at C. While the word deception has a dishonorable connotation in modern life, it is simply strategic common sense to lead your opponent on a false and wasteful path. Deception is completely inappropriate in relating to customers.

IT Fighting. The purpose of deception is to accrue the advantage of surprise. If they believe you will do A, and you do B, they are ill-prepared and you gain advantage, at least during their period of recovery. The applicability of deception to IT fighting has less to do with overtly feeding misinformation than it has to do with sharing no information.

It is common in our industry to be applauded for participating in industry events and sharing stories of what we are doing, how we are doing it, and the results. Case study presentations are very well attended and aggressively sought by conference sponsors. While admirable, these common actions would seem strategically counterproductive. Why reduce your competitors' learning curves by sharing your hard-won experience with them? While it certainly would be inappropriate to deliberately present lies or half-truths at a public event to overly mislead, the alternative is to say nothing. If you view knowledge sharing through the lens of deception, one should only publicly share information on what is unimportant.

The reaction to this type of advice is often quite negative and emotional. It often engenders a response such as, If you won't share, than no one will share and we will have no knowledge exchange and no one will sit on the shoulders of another. As an IT strategist for your company, you are not responsible for the actions of the world. Your problem is, do you enable those who would take your profits to do so more easily or do you leave them to their own devices. If others make the decision to share and in doing so, permit you to better plan for them, that is their strategy.

Strategic Idea: Deflection

Quotation. When you attack, you generally have to ward off an attack at the same time. This is called deflection. (MM)

Description. The notion of deflection reminds us that the game of strategy is a game of overlapping moves and counter-moves by intelligent and purposeful antagonists. One does not only have to act, one has to be able to maintain acting while reacting to the anticipated and unanticipated actions of one's opponents. Nobody has a monopoly on good ideas and, just as you are trying to drive your opponent crazy while delighting your customers, your opponents are trying with equal desperation to do the same thing to you. In a marketplace with multiple capable suppliers, you must parry their actions while proceeding with your own. Deflection is, therefore, a higher form of acting in which you both act and react within the same motion.

IT Fighting. The shortest distance between two points in strategic conflict is often not a straight line. While you proceed toward your objective, it is, as a practical matter, often necessary to divert to match or devalue the superior market actions of your competitors This, again, brings forth the primacy of IT maneuverability. To reach your objective, you may have to alter your path a dozen times. Can IT permit you to act and react as one continuous motion, or are your actions disjointed and friction-full transitions?

Consistent with Sunian strategic thinking, it would seem that those who deflect best, are those who keep their opponents busy deflecting. It is therefore necessary that strategic actions be designed with the intent of periodically calving off value. One should not design acts that only deliver at a final big bang. By delivering interim points of value to customers, competitors are coerced to react to you and those busy reacting to you are not busy creating new value propositions that you must react to. So the height of strategic deflecting is achieved when your opponents are kept busy responding to a barrage of temporary competitive advances from you.

Strategic Idea: Dilemma

Quotation. The best way is to operate along a line that offers alternative objectives. For thereby you put your opponent on the horns of a dilemma, which goes far to assure the gaining of at least one objective—whichever is least guarded. (LH)

Description. Placing your opponent on the horns of a dilemma is one of the great classical strategic ideas. By taking a path that permits you to achieve alternative objectives, you maintain your concentration of effort but your opponent, unsure of your intent, divides her resources to match each possibility. Figure 3.1 illustrates the difference between a person who proceeds directly towards an objective and a person who chooses a path that lends itself to multiple objectives. This approach, as well, maintains a high option value for your decision making, as a final choice of objective can be delayed.

IT Fighting. A dilemma strategy demands mobility of action. It is necessary to abruptly change directions at the last possible moment to minimize the response time of the opponent. If the business is going to use this technique, it would, again, imply the absolute necessity of IT being highly maneuverable. To be able to support a dilemma strategy, it would seem that productivity and flexibility technology and design choices such as objects and databases positioned as decoupled servers would be necessary.

Strategic Idea: Dislocation (Disorder)

Quotation. For success, two major problems must be solved—dislocation and exploitation. One precedes and one follows. (LH)

Description. The idea of dislocation is to take actions that throw your opponent off balance. By virtue of your actions, your oppo-

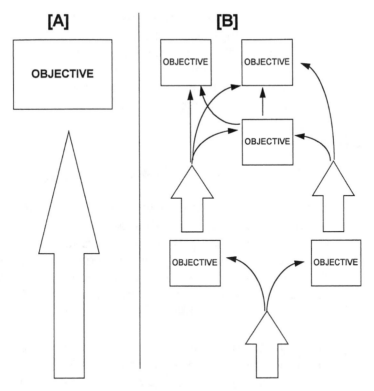

Figure 3.1 Dilemma. If your opponent does not know which objective you will seek, you will be concentrated while your opponent disperses to cope with her uncertainty.

nent finds himself confronted with a sudden, unexpected, and formidable problem. A problem that he cannot ignore. The dislocation has the effect of causing the opponent tremendous friction as he struggles to recover. During this period of time, there is a large window of opportunity for you to exploit the situation since he is stumbling and focused on the distracting dislocation.

IT Fighting. The role of IT is one of being both the means of dislocation and the means of exploitation. The idea would be to do something so unexpected and satisfying to customers, as suggested by the Kano Methodology (Figure 2.9), that it upsets the competitive balance of power. As your competitors stumble to respond, IT is further used to exploit the favorable situation by furthering the original act or presenting additional attractions to the marketplace.

At best, the customer is presented with a series of highly attractive IT-based offerings while the competitors are confronted with a deteriorating set of conditions that compound their friction. The ability to dynamically reconcentrate distributed computing is very important to this type of action since you would rapidly desire to reinforce successes that exceeded your original plan.

Strategic Idea: Efficiency

Quotation. It is best to win without fighting. (ST)

Description. The idea is to win with the absolute minimum expenditure of resources. You wish to avoid time-consuming, financially depleting, and people-exhausting confrontations. If you will recall from our previous definition of strategy, the intent is to find a way short, the shorter the better, of brute force to accomplish one's ends. The most efficient are those who create compelling value propositions for customers while deftly avoiding competition.

IT Fighting. To win without fighting means to offer a continually improving value proposition that cannot be matched by competitors. This means that you have put in place an advantage engine. IT, as the context of the marketspace, will be expected to be that advantage engine.

Strategic Idea: Flexibility (Agility, Adaptability, Dexterity)

Quotation. Be prepared in spirit to change the direction of your attack at any moment. You must be able to shift into any method of attack without having to make a conscious decision. (MM)

Description. Flexibility is an underappreciated rich concept. It means:

- The quality of a system that allows it to respond to change and variety.
- The ability to deal with variance.
- An action a_1 is more flexible than action b_1, if the set of possible actions following a1 includes the set of possible actions following action b_1.

- The capacity to take new/novel actions in response to new/changed circumstances.
- The ability to respond to environmental disruption without disorganization or collapse.
- The ability to reconfigure and remain in alignment with a changing environment.
- The ability to add, modify, or delete without causing disruption.
- The ability to adapt to fluctuations.

Flexibility plus speed equals maneuverability. Flexibility is a core requirement of any information age IT strategy.

IT Fighting. Being flexible sits at the heart of a strategy of potentiality. It is the design anchor for strategic configurations of power. It is by virtue of your superior flexibility (plus speed) that you can, in one continuous motion, move from a position of potentiality to a position of actuality.

Strategic Idea: Focus

Quotation. Focus your concentration on only making the hit. (MM)

Description. Focus is the ability to segregate all the competing demands on your attention into two groups. One group, the points of focus, are those limited items that make a meaningful difference and deserve extended and concentrated attention. The other group consists of those things that are anywhere from negligible to important but do not ultimately make a profound difference. When you focus strategically, you choose what is worth consuming your organization's attention and effort until completion.

IT Fighting. Strategic focus provides the aims for IT fighting. IT fighting will also provide the means to attempt to defocus your competitors. Consistent with the previously discussed ideas of dislocation, deflection, and dilemma, part of focusing is taking actions to disperse the attention of your opponents. So as is true for the notions of concentration and preparation, you are most focused when the act of focusing defocuses your competitors.

Strategic Idea: Foreknowledge

Quotation. What enables an intelligent leader to overcome others and achieve extraordinary accomplishments is foreknowledge. All matters require foreknowledge. (ST)

Description. The Art of War devotes an entire chapter to the subjects of espionage and spying. Mapping this to contemporary times, he was discussing the absolute need for research: market research about customers, the business environment, competitors, technology changes, the economy, and so on. Since all matters require foreknowledge, foreknowledge enables the efficiency and efficacy of all the other strategic ideas.

IT Fighting. In Chapter 2 (Figure 2.22), we discussed the idea that all strategy is constructed on a foundation of knowledge. It will therefore be necessary to use IT to build a knowledge management infrastructure. Knowledge management will consist of all the activities involved in collection, storing, managing, cataloging, indexing, maintaining, sharing, and dispersing knowledge. Knowledge is created both within the company and outside of it. IT knowledge management must extend to external sources such as the government, market research firms, universities and so forth. The idea of knowledge management is recursive. We must use knowledge management to collect and exploit knowledge about IT so that our IT fighting is the most efficient and effective possible.

Strategic Idea: Formlessness

Quotation. A victorious strategy is not repeated; the configurations of response to the enemy are inexhaustible. Water configures its flow in accord with the terrain; the army controls its victory in accord with the enemy. Thus, the army does not maintain any constant strategic configuration of power; water has no constant shape. The end of an army's form is formlessness. (ST)

Description. Formlesseness does not mean that one does not have structure; it means that one can rapidly alter structure. If one is formless, structure in motion, than against what does one defend and against what does one attack? Formlessness creates uncertainty for one's adversaries and enables one to maneuver.

IT Fighting. Formlesseness emphasizes the importance of flexibility to strategy. The best strategic configurations of power will be formless, that is, they will be able to quickly and without friction alter their form. When you can alter your form with alacrity, you can adapt favorably to all challenges presented to you. In Chapter 6, for example, we will present a way of designing an IT organization structure that supports spontaneous self-reorganization so that the IT organizational structure is in a continually evolving alignment with customer needs.

Strategic Idea: Friction

Quotation. When they come out, you go home; when they go home, you go out. When they go to the aid of the left flank, you head to the right; when they go to the aid of the right flank, you go to the left. This way, you can tire them out. (ST)

Description. Friction is the counter force that resists acting. It is the sum of everything that impedes your efforts. The greatest frictional force encountered and the hardest to overcome is normally human friction. Without any technological changes whatsoever, most companies could probably double their performance if they could simply eliminate existing structural and human factors that retard effort. Friction drains you, to the points of depletion and exhaustion, of your energy and resources.

IT Fighting. A strategy of potentiality is contingent on building strategic configurations of power that are friction-free. Friction-free configurations of power enable dramatic maneuverability. They provide the means to provide friction-free interactions with your customers. They also provide the means, through acts of dislocation, deflection, dilemma, concentration and preparedness, to create extraordinary friction for your opponents.

Strategic Idea: Gaps

Quotation. Attack what can be overcome, do not attack what cannot be overcome. To advance irresistibly, push through their gaps. Attack where there is not defense. (ST)

Description. While it is very American/macho to directly confront an opponent, it is generally considered strategic nonsense. Since the paradoxical logic of strategy is that those who achieve the absolute most, do the absolute least, it is much wiser, more efficient, and most profitable to attack market segments that offer inviting opportunity gaps. As others will also recognize gaps, attacking gaps requires speed.

IT Fighting. Gaps are the object of attention and affection of maneuver fighters. They seek points of opportunity that offer disproportionate returns for their effort. As the gap becomes crowded with competitors it is time to move on to another gap. IT maneuverability provides the means to attack information age market gaps.

Strategic Idea: Initiative

Quotation. When opponents are at ease, it is possible to tire them. When they are well fed, it is possible to starve them. When they are at rest, it is possible to move them. (ST)

Description. Initiative means taking actions before another. It often involves making up in vigorous activity what you lack in strength. Initiative puts you in the pleasant position of defining the direction of the game rather than reacting to the movements of others. Initiative is an ambitious and energetic form of execution. The notions of taking and holding the initiative are extremely consistent with wooing customers in the information age. Given the relative ease of switching suppliers, those who take and hold the initiative in meeting evolving customer needs will have a substantial advantage in achieving high levels of customer retention.

IT Fighting. To take the initiative means to do something. To do something means to move. Having moved, it may be necessary to accelerate your movement, change the direction of your movement, or retrace/reverse your movements. IT fighting is, again, built on maneuverability.

Strategic Idea: Leadership

Quotation. Vision (Leadership) is seeing victory before it exists. This is the strategist's (leader's) path to strategic triumph. (ST)

Description. A great deal of contemporary strategy literature focuses on the requirement for a business to have a perspective on the future. You then gather and direct your resources to achieve that perspective. What is happening in the present is a *fait accompli*, a done deal. The strategic battle is not about now but about what you will do now to prepare for tomorrow. Sunian leadership demands not only that you have an attitude about the future, but that you have a plan on how you will win in that future. Deep leadership goes beyond a vision of a future to the results of that future.

IT Fighting. Visionary leadership is what is required to put in place an IT organization capable of engaging in IT fighting. The vision for IT that we have proposed in Chapters 1 and 2 and will refine in future chapters is not a simple linear extrapolation of the way that most companies deploy IT today. Leadership is required to cross the chasm from where you are today with your IT investment and where you will need to be to compete in the information age.

Strategic Idea: Learning

Quotation. Test them to find out where they are sufficient and where they are lacking. Do something for or against them, making the opponent turn their attention to it, so that you may find out their patterns of aggressive and defensive behavior. (ST)

Description. The same thinking patterns that get you into problems will probably not be sufficient to extricate you from them. Learning is the process of absorbing and applying new and different ways to do things. Stupidity is not doing something wrong; the only people who do not do things wrong are people who do not do anything. Stupidity is having an experience, failing to learn from it, and repeating the same set of faulty actions. Learning provides the basis to do things with ever-increasing efficacy.

IT Fighting. An information age company is a learning company. It engages in prototyping, path finder projects, market trials, and experiments to learn. The result of learning is improved understanding and the need to change and tune its products and services. You can anticipate that an information age company will expect to continually revise its systems to be in a greater state of harmony with the marketplace as a result of the constant transfusion of new knowledge.

Strategic Idea: Leverage

Quotation. Roll rocks down a mountain and they cannot be stopped—this is because of the mountain, not the rocks. The people fight with courage—this is because of momentum, not the individuals. (ST)

Description. Leverage is a fundamental principle of strategy. It is the art of doing one thing and receiving cascading benefits from it. The strategic framework of core competencies (Figure 2.17) is constructed on the notion of leverage. Leverage conveys its benefits to all without explicit effort on their part. Leverage is the art of designing multipliers.

IT Fighting. The word salad of leverage consists of words like reuse, sharing, templates, substitution, standards, and layered. It is with leverage that you build your strategic configurations of power.

Strategic Idea: Love of the People

Quotation. Look upon your soldiers as you do infants, and they willingly go into deep valleys with you; look upon your soldiers as beloved children, and they willingly die for you. (ST)

Description. Classical strategy emphasizes the importance of a positive bond between the leader and the led. It recognized the extraordinary effort required to overcome the friction that accompanies every step of effort. The view was that people would only extend themselves and sustain that effort to the continuing necessary level if their commitment to the aims of the leadership exceeded simple and impersonal financial reward.

IT Fighting. Love of The People is a strategic idea in a cause/effect relationship with the previously discussed idea of cohesion. Cohesion, in part, develops from the shared belief of the workers that they are more than technology fodder to their employer. Cohesion begins with the demonstrated attitude of the leadership towards the staff.

Strategic Idea: Maneuver

Quotation. The ability to gain victory by changing and adapting to the opponent is called genius. (ST)

Description. The ability to maneuver, the act of finding the most advantageous way to go, sits at the locus of strategic thinking about conflict. Advantageous means to achieve one's end with the absolute minimum effort—one does this by moving from a position less favorable to a position more favorable to your aims. From this superior position, you can accomplish your objectives with less exertion. The central idea of maneuvering is that to overcome resistance, one must first reduce resistance to a point, through favorable movement, that makes the act of overcoming, at the ideal, a fait accompli.

IT Fighting. The ability to maneuver sits at the locus of a strategy of potentiality. The information age is a war of movement and success will accrue to those who can use IT to continually enhance their value proposition to their customers. In the industrial age, the formula for winning was stable and efficient processes based on economies of scale. IT was the back-office engine. In the information age, the formula for winning is dynamic and effective processes based on mass customization. IT manages the entire life cycle interaction and experience of the customer. Strategic configurations of power are explicitly crafted to enable maneuverability. The market cry by both business and IT leadership to their organizations will be the same—*keep moving!*

Strategic Idea: Mercenaries (Outsourcing)

Quotation. There is nothing outside of yourself that will ever enable you to get better, richer, quicker, or stronger. Everything is within you, seek nothing outside of you. (MM)

Description. The perpetual question is, what must you be competent in? It is increasingly popular for companies to engage in outsourcing as a way to allocate IT requirements to highly competent suppliers and, thereby, alleviate management attention to managing these specialized resources. Outsourcing arrangements vary widely in the domain of services that are off-loaded. The outsourcing contract may vary between only desktop support to IT strategy and systems design. Of increasing popularity is the outsourcing of the maintenance and operations of legacy mainframe systems to permit internal staff to focus on developing new distributed systems. This is called transitional outsourcing.

IT Fighting. In deciding to outsource all or part of the IT function, the following points needs to be especially considered:

- As illustrated in Figure 1.30, IT is elevated to a strategic resource because, in the information age, companies become highly dependent on IT and it has a high business impact.
- As itemized in Table 1.13, the strategic force of IT is not only restricted to convergent industries (communications, computing, and content), but information management industries such as banking, brokerage, and insurance and physical product and service industries such as utilities, retailing, and manufacturing. Everybody, to a large extent, is in the information movement and management business regardless of business they think they are in.
- Exchange in the information age economy shifts to the marketspace from the marketplace (Figure 1.24). Wealth creation is a function of moving and managing bits, rather than moving and managing atoms.

Given these factors, it would seem that if you are going consider outsourcing, a prudent outsourcing strategy would be as follows:

- Outsource legacy systems to enable focus and resources for new systems.
- Outsource low-level operational functions.
- Outsource higher-level IT functions that aren't key variables in determining your IT speed, flexibility, or ability to overcome friction.

While it is certainly tempting, to many, to expediently get rid of the IT headache, this headache is increasingly your business. The fundamental problem with outsourcing such a vital resource, especially the higher-level functions, is agility. The world is changing quickly and IT is the strategic coping mechanism. It is the means through which your business maneuvers in the customer satisfaction, revenue, and market share ether. Outsourced IT is subject to the restrictive terms of your contract. Insourced IT is subject to the evolving judgment of the management team and, ultimately, executive edict. Regardless of the press popularity with outsourcing, you should very carefully consider whether outsourcing will, in fact, make you *better, richer, quicker, or stronger.* For most companies, IT needs to be a core competency, something within you. If you outsource, ultimately, if they are good, they will one day hold you to ransom and, if they are bad, they will one day lead you to ruin. It has never been prudent to turn your strategic configurations of power, your way to win, over to mercenaries.

Strategic Idea: Moral Leadership

Quotation. When directives are consistently carried out, there is mutual satisfaction between the leadership and the group. In ordinary times it is imperative that benevolence and trustworthiness along with dignity and order be manifest to people from the start, so that later, if they are faced with enemies, it is possible to meet the situation in an orderly manner, with the full trust and acceptance of the people. (ST)

Description. The challenge of leadership is not leading when the sea is calm and the sky is blue. The challenge of leadership is leading when the wind is howling and the waves are breaking over the boat. To have a staff that will devote itself to your aims when the waves are breaking over the boat and the wind is howling requires earning the staff's loyalty while the sky is blue and the sea is calm.

IT Fighting. A parallel strategic idea to the previously discussed strategic idea of Love of The People, moral leadership also sits in a cause-effect relationship with the strategic idea of cohesion. There is much more involved in winning than the mechanistic acts of simply attaching communications wires to computer ports. How you engage your staff to share your aims will have a greater effect on your success than the specific technologies you choose.

Strategic Idea: Objective

> *Quotation.* Keep your objective always in mind. (LH)

> *Description.* This is a simple, obvious, and basic strategic truth that is often forgotten. There are many distractions and immediate challenges that can divert you from your goals. It is easy to stray.

> *IT Fighting.* The objective of IT fighting is to enable the business to win through maneuver. You position yourself to be able to maneuver by building strategic configurations of power.

Strategic Idea: Options

> *Quotation.* The following is a philosophical truth. One thing does one thing, two things do four things. (MM)

> *Description.* To have options means to have choice. To have choice means to have freedom of action. Strategists refer to the number of options you have as your strategic degrees of freedom. Without options, there is nothing to decide and one merely proceeds on a predetermined path without any ability to alter one's fate.

> *IT Fighting.* When you build strategic configurations of power, what you are doing is creating future options. You are taking actions now that will permit you to make choices later. Since the turbulence of our times prevents forecasting needs with assurance, the response is to create IT structures that buy you future options.
>
> If you get trapped into the situation where the cost of your strategic configurations of power becomes an issue, in cost-justifying them, like stock options, you should assign to them the additional value that they give you by providing you with future choice. A cheaper IT solution now that cannot maneuver later will ultimately prove dearer than a more expensive IT solution now that permits you limitless adaptability over time. What is the value of choice to your decision makers? As they are confronted with dilemmas, surprise, bold acts, and the need to deflect, they will find the strategic degrees of freedom that you have provided them to be invaluable.

Strategic Idea: Organization Structure

Quotation. Structure depends on strategy. Forces are to be structured strategically based on what is advantageous. (ST)

Description. Organizational structure is the most visible act of strategy to most people. To many employees, the periodic reorganizations are the only aspect of strategy that they actually understand. Designing organizational structure is the last act of strategy and should be explicitly designed to facilitate the strategy.

IT Fighting. Organizational structure is a core strategic configuration of power. It contributes to speed, flexibility, and, most importantly, to the elimination of friction. A model design for an organizational strategic configuration of power will be presented in Chapter 6.

Strategic Idea: Planning

Quotation. It is easy to take over from those who do not plan ahead. (ST)

Description. A plan documents and formalizes the results of strategic thinking. As was shown in Figure 2.19, the planning process consists of the tightly bound trinity of assessment, strategy (the plan), and execution. Plans are subject to change based on learning, experience, and changing times and circumstances.

IT Fighting. Industrial age IT plans were designed on the fixed model of a strategy of actuality. The intent was to achieve precise results. Information age IT plans should be designed to achieve a strategy of potentiality. The intent is to achieve an inexact result, a result that can dynamically support a changing business and a changing IT infrastructure.

Strategic Idea: Positioning

Quotation. In ancient times, those known as good warriors prevailed when it was easy to prevail. Their victories are not flukes. Their victories are not flukes because they position themselves where they will surely win, prevailing over those who have already lost. (ST)

Description. The notion of positioning is that the state of any business area, process, function, competency, and so on, can be modeled or positioned. Positioning models illustrate the state of the position along its critical dimensions and may be expressed graphically, quantitatively, or qualitatively. One may assert that the strategic position of the business at any time, t, is the set of positions for those chosen business areas, processes, competencies, and so on that are fundamental to its strategic success. The notion of positioning is recursive; for example, a position may be expressed as a set of decomposed sub-positions. As was illustrated in Figure 2.20, the intent of strategic planning is provide a plan to move the business from its current set of positions to a more desirable and winning future set of positions.

IT Fighting. It is our assertion that, in the information age, the IT resources are promoted from a factory asset to a strategic asset (Figure 1.30). All businesses, whether they realize it or not, are very much in the information movement and management business. It is therefore mandatory to reposition IT to maximize its utility to the business. The position that maximizes IT's value is a position of potentiality.

Strategic Idea: Preparation (Readiness)

Quotation. Those who face the unprepared with preparation are victorious. (ST)

Description. The notion of preparation or readiness concerns itself with the practical question of executable capabilities. A strategist does not live in fantasy land. The initial act of almost any strategy is to execute the necessary preparatory acts of training, staffing, practice, capability building, and so on. The end of being prepared is a state of readiness. The logic of strategy is planning, preparation, readiness, and execution.

As was true when we discussed the strategic idea of concentration of force, preparedness exists in a state of relative advantage, that is, your advantage is equal to your preparedness less your opponent's preparedness. It is therefore the case that those who are most prepared are those whose preparation devalues the preparation of her opponents. Preparation is strategically most potent when it is associated the complementary strategic idea of surprise.

IT Fighting. When you engage in a strategy of actuality, you prepare and ready yourself for a specific objective. When you engage in a strategy of potentiality, you prepare and ready yourself for anything. In an information age world of constant change, what but anything would be prudent to prepare and ready yourself for?

Strategic Idea: Psychological Conflict

Quotation. Use strategy to thwart the opponents, causing them to overcome themselves. (ST)

Description. It is the view of classical strategy that defeat first occurs in the mind of the opponent. The accumulating successes of your actions present your opponent with not only an actually deteriorating situation but one that psychologically discourages and demoralizes her. The psychological demoralization causes the opponent to take increasingly desperate and imprudent actions that further her own demise. Paradoxically, your best ally may be your opponent who, caught in your tar pit of deep and far-reaching strategy, overcomes and defeats herself by trying to extricate herself through shallow and near-sighted strategy.

IT Fighting. The outcome of a strategy of potentiality is the express ability and intent for the business to be a maneuver fighter and execute Sun Tzu's maxim: *Go forth where they do not expect it, attack where they are unprepared.* A maneuver fighter (Figure 2.21), by the inherent nature of movement, causes psychological distress for her opponents. The constant movement disrupts the opponents' plans, causes them to backtrack, change directions, and feel that they are under a state of strategic siege. Psychological conflict is a byproduct of IT fighting and, by adjusting the tempo and rhythm of the maneuvers, the stress on the opponent can be regulated. By manipulating tempo and rhythm, you restructure time with a disorienting effect on your competitors.

Strategic Idea: Responsiveness

Quotation. It is a terrible shame to die in battle with your sword undrawn. (MM)

Description. The marketspace is crowded with entrepreneurial people who are action-oriented. Nobody has a monopoly on good ideas and it should be anticipated that your competitors will be bold, create dilemmas for you, present you with surprises and, in all possible ways and with great eagerness, try to do to you what you would fancy doing to them. In the marketspace, acting and reacting are indivisible parts of the same motion.

IT Fighting. The strategic idea of responsiveness, again, drives the need for speed and flexibility as the primary design points for your IT strategy. In the information age, IT is your sword and shield. It will be a very costly shame to be overwhelmed in the marketspace with your sword undrawn.

Strategic Idea: Self-Invincibility

Quotation. In ancient times, skillful warriors first made themselves invincible, and watched for vulnerabilities in their opponents. So it is said that good warriors take their stand on ground where they cannot lose. Ground where one cannot lose means invincible strategy that makes it impossible for opponents to defeat you. (ST)

Description. The first strategy is always the same; it is to get your own house in order. Before one tries to grow and win new markets, one should be prepared to defend what one already has. One does this by nurturing a compelling set of advantages that dissuades customers from even entertaining the idea of defecting to competitors.

IT Fighting. In the marketspace, customer touch occurs through the use of hypermedia. A primary focus, if not the primary focus, is applying your IT assets to making each touch experience as convenient, satisfying, entertaining, informative, value creating, and mutually beneficial as possible. The interactive marketspace will give your customer, more than ever before, the opportunity to effortlessly wander. The solution is not to expect them not to consider wandering but to have a way to deal with it. The way to deal with it is to create customer experiences through IT that voluntarily bind them to you.

Strategic Idea: Speed

Quotation. Superlative speed is essential to be able to move in on the enemy. Speed does not necessarily mean being fast, it means being smarter. (MM)

Description. Speed is the rapidity of action. Speed over time is tempo. When you alter your speed, you change the rhythm of the marketplace. It is the view of classical strategy that speed alone can compensate for numerous other failings. The depth of the strategic intent of your superlative speed is the multiplier of the benefit consequences of the speed.

IT Fighting. Speed is a fundamental demand of the information age. A strategy of potentiality is built on speed. Flexibility permits you to direct the speed. The elimination of friction accelerates the speed. All strategic configurations of power are crafted around speed. Strategies of actuality focus and concentrate speed at the point of opportunity in time and space. In all things, speed is of the essence. Speed is the spirit of IT fighting.

Strategic Idea: Strategic Conflict

Quotation. What is valued is foiling the opponent's strategy, not pitched battle. (ST)

Description. Figure 3.2 illustrates a rooted strategy tree. Each level of action is built upon and is dependent on the lower level of action. The notion of strategic conflict asserts that you should take actions to create dislocations at the lowest possible level in the hierarchy. In this way, through one targeted action, multiple dependent actions are structurally invalidated. Strategic conflict is a strategy of leverage. By compromising the utility of the foundation strategy, all the plans and actions that stand upon it collapse.

The target of strategic conflict is often referred to as the center of gravity. The center of gravity is that asset, capability, or strength of the competitor from which its success emanates. Without it, the competitor proceeds without this distinguishing advantage. Centers of gravity cannot normally be challenged directly. One has to use indirection to draw the opponents' attention, resources, and

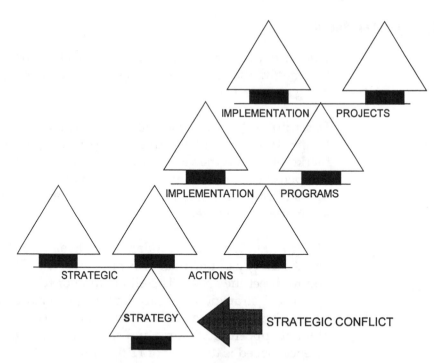

Figure 3.2   Strategic conflict. The aim of strategic conflict is to under-
mine your competitor's root strategy.

energy away from their center of gravity, and through their own
loss of focus and neglect, do to themselves what you cannot do to
them.

IT Fighting. You use IT fighting to move and distract your opponent. If you can make them follow you, they are focused on executing your plans and not their plans. You can always make an
opponent pay attention to you by threatening something they care
about. An opponent who is absorbed with your agenda is an opponent who may let her center of gravity, slowly but surely, atrophy.

Strategic Idea: Surprise

Quotation. In battle, confrontation is done directly; victory is
gained by surprise. (ST)

Description. Surprise has a dual nature. A strategic surprise
excites to the point of delight your customers while it paralyzes the

competitors. It is the unexpected nature of a surprise that makes it so compelling for a customer. It is the dislocating nature of a surprise that makes it so damaging to a competitor. Surprise creates incredible friction for competitors as they rally to respond. If you can maintain a tempo of surprises, you can present your competitors with a rapidly deteriorating situation, which includes the desirable side effect of creating psychological demoralization.

IT Fighting. To surprise means to do the unexpected. The greater the unexpected, the greater the surprise and the greater the benefit. To do the unexpected requires you to move. To move in the information age requires a strategy of potentiality.

Strategic Idea: Timing

Quotation. There are good times and bad times for everything. Always be aware of the possibility of changing timing and rhythm. (MM)

Description. Timing has to do with the market questions of where and when. The same action can be done too soon (the market is not ready for it), at the right movement, or too late (the market window has passed). A strategist is concerned with influencing the time and place where she will engage the marketplace.

IT Fighting. Timing is, in part, a function of speed and flexibility. It is sometimes necessary to accelerate schedules, and sometimes necessary to decelerate schedules, in order that resources be shifted to more favorable opportunities that need to have their timing altered. Timing demands IT maneuverability.

Strategic Idea: Unity of Command

Quotation. One might be quite certain that it is better to entrust an expedition to one man of average prudence than to give to two men of outstanding ability the same authority. (NM)

Description. Unity of command concerns itself with the question of alignment and direction. There must be a shared market agenda, an agenda that attracts customers and dissuades competitors. It is the teaching of classical strategy that this requires *a* leader who leads.

IT Fighting. Creating strategic configurations of power will not happen by simply formulating teams, saying go, and crossing one's fingers. There is a huge abyss between where most IT organizations are today and where they need to be to engage in IT fighting. The IT leader cannot abrogate her responsibility by delegating her leadership responsibilities to faddish team structures. The leader must demonstrate leadership through vision, continual commitment, and the system of rewards and punishments.

Strategic Idea: Vision (Foresight, Anticipation)

Quotation. What the aware individual knows has not yet taken shape. If you see the subtle and notice the hidden when there is no form, this is really good. What everyone knows is not called wisdom. A leader of wisdom and ability lays deep plans for what others do not figure on.

Description. Classical strategy demarcates the great disparity between the strategic skills of the few gifted *aware* individuals and the general population. As is common in all disciplines, the dispersion of strategic skills and abilities across the population is very wide with the greatest density occurring at the cluster of average ability. Modern strategy pundits, who wish to thoroughly democratize strategy and disperse it throughout the corporate proletariat, have yet to come to terms with this unbending truth.

It will, undoubtedly, be of great benefit to raise the strategic acumen of your staff so that their collective abilities will enjoy comparative superiority over your opponents. We will recommend a Breeder Strategy in Chapter 5 to accomplish this objective. Nevertheless, as the great middle progresses to the right of the bell curve, by their own actions, they also inadvertently shift the point of average ability. The rules of mathematics simply do not permit the pundit fantasy that everyone can be above average. So though you will be relatively better than your competition, which is to be fervently applauded, in absolute terms within the boundaries of your own enterprise, your strategically *aware* individuals will still be markedly superior at this specific activity.

If everyone could sing like Whitney Houston, singing like Whitney Houston would be the talent of an average singer. If everyone could shoot hoops like Michael Jordan, performance on the court at a Michael Jordan level would be the talent of an average basketball player. In devising strategy, you must be attentive to all but act based on the strategic merit of the advice. Neither be surprised nor disappointed that strategic skill is not equally distributed throughout your organization. Unfortunately, it really can't be any other way.

IT Fighting. Your ultimate success can only be as grand as your IT vision. If you develop strategic configurations of power that realize a deep and far-reaching strategy, you will win. If you develop strategic configurations of power that realize a shallow and near-sighted strategy, you will continue to muddle through. Unfortunately, it really can't be any other way.

Strategic Idea: Will (Determination)

Quotation. All conditions are more calculable, all obstacles more surmountable, than that of human resistance. (LH)

Description. Classical strategy recognizes the indispensability of will to overcome obstacles. Will is required to valiantly persist in the face of compounding barriers to success. While you may feel that your situation is impossible, you can often take solace in believing that the true situation of your opponent is probably no better. Strategic execution often reduces to a contest of wills.

IT Fighting. Will is an attribute of commitment. The depth of your commitment demonstrates your will to remake your IT organization in the strategic imagery we have painted. Will is required to overcome. If it wasn't hard, there wouldn't be the coveted prize of advantage.

While all these strategic ideas have been purposefully presented in the context of synthesizing information age IT fighting, the approach is wholly suitable for analyzing any situation stamped with conflict. As Miyamoto Musashi said: "Strategic thinking has its own principles and they can be applied to anything that has to do with conflict." The intent of strategic ideas is to guide your abstract thinking into fruitful directions. The underlying idea of all strategic ideas is to win, and winning is the desired outcome of conflict.

CONCLUSION

The following should be kept in mind to fully comprehend strategic ideas:

- The ideas that have been presented are only a representative list. I doubt if a complete list exists. Who would catalog and certify it?
- When thinking about a problem, in theory, the ideas can be combined in unlimited combinations to develop strategic insight. Since, also in theory, the number of combinations of issues that are being reviewed is unlimited, strategic thinking is a boundless activity. In practice, even the best strategist can only think about a few strategic ideas and issues concurrently.
- You are encouraged to select your own strategic ideas. Because nobody else has looked at problems from your lens does not mean that it is not a lens of advantage. As it is in all aspects of strategy, originality is best of all.
- Strategic thinking, in many ways, is to the art of choosing a set of strategic ideas that guides you to insight into the current strategic problem.
- The ability to repetitively choose optimum sets of ideas over time is called genius. Rare genius would consist of dynamically creating a problem-specific set of optimum strategic ideas for each strategic issue. In this way, you inflame insight that cannot be repeated by others.

If you are going to build information age advantage and succeed in IT fighting, you will have to think strategically. Thinking strategically means analyzing and synthesizing your strategic issues in terms of strategic ideas. As is common in achieving excellence in all other intellectual fields, this will demand study, practice, and mentoring.

Having now completed this review of strategic ideas, it should be obvious that recommending a strategy of potentiality for information age IT organizations was neither a casual nor an impulsive act. A strategy of potentiality has its strategic seeds in very fertile soil. All of the following strategic ideas contribute to its strategic logic: action (execution), boldness, concentration of force, contingency, deflection, dilemma, flexibility, formlessness, friction, gaps, initiative, maneuver, options, position, preparation, responsiveness, speed, and surprise. When you engage in a strategy of potentiality, you unite these ideas into a composite act of advantage.

4

Strategic Configurations of Power

A STRATEGY OF POTENTIALITY

A strategy of potentiality is implemented by creating a crafted set of *strategic configurations of power*. A strategic configuration of power is an asset, resource, capability, or process that has been precisely designed to position you for future but unknown actions. It is a carefully designed capacity that fills the Musashi requirement to be able to lay in ready wait in a state of strength and speed but to be able to effortlessly transition, without hesitation, to a state of force and quickness. In this way, you engage the marketspace mayhem without an exact plan of what you will do, but you are confident that you will win by virtue of being able to improvise as the fog of the marketspace lifts.

A strategic configuration of power is the precision engineering of your infrastructure so that frictionless, dynamic, and adaptive maneuvering can take place upon it. Your strategic configurations of power position you so that you can compete across time and prevail over your competitors who have already lost because of their stationary natures.

Sun Tzu described strategic configurations of power:

> A victorious strategy is not repeated, the configurations of responses to the enemy are inexhaustible. . . . Water configures its flow in accord with the terrain; the army controls its victory in accord with the enemy. Thus, the army does not maintain any constant *strategic configuration of power*; water has no constant shape. The end of an army's form is formlessness. One who is able to change and transform in accord with the enemy and wrest victory is termed genius. [emphasis added]

By creating your own IT strategic configurations of power, your responses to the marketspace become inexhaustible.

A strategic configuration of power has four attributes:

- It permits an endless variety of actions.
- It permits you to adapt expeditiously to the actions of others.
- Its only form is a temporary form; it is continuously self-adaptive.
- It is a critical contributor to advantage.

We can further understand the nature of a strategic configuration of power by deconstructing it:

- Strategic means advantage.
- Configuration means elements and the relationships between those elements.
- Power means maneuverability where maneuverability means speed plus flexibility.

A strategic configuration of power, therefore, is the ability to create advantage by being able to craft the elements and relationships of the elements of the source of power to enable unparalleled maneuverability.

It is a sophisticated state of potentiality that enables you to transition to actuality on demand. Candidates for strategic configurations of power are only those capacities that create advantage. It is these capacities that you wish to put in a state of constant motion. In this way, your opponent does not know against what to attack or against what to defend. In Sunian imagery, you are always in a state of *fullness* and your opponents are in a state of *emptiness;* you are always concentrated at the point of need and your opponents are always dispersed.

Strategic configurations of power are created and exist only at the infrastructure level. They provide the resistance-free surface upon which your product teams, marketers, sales force, operations personnel, and so on are free to tactically maneuver to create advantageous disruptions and respond to the thrusts of your opponents. IT strategic configurations of power are, therefore, a set of holistic infrastructure designs that create the necessary foundation for tactical nimbleness.

Rather than strategic configurations of power, most IT organizations today have accidental configurations of nonpower. Their sources of power are haphazard accumulations of procedures and technologies. They enable the organization to muddle through but do not facilitate building maneuver-based advantage. To successfully engage in IT fighting, they must reengineer themselves from a state of accidental configurations of nonpower to a future state of strategic configurations of power.

It is fashionable for modern strategy pundits to criticize traditional strategic planning. They describe alternatives with names like real-time strategy, Nintendo strategy, on-demand strategy, dueling strategy, fluid strategy, and continuous strategy. The powerful imagery conveys the message that strategy must be in a state of motion to remain relevant in a competitive world in motion. They allude to leaders dynamically altering the business in response to global corporate sensors. Everything responds without resistance at levels of perfect granularity to continuous tuning. They paint a captivating picture, but unfortunately they never tell us exactly how this comes about.

I believe that to engage in dynamic forms of strategy, strategy must be segregated into the notions of potentiality and actuality. Industrial age strategy can be equated with a strategy of actuality. One defined a desired future and took the linear logic actions to achieve that future. More often then not, those actions were driven, correctly so, by economies-of-scale thinking

To compete in the turbulent information age, a strategy of potentiality must be executed to put in place a nimble infrastructure upon which tactical strategies of actuality execute. To engage in dynamic forms of strategy, to continuously alter the business from a corporate joystick, you must first put in place a set of strategic configurations of power that permit you to be fluid. If your infrastructure is a frozen block of ice, you cannot engage in real-time strategy and expect to react opportunistically.

One cannot dynamically create a dynamic environment. There is no alchemy. You can, however, create a set of strategic configurations of power that, by virtue of your design, lend themselves to being continually refreshed and enable dynamic behavior upon them. So users will find Java on-demand application environments with Web PCs over Internet networks to be absolutely incredibly dynamic and adaptive, but the infrastructure upon which all that operates will need to be thoughtfully designed to support such dynamic behavior and permit self-evolution.

If you think about it, you will agree that it cannot be any other way. It is one thing to want to be maneuverable; it is quite another thing to be maneuverable. One is but wishful thinking while the other is a calculated act. So one cannot dynamically create a dynamic environment but one can purposefully plan and implement a dynamic environment that, itself, has been infused with the property of spontaneous adaptation.

Consider what the notions of *real-time* strategy and the others really mean. A real-time system consists of a controlling component, with sensory capability, and a controlled component. In response to periodic or event driven data from the environmental sensors, the controller evaluates the data and sends adaptive instructions to the controlled component. The controlled component executes the corrective actions and the cycle continues indefinitely. In real time, precise corrective actions are taken and the system stays in perfect harmony with the changing environment.

While this is a reasonable analogy and excellent model for tactics, it is unsuitable for strategy. Suppose you have chosen a strategy that consists of a set of competencies, processes, vendor relationships, architectural decisions, and product value propositions. Can you fundamentally change these types of things in real time? Can you change your hardware, software and telecommunications vendors every other day in response to some stimulus? Can you staff, in response to your real-time commands, be competent in MVS on Monday, UNIX on Wednesday, and Windows-NT on Friday?

If a baseball team chooses a strategy of slow runners but power hitters, when they are losing a game, can they suddenly, in real time, switch to stealing bases, stretching singles into doubles, hit and run, sacrificing, and bunting? They can certainly switch over time by changing their talent/competency mix, but if speed was not part of their strategy, it can't be dynamically conjured up. Deep and far-reaching strategy and real time are incompatible. Real time is compatible with the notion of tactics, and a strategy of building configurations of power puts in place the infrastructure so that the business can tactically maneuver.

So to enable IT fighting, the IT strategist must focus her attention on crafting strategic configurations of IT power. She should worry less about the specific IT applications that she imagines her company needs, and more about creating an infrastructure that can respond to needs that she never imagined. In this view of strategy, she does not focus on solving specific problems; she focuses on the more powerful act of putting in place the devices to solve everyone's known and unknown generic problems. She must select what are the prized areas that need to be redesigned into strategic configurations of power, decide how they should be crafted, and do it. She must execute her strategy of engineering an environment of potentiality while keeping in mind that it, itself, must be able to spontaneously self-reorganize and grow while creating the necessary ice surface for all the user groups that will be engaged in fast-paced and abruptly changing strategies of actuality upon it.

In this way, like at the beach when the tide comes in, we raise a tide of maneuverability for all. With no extra effort on their part, everyone inherits all the capabilities of the strategic configurations of power as needed. Our strength and speed sit in a state of readiness for the moment of actuality when they become focused and concentrated force and quickness. Our strategy of potentiality is a strategy of tremendous leverage that raises the tide for every employee, for every process, and for every product line every day. In this way, we deploy IT with strategic insight to cope with both the chaotic impact and rare opportunity of the information age.

THE PROBLEM

The information age and the derivative need to engage in IT fighting is further complicated by what has been an extended poor record of delivering strategic value by many IT organizations. Figures 4.1 and 4.2 illustrates annual studies that identify the most pressing strategic issues confronting IT management in North America and Europe. If you review it even briefly, it is evident that the list is most disconcerting. It is like a deck of strategic issues cards are reshuffled each year but almost none are ever discarded. Businesses cannot engage in IT fighting with such a poor report card. You cannot maneuver if you cannot access information, if you don't have an architecture, or if your development is hopelessly slow.

To an information technology strategist, businesses are no more than massively parallel information processing factories. Numer-

ISSUE	'95	'94	'93	'92	'91	'90	'89	'88
Aligning IS with Business Goals	1	2	2	1	2	4	2	1
Cross-Functional Information Systems	2	4	4	6	3	3	7	N/R
Utilizing Data	3	3	4	4	5	7	6	7
Business Reengineering Through IT	4	1	1	2	1	1	11	N/R
Improving the IS Human Resource	5	9	12	5	13	11	8	8
Enabling Change and Nimbleness	6	N/R	N/R	N/R	N/R	N/R	N/R	N/R
Connecting to Customers/Suppliers	7	16	16	20	15	10	N/R	N/R
Information Architecture	8	5	7	3	8	9	5	5
Updating Obsolete Systems	9	7	8	18	N/R	13	N/R	18
Systems Development	10	6	3	9	4	6	13	12
Educating Management on IT	11	18	18	16	14	2	3	3
Changing Technology Platform	12	9	10	N/R	N/R	N/R	N/R	N/R
Using IT for Competitive Breakthroughs	13	15	15	14	12	8	1	4
IS Strategic Plan	14	11	9	10	6	5	4	2
Capitalizing on IT Advances	15	13	14	19	20	N/R	17	N/R
Integrating Systems	16	8	11	13	9	16	12	6
Cutting IS Costs	17	12	5	11	11	10	14	17
Providing Help Desk Services	18	N/R	N/R	N/R	N/R	N/R	N/R	N/R
Moving to Open Systems	19	17	19	N/R	N/R	N/R	N/R	N/R
Improving Leadership Skills	20	20	17	7	10	N/R	N/R	N/R

Figure 4.1   North America strategic issues 1988–1995. The list of strategic issues has remained remarkably stable over the eight years. (Source: CSC Index)

ous streams of information flow into it, the information is massaged, new information is created, and numerous streams of information flow out of it. IT had historically existed to make these information flows happen with maximum efficiency and effectiveness to enable the noninformational business purpose. In the information age, these information flows become the business.

Information flows within a business are exceedingly complex. We model that diversity by using a business diversity box (Figure 4.3). Diversity is defined by four dimensions:

1. Work site diversity: Defines the variable geography of where people work.
2. Work unit diversity: Defines the different types of work groups within which people work.
3. Information diversity: Defines the different forms of information with associated attributes that people require.

ISSUE	'95	'94	'93	'92	'91	'90	'89	'88
Cross-Functional Information Systems	1	4	4	9	7	3	5	N/R
Improving the IS Human Resource	2	8	6	3	6	10	4	7
Business Reengineering Through IT	3	1	1	19	2	1	17	N/R
Cutting IS Costs	3	2	2	8	9	11	16	16
Information Architecture	5	7	4	5	12	6	8	5
Aligning IS with Business Goals	6	3	3	1	4	2	3	2
Systems Development	7	6	11	18	5	9	10	14
Educating Management on IT	8	11	14	12	20	13	5	3
Utilizing Data	9	5	7	4	17	4	7	12
Changing Technology Platform	9	14	9	N/R	N/R	N/R	N/R	N/R
Integrating Systems	11	13	7	12	10	14	14	10
Using IT for Competitive Breakthroughs	12	16	N/R	11	1	7	1	4
Enabling Change and Nimbleness	12	N/R	N/R	N/R	N/R	N/R	N/R	N/R
IS Strategic Plan	14	17	12	2	3	5	2	1
Connecting to Customers/Suppliers	15	19	16	N/R	14	8	N/R	N/R
Providing Help Desk Services	15	N/R	N/R	N/R	N/R	N/R	N/R	N/R
Moving to Open Systems	17	15	9	N/R	N/R	N/R	N/R	N/R
Updating Obsolete systems	18	12	12	16	13	18	N/R	19
Determine the Value of IT	19	20	N/R	20	N/R	17	19	N/R
Capitalizing on IT Advances	20	N/R	N/R	N/R	N/R	N/R	N/R	N/R

Figure 4.2 European strategic issues 1988–1995. This list of issues has also remained remarkably stable over the eight years. (Source: CSC Index)

4. Information technology diversity: Defines the different types of information processing technologies that are used to create, present, move, store, and analyze information (the IT function chain).

In a company of even small stature, the number of permutations and combinations of information flows across these four dimensions become astronomical. These flows, of course, do not remain constant. They are not a still-life picture but continuously revise themselves as required by the business dynamic. So within a business alone, the problem of enabling rich information flows across all the diversity elements is exceedingly challenging. What happens to this maze when we add the value chain?

A business does not exist as an isolated entity. It participates with other trading partners in a value chain. As shown in Figure 4.4, each partner, supplier, regulator, distributor, financier, insurer,

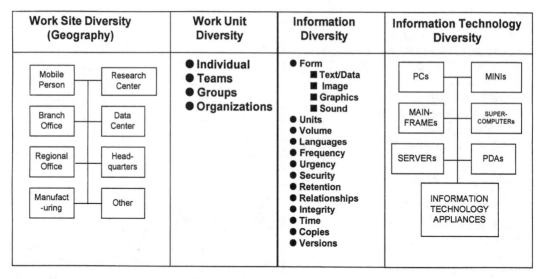

Figure 4.3   Business diversity box. The variety of information flows within a business is a function of four variables.

consumer, and so on first has its own proprietary diversity box with all its private information flow complexities, and secondly must interface diversity boxes across the value chain. The attempt to move information across the value chain information diversity boxes is difficult because of:

- The proprietary nature of each one.
- The dynamic changes of information flow.
- The uncertainty of what flows will be needed next.
- The state of flux.
- The continuously shifting combinations and permutations of flows.

A pessimist would say that it is a tribute to the heroic efforts of staff that any information at all flows between companies.

The information age promotes this picture (Figure 4.4) to center stage. In the industrial age, these information flows were adjunct to the mission of the business. They were an expense that you had to do to get the real product out the door. In the information age, for many companies they are the business or at least a critical component of it (Table 1.13). In addition, besides rising IT prominence, the

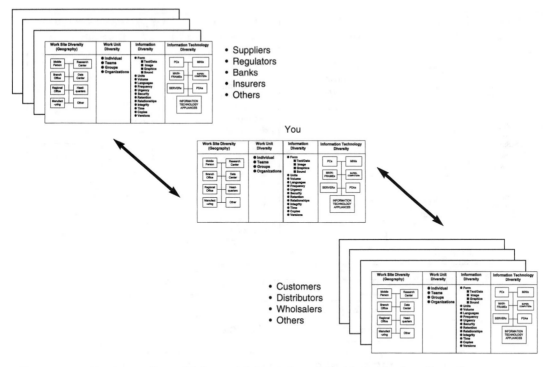

Figure 4.4 Business diversity box and the value chain. Information flows have to cross the business diversity boxes of each trading partner.

hyper-nature of the marketspace raises the level of turbulence, competitive fervor, and change, which makes the flows more unpredictable and chaotic than ever. So to engage in information age IT fighting means to manage in a superior and dynamic manner the information flows both within and across information diversity boxes.

What we are suggesting by a strategy of potentiality is that you create advantage by building your business diversity value chain upon a foundation of IT strategic configurations of power (Figure 4.5). By virtue of the strategic configurations of power that have been explicitly designed to support information-based adaptive maneuver, you are in a better position to compete then your competitors. You can further optimize your strategic configurations of power by overlapping them with your trading partners.

You exploit your strategic configurations of power to make life miserable for your competitors while exciting your customers. You

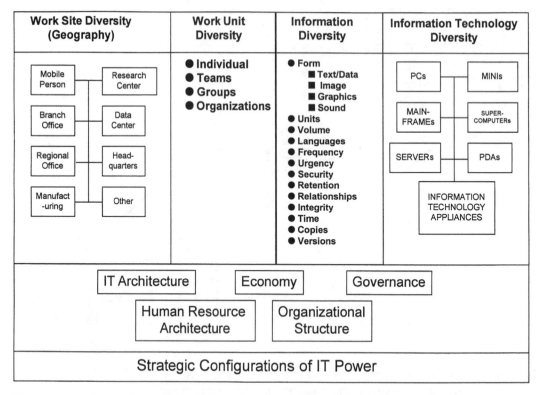

Figure 4.5   **Strategic configurations of power. Your business diversity box must rest upon your strategic configurations of power.**

use them to deliberately disrupt the status quo to your advantage by:

- Changing information-based value propositions.
- Manipulating the tempo and rhythm of change.
- Rapidly attacking emerging but unexploited market niches.
- Preempting competitor moves with your own announcements to which they must respond.
- Performing acts of mass customization.
- Being first to market.
- Surprising your competitors with acts of collaboration that they cannot duplicate.
- Attracting the best combination of value chain partners by virtue of your superior methods of value chain collaboration.
- Rolling out a continuous stream of temporary advantages.

You disrupt the environment by being able to *go forth where they don't expect it and attack where they are unprepared.* You fracture the cohesion of your opponents' processes and plans by creating a turbulent and deteriorating situation with which they cannot cope while, concurrently, satisfying your customers. Your prowess enables you to defeat your opponents psychologically as they become discouraged and quarrelsome as they keep falling hopelessly further and further behind you.

Figure 4.6 summarizes our strategic intent. Against a game board of the three standard business objectives of customer satisfaction, market share, and revenue/margins, the business will be free to move in any direction at will because its IT infrastructure is not an

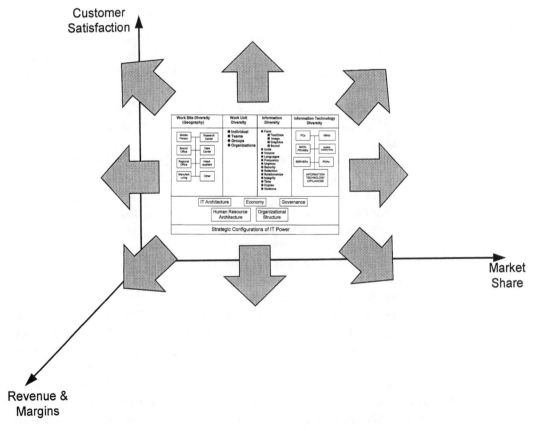

Figure 4.6   **Maneuver. Upon an infrastructure of strategic configurations of power, the business will be free to maneuver.**

accident; it is has been carefully constructed upon strategic configurations of power. A business that can execute Figure 4.6 is a business engaged in IT fighting. It is an information age predator to be feared.

STRATEGIC CONFIGURATIONS OF IT POWER

Strategic configurations of IT power are those selected and engineered infrastructure elements that permit frictionless, dynamic, and adaptive maneuver to take place. They are the crafted acts of potentiality that enable IT fighting. They are by definition high-leverage actions.

As itemized in Figure 4.5, we suggest five sources of interlocking power:

- IT architecture: The definition of the IT elements that will be used and the manner in which they interoperate.
- The economy: The manner in which the IT organization engages in transactions with its customers and between intra-organizational units.
- Governance: The policies and rules through which decision making is made between the IT organization and its customers.
- Human resource architecture (people): The policies used to promote commitment and effort towards a shared agenda by the IT staff.
- Organizational structure: The way that IT organizational units are structured and relate to each other.

Each IT organization will have to choose its own set consistent with its own unique set of needs. I believe these five to be a good reference model and starting point.

Some strategists propose rules of thumb that to be successful, strategic initiatives must be focused and limited to the two or three primary critical issues. Otherwise, you will disperse your attention and by trying to succeed at all, you will succeed at none. I believe that organizations are not impersonal and statistical rules of thumb; they are singular entities that have their own distinct challenges. You must do what is necessary to win whether that means doing one thing or doing 50 things. The marketspace does not care about arbitrary and impersonal rules of thumb.

The first thing that should strike you about my proposed strategic configurations of power is that even though we are developing IT strategic configurations of power, most of them are nontechnical sources of power. Many IT people believe that IT strategy should be constrained to only embrace technology. This is the result of functional decomposition thinking, not strategic thinking.

If you will recall from our discussion of strategic thinking in Chapter 2 (Figure 2.4 et al.), synthesis, not decomposition, sits at the heart of strategic thinking. Synthesis permits seeing properties present in the whole but not present in the parts. Thinking about IT strategy and limiting your plans to only technology issues means that you ignore the linkages.

IT technologies are managed in complex relationships with other functions such as those that we just listed. For architecture to work as a strategic configuration of power, it is necessary that the organization's structure, governance, and so on all function in linked harmony. Figure 4.7 more accurately depicts the linkage nature of the sources of power than Figure 4.5. So though it is tempting to sim-

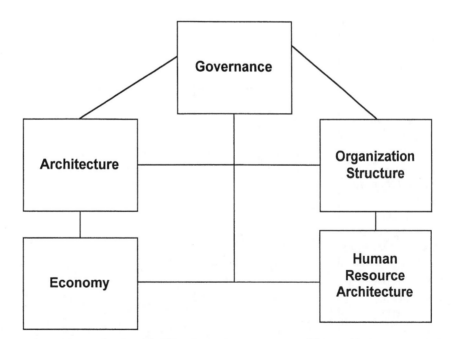

Figure 4.7   Revised strategic configurations of power. Configurations of power are tightly linked to each other.

plify and focus the strategic configuration of power effort just on architecture, you will discover to your chagrin that it is inadequate and that your sources of power must be more holistic. You must decide, do you wish to develop strategic configurations of power or do you wish to do an architecture project? They are not the same thing.

We will now provide an introduction to four of the five sources of power. The fifth, organizational structure, will be covered in Chapter 6. I have covered most of these subjects in depth in my other strategy books. It will be our purpose here to provide an overview of the key issues and provide appropriate references to more detailed explanations for the interested reader. Table 4.1 pro-

Table 4.1
Strategic Configuration of Power Reference

	IT Architecture	Economy	Human Resource Architecture	Governance	Organization Structure
Implementing Client/Server Computing: A Strategic Perspective	x				x
The Art of Strategic Planning for Information Technology	x	x			x
Practical Steps to Aligning Information Technology with Business Strategies	x		x		
Cost-Effective Strategies for Client/Server Systems	x			x	x

You can learn more about strategic configurations of power of interest to you by selecting the marked columns for each subject. All titles by Bernard H. Boar.

vides a reference list for more details on these sources of power from my other strategy books. Organizational structure has been separated out because, based on my consulting experiences of the last year, it remains a very visible and difficult issue that requires in-depth coverage.

Strategic Configuration of Power I: IT Architecture

An IT architecture is a series of principles, guidelines, or rules that guide an organization through acquiring, building, modifying, and *interfacing* IT resources throughout the enterprise. IT resources include equipment software, communication protocols, application development methodologies, database systems, modeling tools, IT organizational structures, and so on. With the migration to network computing environments (client/server, peer-to-peer, distributed objects, distributed processing, etc.), an IT architecture most importantly defines and demonstrates the interoperability, scalability, and portability of applications and their subcomponents across the architecture. An architecture should preserve IT investment as underlying technologies change.

Architecture is the classical case study of a strategic configuration of power. Since applications execute upon the data and processing components of the architecture, the maneuverability of the applications is directly enhanced or constrained by the foundation architecture decisions that are made. If architecture is performed at an application level, maneuverability is constrained to that level. On the other hand, if architecture is done at an enterprise level, all applications are postured to relate to each other through architectural coherence.

Figure 4.8 provides a taxonomy of business systems. The business applications are those applications that operationally *run* the business on a daily, weekly, monthly, and so on basis. The payoff from these applications is operational performance; they are cost-, productivity-, and efficiency-driven. The about the business applications are those applications that both provide information about the business and *analyze* the business. They are retrieval-, analysis-, report-, what-if, and information-sharing-oriented. The payoff from these applications is improved knowledge about the business, improved decision making, and information exchange.

Of particular interest in Figure 4.8 are info-transactional systems. These are a new generation of systems that provide the user with a

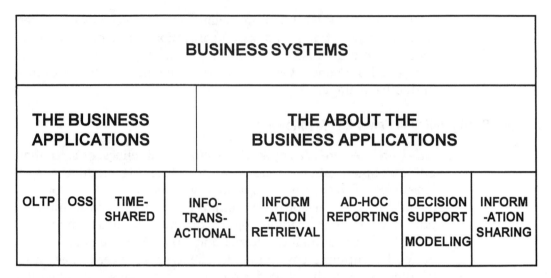

Figure 4.8   Business systems. Business systems can be classified into those that run the business and those that analyze the business.

rich mixture of information retrieval and transactional capabilities. It is the model for emerging information age applications where a user can engage in extended environment navigation, information retrieval and analysis, and then execute a structured transaction. These systems are also distinguished by the common usage of hypertext and the emerging use of hypermedia.

Figure 4.9 is a typical architecture definition matrix. It provides a broad boundary of what a comprehensive architecture should embrace. It is my view that the conceptual architecture that you want to catalog in such a matrix is the Reach, Range, and Maneuverability architecture that we introduced in Chapter 2 (Figure 2.18). Such an architecture provides what you require of an architectural strategic configuration of power:

- It provides the application portfolio with broad and inherited reach.
- It provides the application portfolio with broad and inherited range.
- It provides the application portfolio with broad and inherited maneuverability (scalability, portability, interoperability, and reconfigurability).

	INVENTORY	PRINCIPLES	MODELS	STANDARDS
INFRASTRUCTURE (PROCESSING)				
DATA				
APPLICATIONS				
ORGANIZATION				

Figure 4.9   Architecture matrix. The matrix defines the contents of a complete architecture. (Source: CSC Index)

A reach, range, and maneuverable architecture provides a context to understand what the elements of the architecture are, and, as is basic to any strategic configuration of power, what the relationships of those elements that promote maneuverability are.

Figure 4.10 decomposes a reach, range, and maneuverability architecture into its data architecture and processing architecture components. As is generally agreed by professional data architecture practice, the data architecture partitions databases into production subject databases that run the business and data warehouse decision support databases that are used to analyze the business. Structured extracts are taken on a scheduled basis from the operational databases and merged with foreign data sources to create the data warehouses. The data assets are purposefully decoupled from the business applications that use it. This makes them available as a server for whomever.

Figure 4.11 shows a logical view of what a processing architecture looks like. The notions highlighted by that illustration are as follows:

- Software should be divided into the three layers of presentation (PN), processing (PR), and data (DT). This decouples soft-

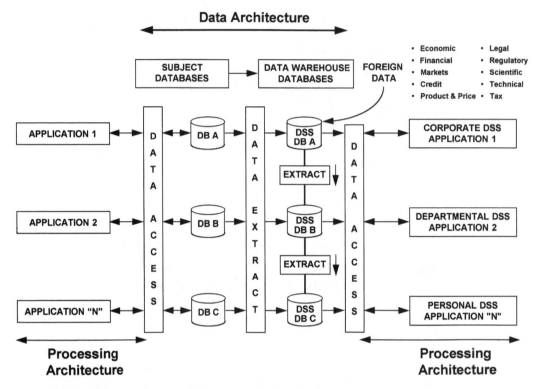

Figure 4.10   Data architecture plus processing architecture. A reach, range, and maneuverability architecture can be decomposed into a data architecture and a
processing architecture.

ware into distinct elements that can individually be positioned across the architecture based on evolving needs.

- The software layers are allocated to and run on platforms. A
platform is any type of information technology device.
- Software layers are written in any number of programming
languages. The software layers interoperate among themselves by invoking services though standardized application
program interfaces (APIs). The services (remote procedure
calls, data transfer, data access, distributed transaction management, messaging, etc.) hide the complexity of moving data
across platforms and move the information over transport
providers that use selected communications protocols.

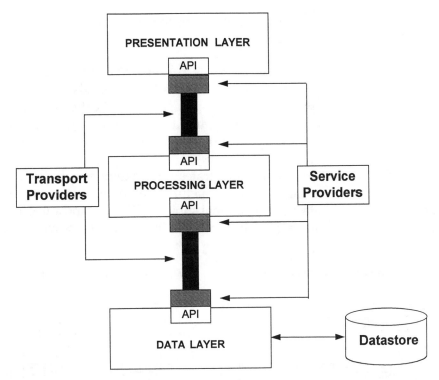

Figure 4.11 Processing architecture. The processing architecture divides software into layers and connectors between these layers.

This way of configuring a processing architecture meets the needs of a strategic configuration of power because of the following:

- It is modular. It divides the elements of the architecture into discrete pieces that can independently be selected, substituted for, and integrated.
- It emphasizes the horizontal relationships of the components. Many architectures are designed as simple or layered parts lists. This presentation of architecture does not communicate the relationships of the components, which is fundamental to being able to maneuver.
- It provides the basis for understanding the supported possibilities of movement. One can itemize against these types of

drawings the portability, scalability, and reconfigurability alternatives.

The defined architecture must be complete. By complete I mean that the architecture definition must also include the operational support components. Business applications must be operationally manageable. Many architectures ignore the operational dimension. Business applications that cannot be production-managed are useless.

Figure 4.12 illustrates the prize of a well-designed reach, range, and maneuverable architecture. As a consequence of decomposing data into operational subject databases and subject data warehouses and partitioning software into three layers with well-defined inter-

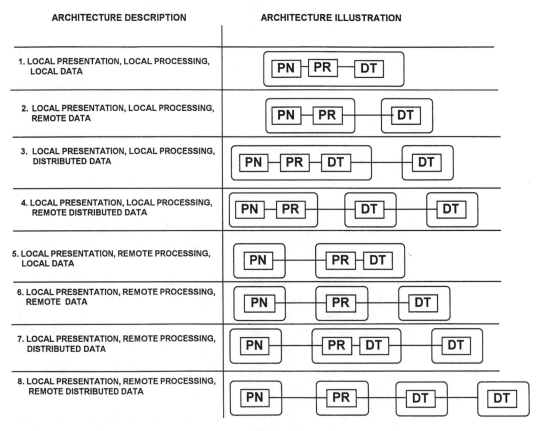

Figure 4.12   Architecture primitives. A thoughtfully designed reach, range, and maneuverability architecture creates 32 building block sub-architectures.

faces, your architecture is an elastic compendium of 32 building blocks. Any of the primitive 32 primitive architectures can be mapped into the others. Since these 32 primitive structures can endlessly be linked with each other via the authorized APIs and service providers, the adaptive designs available to you becomes limitless.

This is admittedly a brief overview of the design of an architectural strategic configuration of power, but it makes the following key points:

- Architecture is the perfect candidate for a strategic configuration of IT power. It is difficult to imagine IT being able to permit maneuverability without architecture being the primary member of the power set.

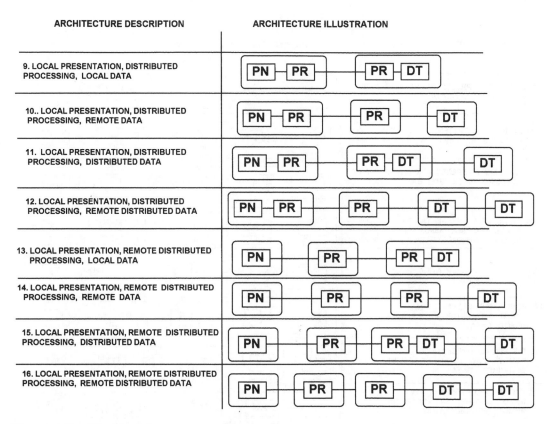

Figure 4.12   Continued

(continued)

- Architecture to offer maximum power must be done at a global level. In this way, you posture yourself for whatever across the business.
- All architectural designs are not equal. Decisions have severe beneficial or detrimental consequences. You must focus on what the elements are to be and how those elements are to relate to each other.

When you implement architecture as a strategic configuration of power, your 32 building block sub-architectures can translate into each other and be endlessly linked to each other. In this way, you meet the Sunian admonition that the *configurations of response must be inexhaustible.*

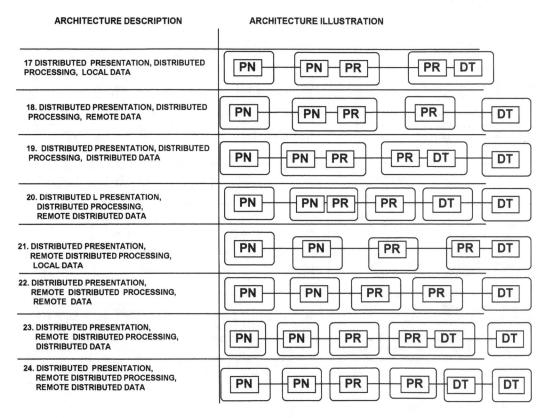

Figure 4.12   Continued

It should therefore be obvious why traditional monolithic host-centered computing architectures are in decline. A host-centered architecture is limiting yourself, by design, to only one of the 32 choices. While at some moments of time, such a configuration may be advantageous, why limit yourself to be permanently bound to it? By implementing an architectural strategic configuration of power, placing presentation, processing, and data on one platform becomes an option, not a limitation.

I remain astounded at the persistence of the Mainframe Preservation Society in resisting the mandatory move to distributed architectures. IT fighting dictates maneuverability, and traditional host-centered architectures are, by intent of design, the absence of maneuverability. Your strategic configuration of IT power must

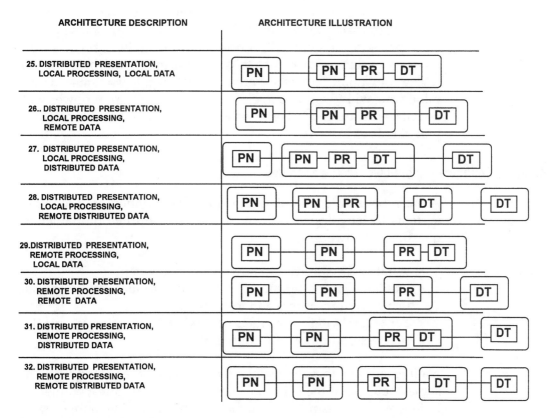

Figure 4.12   Continued

posture you so that the business can *go forth where they don't expect it and attack where they are unprepared.* This falls into the domain of modular distributed architectures with well-defined and standardized interfaces.

When you think about a program to create strategic configurations of IT power, quickly turn to architecture. Most enterprises today have a random collection of processing elements without any allusion of a purposeful grand intent. To the contrary, application project teams argue to the death why they absolutely must have their own unique everything. If you do not reposition your architecture as we have discussed, your opponent's strategy is translucent. Since you are concentrated and stationary, they know exactly what you can and cannot do. They will revise their software systems to continuously change the value proposition to the consumer. The growing impossibility of duplicating the functionality at all, yet with comparable speed, will break you.

So you have much to do. You must not only design your architectural strategic configuration of power, but you must also put in place processes to evolve it, processes to maintain it, processes to assure compliance, processes to communicate it, and processes to review deviation requests. Perhaps most of all, you must determine your will to enforce it, else your configuration of power will be but shelfware and become yet another disappointing configuration of failure.

Strategic Configuration of Power II: The Economy

A business is an economic entity and, like a nation, its economic systems for creating wealth must address the three fundamental questions of any economic system:

- What will be produced, how much, and when?
- How will it be produced, who will produce the products, using what resources and technologies?
- For whom will the products be produced, who will receive the products, and in what proportions?

Nations answer these questions by choosing an economic system somewhere along the continuum between laissez-faire, completely unfettered capitalism, and extremely central-planning, bureaucratic communism.

Analogous to a nation, every business must also design its economic systems. Its economic systems define the rules for economic exchanges (goods and services) between the business and its external customers (the external economy), the IT organization and its business unit customers (the business economy), and the rules of economic exchange (goods and services) within the IT organization itself (internal economy). Figure 4.13 illustrates these three complementary economic systems. Since the fundamental goal of an economic system is to create wealth through voluntary collaboration of parties, the design of both the business economy and the internal economy is a critical strategic configuration of power. It is a critical strategic configuration of power because it orchestrates how efficiently and how cooperatively people will work to meet their customer's needs. The economic system is the primary means of promoting alignment of IT products and services with business unit customer needs. An economic configuration of power is a strategic configuration of power that promotes extraordinary alignment between the providers of IT products and services and their customers.

In the television series "Star Trek: The Next Generation," there is an alien called Q. Q has remarkable powers that defy the galactic

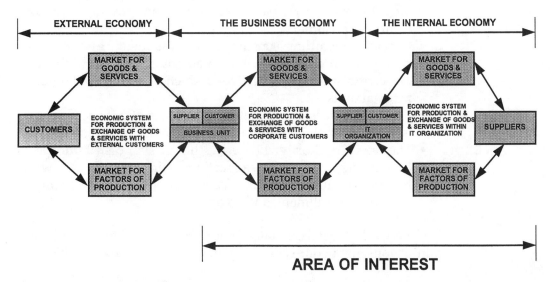

Figure 4.13 IT organization and economic systems. Every business has three interrelated economic systems.

laws of physics. In one episode, Q makes the statement: *"It is difficult to work in teams when you are omnipotent."* The average organizational unit is certainly not omnipotent in the way that Q is, but it
is omnipotent when the economic system does not, with its invisible hand, gently and not so gently push it to collaboration. If the
economy promotes monopolistic behaviors, the customer is not
served because the service provider optimizes its own well-inten-
tioned but selfish interest. In a poorly configured IT economy, each
IT organizational unit, armed with its annual budget, is omnipotent because they do what they wish without incentives to collaborate and align. How can you maneuver your systems, your
technologies, and procedures when each organizational unit is an
omnipotent Q?

Both the business economy and the internal economy need to be
explicitly designed to promote speed in the delivery of products
and services and adaptability in the delivery of products and services. They must be designed to align IT assets with the needs of its
customers. If you choose a central-planning model to govern your
economic transactions, then your business and internal economies
will work something like this:

- All decisions will be based on the decisions of central planners. Success will be a function of the wisdom of the planners,
  the information they base decisions on, and the shared needs
  of all the consumers.
- Decisions regarding consumption, investment, resource allocation, and production will be made by the central authority.
- The central authority will give production orders to all organizational units.
- Production orders will include all factors of production, that
  is, what technologies and methodologies are to be used.
- The central authority will decide the rules for distribution.
- Consumers will accept allocations without any say with
  regard to quality, terms and conditions, styling, cost, prompt-
  ness, need fulfillment, and so on.

If you select a laissez-faire model to govern your economic
transactions, then your economy will work something like this:

- All decisions will be based on the marketplace dynamics of
  market-driven producers and self-interested consumers. Suc-

cess will be a function of balancing producer revenue motives with consumer value/cost judgments.

- Producers must anticipate what goods and services consumers will want, at what value proposition, and in what quantities.
- Each producer must select the factors and methods of production that yield products must be attractive to consumers.
- Consumers will select products based on tradeoff between key buying factors.
- Advertising, marketing, and sales are used to educate consumers.
- Production will be adjusted to meet actual demands. The producers must spontaneously reorganize themselves to cope with the favorable or unfavorable consumer reaction to their offerings.

Most IT organizations participate in a haphazardly designed set of economic systems. They have randomly accumulated asynchronous economic rules on a tactical basis with the result that both the business and the internal economic systems often work against the goals of maneuverability and alignment.

It is important to acknowledge that the economic system is so critical to each employee's welfare, that more than any other factor, it governs people's behavior. It, unlike many actions that management takes, cannot be ignored without peril. So, though exaggerated, but only slightly so, as you design your economic systems, you posture yourself to be maneuverable and aligned, or stationary and misaligned. As you design your economic systems, you create a configuration of power to promote the maximum wealth creation by your IT resources.

Among many design choices, you must consider the following design points in formulating your economic strategic configuration of power:

- Allocation System: How is market demand governed? Does a central committee decide project allocations or do users make purchase decisions?
- Market System: Are users free to choose their supplier or is the IT organization a monopolist? Is the IT organization free not to supply internal customers? Can it sell to external clients? To what degree is the choice of technologies regulated?

- Resource (Budgeting) System: Do users control their IT budgets or are they taxed for services? Does the IT organization get a budget or earn revenue? Can the IT organization grow or contract based on demand or is its size used to throttle IT demand?
- Supplier System: Does the IT organization act as an order taker or operate as a competitive business?

In practice many business and internal economic systems are highly dysfunctional; they work against speed, quality, alignment, and adaptability. Numerous business economies are best described as communist, while it is common to observe internal economies that are best described as feudalistic. The external business economy has to compete in a feverish free market. Is it surprising that those who face the customer everyday are frustrated with IT unresponsiveness when they must react to a free-for-all marketspace while their IT service provider engages in stodgy economic communism or inwardly focused feudalism?

Among the common dysfunctions that result from poorly designed economies are:

- User needs fulfillment is a highly politicized process.
- An impersonal bureaucracy decides priorities.
- The IT budget creates an artificial cap on demand.
- The IT organization is shielded from competitive pressures.
- The IT organization is immediate supervisor focused.
- User organizations cannot dynamically shift resources.
- There is little motivation for IT organizations to innovate.
- IT billing is indecipherable.
- There is no nimbleness in the process.
- The IT organization is not subject to benchmarking or competition.

Let me share some actual examples of such economic dysfunction. In one company, the users negotiate an IT budget but are restricted to buying from the corporate IT organization. The budget of the IT organization is throttled to control expense and is often set below the amounts authorized to the consumer organizations. The result is a marketplace that becomes an auction with excess consumer dollars chasing too few IT resources. The IT units are put in the favorable position of being able to choose what they want to do based on interest and politics and the users, who have money that they can't spend, grow more resentful of the IT organization every day. This is not a configuration of power; it is a configuration for promoting disharmony and conflict.

In a second company, the funding of IT is done as an allocated tax. Day-to-day IT is therefore perceived as free. The people who receive IT services are not the same people who pay for them. The result is that the payer always feels that she is paying too much—after all, she gets no personal benefit for her tax payments—and the consumer is always screaming for more—after all, it is free. As it is true in your personal lives, for an economy to work towards satisfaction of all parties and for considered tradeoffs to be made between needs and cost, those who benefit must also be those who pay. So what we have here is a configuration of economic power that results in the users being perpetually dissatisfied with their IT provider due to the economic structure.

A final case exemplifies a most common situation. The IT organization is organized into technological smokestacks. Operations, planning, and technology support each receive their own budget. Each group bitterly complains about the lack of cooperation form the others. Systems support does not wish to support what planning promotes, operations does not wish to run what the developers develop, and operations does not wish to install the new system releases per support's plans. This culminates in gross customer dissatisfaction with their service provider as what they want is systems, not to referee IT internal bickering. Prefunded for the year, each has absolutely no motivation to cooperate with the other. Collaboration, when it does occur, is a result of edict, I.O.U.s, favors, shifting coalitions, and politics. How quickly their behavior would turn if they had to offer joint proposals to customers to earn revenue.

How could you use the economic system to favorably alter organizational behavior? Consider the following:

Economic Issue 1. Middle-level IT managers do not voluntarily cooperate with each other. Rather than sharing their resources and concentrating them at crucial points of immediate need, they hoard their staffs because their bonuses are based on their individual performance.

Economic Resolution. Change the bonus formula so that 25% of each manager's bonus is based on their performance and 75% is based on the group's performance.

Economic Issue 2. Developers do everything that they can to avoid using the strategic IT architecture.

Economic Resolution. Estimate the expected productivity increase per project to be realized by using the architecture. Lower the recovery billing rates that developers may charge users by that percent. Developers can make up the shortfall by using the architecture or finding another way to improve productivity by the reduction factor. In the latter case, find out what they did and repeat the rate reduction process with the new productivity factor. Eventually, they will run out of innovations and they will use the architecture and, as an unexpected bonus for you, they will have created all kinds of productivity improvements.

Economic Issue 3. You wish to improve productivity through the implementation of object-oriented programming and need to populate a reusable object library. It is your expectation that through the use of shared objects, you will significantly improve the quality, the speed, and the cost of software development.

Economic Resolution. Share the productivity improvement with the development staff. Create a unit to own the reusable object library called Objects Inc. Objects Inc. will pay development groups in the form of education credits, computer show attendance credits, dinners, and annual bonuses for objects that are submitted to and accepted by Objects Inc. Development groups will also be paid a three-year royalty in the same manner as the original payment based on usage by other development groups. Development groups that use objects from Objects Inc., other than their own objects, will likewise receive payments for the usage.

Figure 4.14 shows a comparison of varying economic governance choices. Should you throw up your hands and solve all your problems by outsourcing? On this subject, Machiavelli said the following 500 years ago:

> The arms on which a prince bases the defense of his state are either his own, or mercenary, or auxiliary. Mercenaries and auxiliaries are useless and dangerous. If a prince bases the defense of his state on mercenaries, he will never achieve stability or security. The reason for this is that there is no loyalty or inducement to keep them on the field apart from the little they are paid and that is not enough to make them want to die for you. I conclude therefore, that unless it commands its own arms, no principality is

secure, rather it is dependent on fortune for there is no valor and no loyalty to defend it when adversity comes.

If in the information age, you are going to engage in IT fighting, bits will replace atoms, the marketspace will replace the market-place, and IT is elevated to a core competency (it is the business for convergent and secondary industries in Table 1.13), why would you turn it over to mercenaries? Perhaps it will make sense to turn over tactical operations for non-core systems or do transitional out-sourcing to enable you to focus your staff on moving to emergent technologies, but you must maintain control of your IT strategic configuration of power.

I know that this is in opposition to conventional wisdom and that the outsourcing industry is thriving. Nevertheless, I cannot help but feel that if they are successful, they will one day hold you to ransom, and, if they are incompetent, they will bring you to ruin. Viewed this way, creating a strategic configuration of economic power is a much more appealing alternative.

Economic Attribute	Economic Governance System			
	Free-Market	**Outsourcing**	**IT Monopoly**	**Regulated IT Utility**
Allocation	Customer Chooses	Contractual	Committee	Customer Chooses
Market	Customer Chooses	Outsourcer	IT Organization	IT Organization
Budgeting	Customer Controls	Contractual	Corporate Tax	Customer controls
Supplier	Customer Selects	Outsourcer	IT Organization	Control Board
Sovereign	Customer	Contract	IT	Business
Architecture	Each Project	Contract	IT	Control Board
Governance	Market	Bilateral	Unified	Bilateral

Figure 4.14   Alternative economic governance. In practice, the choices of economic design are limitless.

You should not be diverted by expedient solutions that are not solutions at all, and proceed to build an economic strategic configuration of power. Your game plan should be as follows:

- Model the current business and internal economies.
- Identify all dysfunctions that prevent maneuverability and alignment.
- Model alternative new economies.
- Evaluate each choice.
- Select new economies.
- Implement boldly.

This is a formidable and nontrivial task. There are many vested interests in your current economic systems and those who are enriched by them will not give up their gain without a confrontation. Resistance will be uncompromising and endless reasons will sprout forth explaining why you can't change this and absolutely can't alter that. Be strong and of good courage. Persist. A strategic configuration of economic power is a *path to strategic triumph.*

Strategic Configuration of Power III: Governance

IT organizations are social, economic, political, and cultural institutions. As is the case with any institution of their size and complexity, they require governance. Governance provides a set of polices, goals, themes, roles and responsibilities, decision-making procedures, conflict resolution procedures, and so on that permit both stability and growth. Governance is embodied in a governance document that outlines these issues.

Governance is a strategic configuration of power because it promotes collaboration while eliminating friction. It promotes collaboration by clarifying intent, standards, and procedures. It eliminates friction by providing a clear definition of responsibilities and processes to adjudicate conflict. You cannot be maneuverable if every decision requires unanimous approval or if every standard is reopened for debate for each project. You cannot be fast and agile if it is ambiguous what should be used or it is unclear who is responsible for funding or if you are subject to retroactive jeopardy after having gotten what you believed to be the necessary deviation approvals.

An IT organization is a living organism. Procedures that did work grow dated, new technologies have to be added to the technology portfolio while others need to be grandfathered in an orderly way, objectives change, and a delicate balance has to be maintained between the needs of the many (standardization) and the needs of the few (customization).

One form of government an IT organization can adopt is a centralized dictatorship. While orderly, it squashes innovation and participation, and stunts growth. The dictator has to be everywhere and make every decision. At the other extreme, an anarchistic organization yields technological chaos. Everybody optimizes their components but nobody integrates the whole. We would submit that a governance model based on a simple constitution is best for an IT organization, just as it is the best alternative for a society.

Underlying the view of governance as a strategic configuration of power is the belief that the orderly management of technology is more important than the specific technologies managed. Orderly management lubricates movement. Anarchistic IT organizations spend the majority of their time (and money) arguing over which instance of a technology they should use this time. Endless studies, vendor presentations, consulting reports, benchmarks, and meetings are called friction. They preempt maneuverability.

A governed IT organization is more concerned with the questions of what are the technologies we need to win and less about which one among many acceptable candidates is chosen. Dictatorial IT organizations prescribe a way. Governed IT organizations prescribe both a way and a way to change the way. So governed organizations are results-oriented and have a sense of urgency to get on with it, while nongoverned organizations are technology-oriented and want to endlessly quarrel about technologies.

A governance document would cover the following major topics:

1. Vision: A compelling statement of the long-term strategic intent of the organization. For example: It is our strategic intent to enable the business to win in the marketplace thought a ceaseless quest for perfect reach, perfect range, and perfect maneuverability.

2. Mission: A statement of the grand task of the organization. For example: It is our mission to manage our information technology resources so that the business can win in the marketplace every day, with every transaction with every customer. Through the superior deployment of information technology we will

impress our attitude on the marketplace and prevail over our competitors who have already lost.

3. Objectives: Measurable and dated results that are to be achieved over a planning period. For example: Over the next three years, it is our objective to:

   • Reduce the unit costs of operational services at an annual rate of x%.
   • Increase the function points/dollar at an annual rate of y%.
   • Increase customer satisfaction by n% over the time period.
   • Maintain a xx% share of all user IT expenditures.

4. Strategic Themes: Identify the strategic ideas that should strongly influence and provide a guiding background for all decision making. Strategic themes attempt to address the problem of influence at a distance. Figure 4.15 illustrates how a magnetic field works. Magnetic fields engage in action (attraction and repulsion) at a distance between magnetic poles. Though the poles don't physically touch, their magnetic fields influence each other.

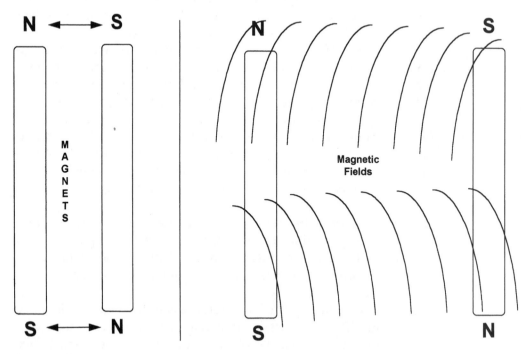

Figure 4.15 The physics of strategic themes. Strategic themes provide the equivalent of a gravitational field.

Management has the same conceptual problem. They can't be everywhere and make every decision. They need to provide influence at a distance. This is done by broadcasting strategic themes that share their intentions. The themes inform the employees what the leadership would take into consideration if they were present. This permits dispersed employees to be empowered and apply their judgment in synchronization with overall strategy.

For example: All decisions should be guided with concern for speed, agility, customer satisfaction, affordability, and operational excellence.

Or: All decisions should be guided with concern for cost reduction and containment, preservation of legacy systems, leveraging of existing skills, and adherence to established operational standards.

Obviously, each of these sets of strategic themes send very different messages to the IT community.

5. Principles: Statements of beliefs that bound and direct decision making. Some are specific; others provide broad guidance in the forms of values and concepts that require situational judgment in their application.

    For example: 1. Security procedures will be enacted to control access to all information processing systems. 2. Data will be administered as a corporate resource and subject databases will be built as a shared resource for all authorized users. 3. For nonstrategic systems, purchased software will always be preferable to internal development.

6. IT Organization Roles and Responsibilities: A statement of roles and responsibilities by logical function. For example: Development management will be responsible for adhering to all architectural rules and guidelines subject to deviation procedures.

7. Customer Relationship Management: A definition of the rules and guidelines for dealing with clients. For example: This section might include user roles and responsibilities, funding producers, system acceptance criteria, operational customer satisfaction measurements and service level metrics, and IT responsibilities for user-procured IT assets.

8. Supplier Relationship Management: A definition of the rules and guidelines for dealing with vendors. For example: This section might include vendor performance criteria, vendor selec-

tion criteria, vendor quality and partnering initiatives, and support guidelines.

9. Committee List, Procedures, and Enforcement: A definition of standing committees, their domain of empowerment, their operating procedures, and how they enforce their decisions.

For example: The architecture review committee will be responsible for overseeing the evolution of the corporate architecture. Representation will include delegates for all functional IT organizations as well as user organizations. Violations of architectural guidelines will be handled by the assessment of a pollution tax at a cost set by the IT auditing function. Deviation requests will be managed by the Architectural Review Board that reports to this committee. All architecture deviation requests will receive a written response within two to four weeks of request.

Governance has the synthesis quality to serve as the integration power for all the other powers. Architecture, economy, and human resources could all be managed and integrated as governance committees. In this way, there is a place to resolve differences and promote synergy.

If for no other reason, constitutional governance is a mandatory strategic configuration of power because of its ability to reduce friction and lubricate the organization. The end of a bureaucratic and dictatorial governance structure is stagnation. Left to their own devices, bureaucracies pass through conservatism and become retrogressive. The end of an anarchistic structure is chaos. Constitutional governance provides a means to enable dispersed execution with coordinated purpose.

Strategic Configuration of Power IV: Human Resource Architecture

Of all the subjects covered in *The Art of War*, the topic that earns the most coverage is winning the *loyalty, devotion, and love of the people*. Sun Tzu said: "Because he regards his men as infants, they will march with him into the deepest valleys. He treats them as his own beloved son and they will die with him." He understood that if you were going to ask people to undergo incredible hardship to the point of dying for you, they must share a deep personal commitment to your aims. Commitment yields belief, belief yields effort, and Herculean effort yields incredible results.

A strategic configuration of human resource power consists of polices, human resource systems, corporate ethos/culture, and attitudes that seek to convert meaningful values into winning behaviors. Most IT staffs are quite jaded and cynical. They are tired of strategic programs du jour and their hard-earned perception that their management believes deeply in little, especially them, and is committed to less. Adaptive maneuver cannot take place when those who must do the maneuvering are at best unenthusiastic and at worst are trying to get even. Nothing has done more to destroy whatever strategic configuration of people power that organizations had than the mindless downsizing that has convinced even the most devoted employees that they are nothing more than throwaway tissues to their employer. How can you build a strategic configuration of power that requires cohesion, hustle, passion, devotion, commitment, espirit de corp, and camaraderie when any reasonable person has to conclude that their employer equates them to an interchangeable and mindless cog?

The types of behaviors that are needed to fuel your configuration of power are:

- Learning: Your employees must be rewarded and given the opportunity to keep increasing their skills both within their current profession and new fields of opportunity.
- Mastery: Your employees need to be rewarded and encouraged to achieve and maintain personal excellence.
- Service: Your employees must be dedicated to servicing the needs of your customers.
- Innovation: Your employees must feel free to take calculated risks to discover new and improved ways to do things.
- Ownership: Your employees must feel a deep personal commitment to get things done. It is their problem.
- Initiative: Your employees must take preemptive actions in their own recognizance to prevent problems rather than only reacting to them.
- Quality: Your employees must understand that the output of the next person is only as good as the input they provide.
- Speed: Your employees must understand that in all things speed is paramount. Speed alone compensates for numerous other failings. Hustle is a valued trait.
- Respect: Your employees must treat each other as they would like to be treated.

- Collaboration: Your employees must work together to accomplish shared aims. Once a decision is made, effort is expended at achieving the goals rather than proving the decision wrong.
- Receptivity to change: Since the employees trust management, they must be willing to risk change without putting up incredible levels of resistance.

These are the types of behaviors that you must configure your personal systems, policies, and cultures to grow.

The following specific actions can be taken to achieve, in part, these winning behaviors:

- Develop programs to create specialist generalist. Freed from the bondage of only knowing one thing, employees will become more open and receptive to new and different ideas.
- Create teams on the basis of open orders. Open orders specify what needs to be done but leaves it open as to how it is to be done. While this maintains overall strategic coordination, authority, and responsibility, it leaves plenty of room for team members to exercise their intelligence, experience, and be innovative in problem solving without having somebody looking over their shoulders and second-guessing every decision.
- Create flatter organizations. Fewer decision makers yields faster decisions, forces managers to focus on what matters, and encourages pushing down decision making and responsibility by necessity.
- Fund problem owner budgets. Let them buy the assistance they need rather than go around the organization begging and pleading for it.
- Align your reward systems with your stated policies. If you believe in teams, reward at the team level.
- Demonstrate commitment. Publicly reward those who demonstrate the desired behaviors; don't reward employees who don't.
- Make examples. If you wish to promote innovation, promote someone who fails. If you wish to promote collaboration, demote someone who doesn't. They are all watching and judging your sincerity. If they can trust you, than they will devote themselves to you.

A strategic configuration of people power has the mixed fortune of being both the most important configuration of power and the hardest to achieve and sustain. There is, however, no alternative. You can distinguish an IT organization that has achieved a configuration of people power because they proceed forward with passion and zeal, and without friction, resistance, or drag.

Conclusion

Procedurally, the implementation of strategic configurations of power are the same as any other strategic initiative. You must:

- Model the current position of the source of power.
- Model a winning position for the source of power, the desired future state.
- Define a set of strategic actions that will move you between positions.
- Develop both a change plan and a commitment plan to overcome the inevitable resistance to such massive change.
- Allocate programs and projects to execute the strategic actions.
- Assign champions and owners to get the job done.
- Communicate, participate, and educate to reduce friction and drag.
- Forge political coalitions to secure a critical mass of support.
- Deploy a strategy control process to oversee the progress of the actions.

What is different is that you must manage all the initiatives holistically so as not to lose linkages and it must all be done under the overarching theme of maneuverability.

All of these initiatives must include a benchmarking component. Speed and flexibility are measurable but they are only meaningful as relative measures. What matters is that you are more maneuverable than your opponents. You can only know that through benchmarking.

This set of strategic configurations of power are certainly not the only possible sets. Other candidates could be your operational processes, your supplier relationships, knowledge management, application development, core competencies and, of course, strategy development. One could argue that, recursively, strategy formulation and execution are the most critical strategic configuration of power because it is the configuration of power from which all other powers are born. In Chapter 5, we will discuss Breeder Strategy as a way to improve the entire organization's strategic competence.

I find it necessary to contradict myself. In one of my earlier books, I said that if there was only one initiative that the IT executive could undertake, that initiative should be architecture. Yes, architecture is incredibly important but it is not the most important configuration of power. I was too influenced by my technology roots.

The most powerful of the strategic configurations of power remains people. Nothing will be accomplished without the sustained and Herculean efforts of your staff. In the Knowledge Society, how could it be otherwise? So more than ever, you must work on developing an organizational espirit de corp that aligns the hearts and minds of your staff with the aims of the business. All ages are first and foremost people ages.

CONCLUSION

Strategic configurations of power are not easy to build. They do not provide instant gratification; they do provide a long-term infrastructure for success. It requires persistence, will, commitment, and the ability to overcome countless obstacles including the vocal corporate chorus of Cassandras of doom and gloom.

It is well worth the labors. Without such an investment, you cannot execute a strategy of potentiality. If you cannot execute a strategy of potentiality, you cannot engage in IT fighting. If you cannot engage in IT fighting, you cannot win in the information age. In this way, you blaze a path to strategic triumph. Always remember, the struggle you are engaged in is a struggle for advantage. Advantage never comes easily.

The heart of a strategic configuration of power is in its ability to enable maneuverability. You make yourself maneuverable by designing in speed and agility, and designing out friction. You cannot compromise on this issue. The power in strategic configurations of power is not to be found in physical strength or size; it is found in flexibility and speed. These two design points cannot be compromised else you will create, to your own misfortune, a strategic configuration of rigidity and sluggishness.

Flexibility (a.k.a. nimbleness, agility, adroitness, dexterity, etc.) and speed (velocity, alacrity, swiftness, dispatch, etc.) are fundamental principles of strategy. Sun Tzu said about speed:

> Some win through speed. . . . Use swiftness to wear them out. . . . Get the upper hand through extraordinary swiftness. . . . Be as fast as the lightning that flickers before you can blink you eyes. . . . Speed is the essence of conflict. . . . It is necessary to proceed quickly, it won't work if you hesitate. . . . Outspeed them. . . . *Speed is the essence of strategy.* [emphasis added]

Sun Tzu said about flexibility:

> Adaptation means not clinging to fixed methods, but changing appropriately to events. . . . Victory adapts is form endlessly. . . . The configurations of responses to the enemy are inexhaustible. . . . Travel by unexpected routes and strike him where he has taken no precautions. . . . Adaptive maneuver must be limitless.

Musashi added: "Be prepared in spirit to change the direction of your attack at any moment; superlative speed is essential to be able to move in on the enemy."

Speed and flexibility are not subject to the contradictions of strategic paradox. You can never be too fast nor too flexible. The end of being fast is not being slow and the end of being flexible is not being rigid. The end of being maneuverable is strategic triumph.

Strategic configurations of power provide the business with *option value.* Decision makers always are faced with three complementary problems: what do I want to do, what can I do, and when can I do it? Strategic configurations of power posture the IT weaponry so that the answers to the latter two questions are always, respectively, whatever and now. After all, in a world of global IT fighting, what other reply would be acceptable? Our strategic configurations of power prepare us for whatever, because what less would be worth preparing for? In this way, we have fulfilled Sun Tzu's enduring admonition: *"Those who face the unprepared with preparation are victorious!"*

The information age creates a period of unique historical competitive fervor. It is a war of all against all. At its essence, it is a contest of frenzied and abrupt movement. Design your strategic configurations of power appropriately; else your customers will abandon you, and your competitors will ruin you by virtue of their infinite adaptive maneuver against your industrial age artifact methods.

Nevertheless, some hesitate. They are concerned that constructing strategic configurations of power will be costly; how do you justify such an investment when cost containment and cost reductions are the prevailing strategic actions of our times? The answer is yes, you will need to invest, but there is every reason to anticipate saving money as well as making money. A major thrust of strategic configurations of power is the elimination of friction. At most companies, 10 units of effort yields only three or four units of output. The remainder is dissipated in overcoming the omnipresent friction. The simple act of lubricating the business will yield tremendous productivity improvements. How much more productive will you be when speed and agility further improve productivity?

Do not build your information age strategy based on the shallow and near-sighted logic of accounting. More of the same effort will not even be enough to uphold a constant level of mediocrity. Strategic configurations of power provide a deep and far-reaching strategy that will enable you to win even before you fight. Musashi said: "The only reason a warrior is alive is to fight, and the only reason a warrior fights is to win. Otherwise, why be a warrior. It is easier to count beads." You are no longer a CIO or VP of IT or Director of Information Systems, you have become an IT warrior who engages in IT fighting. Warriors do not count beads. You have become the highest type of warrior, an *aware* individual. Do not continue business as usual, the easy but destructive path to stagnation. Win through a deep and far-reaching strategy of strategic configurations of power.

5

Breeder Strategy

PROBLEM AND OPPORTUNITY

In Chapter 2, we asked the question, where does strategy come from? Our answer was that strategies are the harvest of strategic thinking. If we repeat this question recursively in an attempt to discover the first mover, we now ask, where does strategic thinking come from? The answer is that strategic thinking is accomplished by people. It is the creative output of individuals, who through a natural gift of intuition or training, mentoring, study, and experience have mastered the art.

Prior to the information age, strategic thinking and strategy formulation was formally limited to the top of the corporate hierarchy. Senior management developed, managed, and communicated strategy. The rest of the organization was responsible for the tactical details of implementation. There is a great deal of controversy over the wisdom of this strategy model but, for better or worse, it is an accurate portrayal of what was done in practice.

Many changes have occurred that challenge the continued wisdom of this approach. The following interlocking events have raised the question of whether it is now prudent to deconcentrate strategy and disperse strategic thinking and strategy formulation throughout the entire organization and, especially, to those units who face the customer:

1. *Hierarchy failure:* Strategic planning, under the command and control structure, has not worked nearly as well as hoped for or needed. One just needs to chart the changing fortunes of once great companies to see the paucity of strategic acumen. As the

issues in the strategy mix have grown—globalization, techno-logical discontinuities, consumerism, hyper-competition, merg-ers, acquisitions, spin-offs, and accelerated cycle times—it has become more evident that a few remote executives do not have all the answers and, in many cases, are too far removed from the mayhem of the marketplace to truly hear and understand the voice of the customer.

2. *Democratic organizations:* In response to competition, the need for speed and agility, the recognition that the hierarchy does not have all the answers, the rise of process management as the pre-ferred organizing structure, social/cultural demands by employ-ees for more say, and information age technologies that facilitate collaboration and promote the knowledge organization, many organizations are moving to more democratic structures. Though they go by many different names such as participation management, teams, self-managing work groups, and empow-erment, they all share the same fundamental idea that decision making should be pushed down, placed closer to the customer, and put in the hands of those who know and do the work.

3. *The information age:* Strategic thinking and strategy are a response to conflict. Without conflict, business reduces to a problem of efficient administration. Strategy and strategic thinking become of interest when, and only when, competition arises. If you have a monopoly, your strategy is maintaining the monopoly. As we have discussed, the nature of the information age creates an incredibly contentious environment. As the tempo of the game quickens, speed and flexibility of response, not hierarchical posi-tion, become crucial. Sun Tzu said:

> As a rule, you need to change tactics a hundred times. To talk about government orders is like going to announce to your superiors that you want to put out a fire. By the time you get back with an order, there is nothing left but ashes.

The competitive nature of the information age propels strategic decision making to the point of action. It propels it to those who know what's happening.

The resulting notion that emerges from these three concurrent events is that strategy and strategic thinking should be dispersed and executed throughout the organization. By dismantling the command and control of the hierarchy, those closest to the customer and the situation will be empowered to strategize and act. To put it in the fighting words of the times: *Everyone and anyone is to be a strategist.*

As one proponent of dispersing strategy formulations states:

> Strategic management is a task for the whole organization all the time, not the province of specialist or a once yearly undertaking.

What they believe is that the aggregate decisions of many associates, exercising individual judgment, even if frequently mistaken, is likely to do less harm than the detached decisions of a hierarchical management and, in any case, through proximity of seeing the results and hustle, will be corrected briskly.

While this is all very liberating and promoted with enthusiasm by the advice community, it does raise three serious questions to the attentive observer:

1. *Synthesis:* As you know, the heart of strategic thinking is not decomposition, but synthesis. The dispersal of strategy responsibility raises question about how holistic thinking and action will be accomplished. Who will see and synthesize the whole picture and speak and think for the whole?

2. *Quality of strategy:* If the few in the hierarchy couldn't do it well, why should we expect that the masses will? If strategy and strategic thinking becomes everyone's responsibility, how does it happen that everyone is an able strategist? Popularization of anything normally results in the creation of a large group of average people. When a large group of people do anything, the result is a huge cluster at the center of a bell curve. We want strategic excellence. Rather than improving the situation, the great transfer of strategy to the organizational rank and file could just as well result in mass strategic mediocrity.

3. *Suitability:* IT professionals, by virtue of their training, nature, interests and dislikes, will not necessarily make very good strategists. The following is a list of qualities one would normally associate with a capable strategist:
   - Holistic thinking: The individual views problems from multiple perspectives and integrates those perspectives.
   - Abstract thinking: The individual is comfortable dealing with conceptual ideas.

- Acceptance of ambiguity: The individual can accept that she will always have to analyze, synthesize, and make decisions based on inadequate and incomplete information.
- Ability to work with models: The individual is comfortable analyzing the real world through abstract models of it.
- Interpretation of metaphors: The individual is able to translate metaphors and aphorisms into practical meanings.
- Open-mindedness: The individual can cast aside her views and consider new and contradictory positions without prejudice or bias.
- Humility: The individual feels the responsibility and burden of the consequences of her duties and is humbled by it.
- Research orientation: The individual is interested in continually learning and improving her strategic acumen.
- Curiosity: The individual's favorite words are why and how.
- Multi-axial thinking: The individual can think in multiple dimensions at a time.
- Paradoxical thinking: The individual can cope with the discomfort of paradox.

Are these the characteristics of your average IT team member? While there is much to be optimistic about in the dispersal of strategy and strategic thinking, there is also reason for caution and concern.

BREEDER STRATEGY

My response to this issue is what I call a *breeder strategy*, a bold action to distribute strategic thinking capabilities across the enterprise. If we are going to dispose of the command and control model, we must not replace it with a substitute form of mediocrity but with a superior capability. The superior capability is an organization with dispersed strategy responsibilities that has created excellence in breeding strategy. By a breeder strategy, I mean a deep and far-reaching competence in strategic thinking, strategy formulation, strategy execution, and the ability to continually procreate new strategies in harmony with changing times and circumstances.

Sun Tzu set the objectives for a breeder strategy:

Victory over the multitudes is unknowable by the multitudes. Everyone knows the forms by which I am victorious, but no one knows the form by which I ensure victory. They know the traces of attainment of victory, but do not know the abstract form that makes for victory. Victory is apparent to all, but the science of ensuring victory is a mysterious secret, generally unknown.

It is the objective of a breeder strategy that as many people in your organization as possible master *the abstract forms and mysterious secrets that make for victory.*

The idea is to create an army of awesome strategic thinkers, a cadre of imaginative thinkers who are not constrained by what has been or what is. Competitive superiority is not about winning today's contests, it is about prepositioning to win tomorrow's contests, contests that are most often not simple linear extrapolations of the present. Accounting logic will provide you with a score card but it is strategic thinking that will tell you the opportunistic paths to follow. How much more sweeping the possibilities when we increase the community of people who can fruitfully engage in the *mysterious secrets.*

The dispersal of strategy responsibility, without a plan on how you are going to educate and elevate the acumen of the new strategists, is magical thinking. Magical thinking occurs when you think something and you believe that that makes it happen. Declaring everyone a strategist is exciting for the moment but unless one takes pains to train and mentor the newly sprung army of junior Sun Tzus, the results will be next year's strategic planning problem. You will create a muddle larger than the one that you had hoped to escape.

A breeder strategy, on the other hand, has the raw potential to make strategy a strategic configuration of power. If you have dispersed strategic excellence, and numerous individuals and teams throughout your business can engage in creative strategic thinking and action on a daily basis, you will have created a Sunian organization. Sun Tzu described strategists as follows:

They do not wander when they move. They act in accord with events. Their actions and inactions are matters of strategy. . . . A leader of deep wisdom and ability lays deep plans for what others do not think about.

An entire organization of people who do not wander, who act in accord with events, and whose every action spurts strategy, is an organization that has turned strategy into a strategic configuration of power.

A breeder strategy is a long-term infrastructure strategy to raise the tide of strategic perfection throughout the organization. It consists of four complementary actions:

- *Education:* Most of your staff probably has little or no formal education in strategy. It will be necessary to provide formal foundation education with ongoing special topic seminars as the students achieve advanced readiness. Nobody would expect a database administrator to be able to do logical database design, physical database design, and production operations design without extensive formal education. Strategic thinking is a much more difficult subject. If you are not willing to train your people, do not expect the dispersal of strategy responsibility to accomplish anything other then dispersing mediocrity.

  Basic strategy education can be accomplished in a one-week course. Subjects covered would include: strategic thinking, strategic frameworks, strategic planning methodology, schools of strategic thought, classics of strategy, and case studies. More advanced courses would focus on special subjects such as positioning, change management, alignment, or use of a sophisticated framework such as the Five Forces analysis method of Dr. Michael Porter of Harvard. Special seminars would consist of group discussion of the classics of strategy such as *The Art of War* and *The Five Rings* and relating the studied sections to current business problems.

- *Study:* A strategist becomes a student of strategy. The reward and recognition system must encourage continual learning and further mastery of the art. Employees must be encouraged to join professional associations, attend strategy conferences, read strategy books and journals, and participate in industry consortia concerned with strategy issues. You must study because study increases your receptivity to learning and understanding the deeper teachings of the great masters. Musashi said:

  > Remember that what I say and how you perceive what I say can be completely different depending upon your *awareness* of yourself and the level of skill that you have attained. The need for constant study and thought is essential for understanding the way of the warrior. [emphasis added]

Study helps create *aware* individuals. Aware individuals see what others do not see, know what others do not know, and perceive the formless. This is optimum return for your breeder strategy investment.

When I conduct strategy workshops with clients, I sometimes ask that to do the "I wish" exercise. When your team engages in "I wish," you make a list of the five key things you would most wish for your business. People wish for all sorts of things. Most often, they wish for the gifts of collaboration, leadership, speed, and alignment. If I was ever on an "I wish" team, my wish would be different. I would wish for awareness.

- *Mentoring:* Strategic thinking is very hard. Having a mentor makes the seemingly impossible possible. Promising strategists should be culled out and assigned to your best strategist for tutoring and development. When you start a breeder strategy, you will not know who will excel. As time progresses, it will become evident who is thriving and who is dog-paddling. You must reinforce success. Through mentoring, you can accelerate the mastery of your junior people.
- *Practice:* Reading and talking about strategy can only get you so far. As is true with mastering any discipline, it is necessary to be a practitioner. Your aspiring strategists need to be given assignments appropriate to their development to stretch and grow their skills. Briefings, presentations, analysis, and so on should all provide opportunities to exhibit their growing strategic acumen.

One of the most noticeable things about organizations that have trained their people in strategy is how the daily debates changes. All work takes on a strategy flavor. The language, the frameworks, and the way of thinking permeates the organization and changes their approach from whatever was being done to a strategic approach. Emotional technology arguments become S-curve discussions. Scattered thinking debates on what to do turn into collaborative Kano sessions. It is an amazing thing to observe.

I never cease to be amazed at how money is spent on things of much less enduring value while a breeder strategy is deemed controversial. How better can your spend your money then by raising the tide of strategic excellence of your business? Many organizations averaged two weeks of training per employee on total quality management and other passing strategic fads. What they got for their money was people trained in one, and only one, specific strategic action. This strategic action was being co-executed by all their competitors and, at best, would yield competitive parity. Having spent all that money and time, all that happened was that the bar got raised for all and all were prepared to reach the new height. If you spent two weeks training all you employees on strategy, as you did for specific strategic actions, you would have a group of people who on a daily basis would begin breeding strategy distinct to your business. Is that not a far more superior result?

All your employees will not achieve the same level of excellence. As is true with everything else, there is a distribution of achievement based on many factors. So some will do better and lead, and the rest will do better than they did before. The bell curve will still be a bell curve but it will have shifted dramatically to the right. You should anticipate that your staff's skills will be distributed across the following four levels of attainment:

- *Indifference level:* These staff members are disinterested to the point of overt negative reactions. They prefer to deal with pressing substantive problems of the immediately in your face variety. While there will be little practical gain from their education, they, nevertheless will absorb some of the education and, in spite of their negativism, will understand your future strategic actions better than before.
- *Cognitive level:* These employees will understand and be interested in the material but will have practical problems in applying what they have learned. Thinking within the strategic bubble (Figure 2.8) is not easy. Their appreciation of strategy will drastically reduce friction as they will comprehend the intents your future strategic initiatives.
- *Execution level:* These employees will both understand what they have learned and be able to apply it. They will provide the greatest part of the rising tide as they will internalize what they have learned and apply it to all their endeavors.
- *Gifted level:* These employees, few and far between, will be exceptional strategists. They will reach a level of intuitive strategic grace where they will sense the most subtle linkages of the cause-and-effect web of relationships. Having employees who can function at this level of excellence is a prize that should be closely guarded.

Competitors will not like to compete against a business that is executing a breeder strategy. They will not relish competing against such a company because who wants, on a daily basis, to compete against team after team of people who think in terms of friction, speed, disruption, paradox, concentration, surprise, maneuver, commitment, alignment, and so on in everything that they do. As your dispersed strategic excellence grows in force, the strategic distance between you and your competitors expands and their ability to maintain your tempo of action will decay. They will be subjected to an ever-intensifying, deteriorating situation that will place constantly increasing stress on all their planning and delivery systems. At best, they will come to realize that they are confronting a formidable opponent, lose heart, and turn their market attentions elsewhere.

A breeder strategy is not susceptible to strategic paradox. Good strategists, who continue to study, practice, and learn do not turn into bad strategists. One does not become a good strategist by being a bad strategist. The end of a well-executed breeder strategy, over an admittedly extended period of time, is a strategic configuration of power. Your dispersed strategic competence results in every action being strategy-rich. You will no longer wander when you move.

If you will recall from Chapter 2, the struggle is the struggle for advantage. The objective is to find a way short, the shorter the better, of brute force, to accomplish your aims. A breeder strategy is a way to create advantage, not as an episodic event, but as the daily routine. It is a deep and far-reaching response to the challenges of the information age. Imagine an entire organization where *every action and inaction is a matter of strategy.* Such an organization would be truly awesome, an organization that can cope with the unknowable as well as the knowable.

Before concluding, we can also investigate the logic of a breeder strategy from a very simple and pragmatic perspective. Let us assume that the information age blooms more or less as hyped. Perhaps time will show, that rather than being overhyped, the impact of convergence has been underhyped. In the forthcoming years, all information, regardless of form, is on-line and readily accessible by point and click from robust desktop browsers. Global networked interactive multimedia has become a reality. Your employees have instant access to anything and everything they need. The digitized multimedia databases of the world are at the mercy of their high performance search engines that can search not only based on word strings, but can locate information based on sounds, partial images, video clips, and so on. Information is available to anyone, anywhere, and in any form.

The problem is, of course, that the exact same information (less your secured corporate digital libraries) is also available to your competitors. The hierarchy of interest to you is data, information, knowledge, and wisdom. Each begets the next. The raw availability of more information does not necessarily increase the ability to create knowledge or wisdom. It may, in practice, have the reverse effect as the average employee is overwhelmed by the seemingly unlimited hypermedia to choose from. Rather than being able to create new knowledge, they become lost in a rat's maze of information as they are unable to cull out the subtle and buried webs of advantage.

The availability of mass information to all has the natural effect of just creating a higher but still level playing field. To acquire advantage, it is necessary to take actions that elevate and distinguish your employees' abilities to interpret the information in a superior manner. The creation of new knowledge and wisdom requires insightful analysis and synthesis of the information. This is where strategic thinking is invaluable. Strategic thinking can provide a powerful zoom lens through which your employees synthesize the newly available information in ways more creative than your competitors. Access to more information alone is of limited value, you must raise the tide of everyone's competence in strategic interpretation. You can accomplish this pragmatically through a breeder strategy.

CONCLUSION

In the Star Trek progeny that has followed the original series, there is a computer simulation playhouse called the holodeck. The holodeck can simulate, in complete detail, any fantasy that you wish. It simulates your story with all the accompanying props, dialogue, and actions in perfect lifelike response to your actions.

The holodeck is the ultimate entertainment product. It is the ultimate entertainment product because, unlike in real life, your holodeck lifelike actions have no real life consequences. When the simulation period is over, regardless of what you did or didn't do, absolutely nothing really happened. It was all wonderful make-believe. So the holodeck creates a fantasy world where actions have no consequences. You can do it over and over again, without any harm to anyone or any negative repercussions, until you get the exact outcome you seek.

We, unfortunately, do not live in an Eden-like holodeck world. In real life, actions and inaction do have real consequences. As we all know, all too well, it really does matter what we do or don't do; actions have consequences. If we could live in a holodeck world, strategy would be superfluous, but we don't. Therefore, what we are suggesting is that since we must conduct ourselves in a real world where real actions result in real consequences, a breeder strategy is an artful action. It is an artful action because the consequence of a breeder strategy is that the strategic utility of our staff's actions improves dramatically with a corresponding increase in the utility of the consequences of their actions.

A breeder strategy satisfies the imposing standard that Sunian strategy must be deep and far-reaching because it results in procreating an entire community of people who can create deep and far-reaching strategies. What could possibly be a deeper and more far-reaching action than an action that multiplies deep and far-reaching actions?

So I believe that companies, ultimately, will have but two choices. You can continue to execute mass market strategic advice or you can breed your own advice. In the former case, you do what everybody else does and engage in a game of who can do the same thing a little bit better. In the latter case, you do a customized set of actions that are designed and executed by you for only you. It may not work, but it certainly is well worth the try. Companies have poured millions into ideas that had much less potential of a comparable payoff. What could yield a larger payoff than strategy as a strategic configuration of power?

So it is my contention, that in the knowledge society, the first knowledge is strategic thinking. It is the business knowledge that enriches all other business knowledge. When you proceed in going about your daily business on a subconscious foundation of the strategic ideas that we reviewed in Chapter 3, everything you do is strategy-intensified. Advantage is integrated at the heart of every decision. If knowledge, your people, and IT are the basis of winning in the information age, then strategic thinking is the required catalyst to kindle the desired interaction to produce winning results. Strategic thinking provides the missing nexus between improved means (information age technologies) and improved ends (market share, revenue, and customer satisfaction).

EPILOGUE

In the play "Amadeus," Salieri, the antagonist of Mozart, is revered by the classical music audiences of Vienna, and Mozart is shunned. Mozart's music is chastised for having *too many notes*. Salieri, however, knows the stark truth that Mozart is the vastly superior composer. Toward the end of the play, Salieri, paradoxically, rejects his own fame, criticizes the uneducated rejection of Mozart by the public, and bemoans the mediocre taste of the music going public when he laments: "What does it mean or matter to be viewed as distinguished or undistinguished by those who, in all truth, are hopelessly unable to distinguish?" Salieri, cursed with musical knowledge, understood the vast difference between what an audience of average musical acumen would applaud and what a knowledgeable audience would applaud. Had Vienna audiences been students of music rather than simple consumers of music, they would not have had it backwards and would have been able to distinguish the genius of Mozart from the mediocrity of Salieri.

In the information age, our employees have to be able to distinguish. The problem will not be the availability of information; the challenge will be the compiling of the relevant slivers, fragments, and shreds that create knowledge and wisdom. They cannot be just simple consumers of information, they need to be students of strategy who can see in the information what others do not see. They need to see in the information what has not yet taken shape or form. They need to sense with strategic insight what is invisible to the less prepared. They need to be aware individuals. You need a breeder strategy to attain this.

6

IT Organizational Design for the Information Age

STRATEGY AS ORGANIZATION STRUCTURE

In February 1996, both the IT industry newspapers and the popular newspaper media published news columns to the effect that Microsoft was reorganizing for the second time with two weeks. As the *Wall Street Journal* headline said on February 21, 1996, "Microsoft Reorganizes to Sharpen Focus on Internet, Raising 3 Officials' Profiles." Once again, the restructuring of a business was gaining widespread attention.

To most employees, strategy is equal to organizational structure, or more precisely, the changing of organizational structure. While they are most often not privy to the grand strategy of the business or are presented with only isolated and disjointed pieces of it, they very personally observe and feel the impact of reorganizations. For most people, the announcement of another reorganization is the start flag of business strategy going into motion. Organizing and reorganizing to align and realign is the most common and visible sign of strategy to the organizational rank and file.

Sun Tzu said: "Structure follows strategy. Forces are to be structured strategically based on what is advantageous." Sun Tzu recognized then, as astute strategists do today, that organizational structure is critical to facilitating strategy. The organizational design defines the structural distribution of resources that will be needed to be mobilized to execute your strategy. How will you be able to execute if your organization's structure stands in direct opposition to your efforts?

Information age IT organizational design has the following pressing objectives:

- Heightened collaboration: The design should promote the various organizational units to work harmoniously together towards the shared competitive aims.
- Speed in everything: The design should enable the business to execute all actions with swiftness.
- Responsiveness: The design should permit the business to promptly react to changing times and circumstances.
- Flexibility: The design should permit the organization to be adaptive.
- Innovation: The design should leave room for people to be innovative in solving customer problems.
- Permeability: The design should enable new ideas to enter and disperse throughout the organization. It should enable the business to learn.
- Leverage: The design should permit the business to achieve economies of scale and reuse where appropriate.
- Execution: The design should facilitate doing. It should lubricate action and eliminate the exhausting resistance of friction.
- Spontaneity: The design should permit the organization to dynamically evolve to stay in harmony with the changing environment. This is called spontaneous self-reorganization.
- Accountability: The design should make it clear who is responsible for what.
- Authority: The design should make it clear who has the authority to make decisions and allocate resources.
- Control: The design should balance spontaneity with the need for control.

Strategy is, to a large degree, not a problem of managing a large group but a problem of orchestrating advantageous coordination across groups. It is not surprising, therefore, that we have included organizational design as a strategic configuration of power. It is mandatory that the organization be designed with speed, flexibility, and the alleviation of friction so that the business can maneuver to engage in IT fighting.

Organizational design remains an art. It is usually necessary to select a strategic dimension that is most relevant to the current times and circumstances (geography, function, process, market, etc.) as dictated by your strategy. The selected dimension is set as the anchor of the design and the remaining design choices are made by revolving them about this primary factor.

Of particular concern in designing organizational structures is the elimination of friction. In most organizations today, if nothing was done but eliminate the massive organizational drag on action, most organizations would experience tremendous increases in productivity. The retarding resistance of organizational friction to doing slows any and all actions yet alone the execution of bold actions, actions of indirection, or surprise maneuvers. So what must often be overcome in redesigning IT organizations to permit graceful maneuverability is to remove the ingrown structures that promote friction.

The history of IT organizational design is the history of a structure in place, the whistle blows, a game of musical chairs ensues, a new structure is created, and the game continues until the next whistle. As organizations strive to balance stability and productivity against flexibility and innovation, they periodically restructure in mass to respond to the environmental stimuli. We will suggest that an IT organizational structure that mixes the ideas of minibusinesses and the internal marketplace can provide a dynamic balance, replace episodic restructuring with continuous restructuring, and position the IT organization in the desired state of potentiality.

Lastly, we would like to reemphasize that structure follows strategy and is not strategy but the facilitation of strategy. In general, organizational restructuring is the last issue to be addressed when developing a strategic plan (Figure 2.19). One first focuses on what is to be achieved and the required actions to accomplish your ends and then, and only then, does one address how to organize to facilitate those ends. Setting an organizational structure in place before you have completed your strategic thinking unnecessarily constrains your degrees of freedom. Organizational design is the first result of strategy, not the aim of it. It is common among the organizational multitudes to believe that the reorganization that they are going through for the nth time is literally the business strategy. If they are right, you are probably in a great deal of trouble.

BASIC AND ALTERNATIVE ORGANIZATIONAL DESIGNS

The challenge of designing an information age organizational structure for the IT organization exists at two levels. These levels may be referred to as the macro and micro design problems. The macro problem addresses the problem of the number of IT organizations, their roles and responsibilities, their placement relative to the business units they serve, and their governance relationship to other IT entities within the business. The micro problem addresses the question of how a specific IT organization should internally organize itself to efficiently and effectively deliver its products and services to its customers.

The Macro Problem of IT Organizational Structure

Figure 6.1 illustrates the macro problem of IT organizational design. The basic organizing unit of the modern enterprise is the strategic business unit (SBU). A strategic business unit is the foundation building block of a global enterprise structure and has the following characteristics:

- It is a collection of related business.
- It has a distinct mission.
- It serves well-defined markets.
- It has a distinct set of competitors.
- It has the resources and opportunity to deliver value to its market.
- It has a distinct management team.
- It has profit and loss responsibility.

The distinct business units may cooperate extensively with each other or be quite independent in their actions. We refer to the degree of collaboration as a strategic position along a continuum between a pure union or a pure multistate strategy. In a union strategy, the business units collaborate extensively in terms of sharing and leveraging processes, competencies, product development, marketing initiatives, and so on. In a multistate strategy, each business addresses its marketplace unilaterally. The design point for the union/multistate decision will be strongly influenced by the following factors:

- Market position: To what extent do market segments across SBUs and product lines overlap? To what extent will the business share brand names, advertising, customer image, and other marketing elements across products/markets?

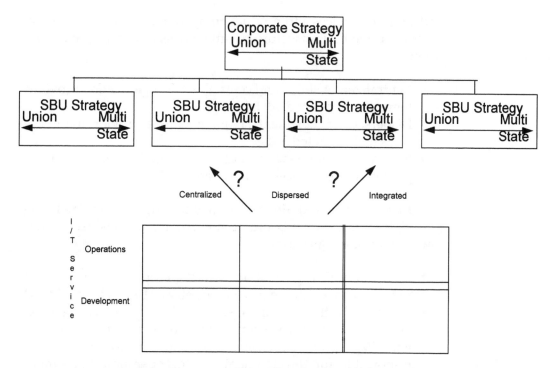

Figure 6.1 Macro organizational design. The business can define its macro structure for the delivery of IT services through a centralized, dispersed, or integrated design structure.

- Product/service position: To what extent is their synergy between SBU product lines?
- Competitive moves: To what extent is advantage accrued by linking competitive moves across SBUs?
- Cost position: To what extent does cross SBU collaboration lead to cost advantage, that is, reuse, leverage, economies of scale?

After analysis, a business takes a considered position somewhere along the continuum between the extremes of a pure multistate or a pure union.

Against the background of this macro organizational structure of the business, a corresponding IT organizational structure must be designed. An IT organization provides two broad sets of products and services to its customers—life-cycle application development and support services and production operations. For each of these, there are three basic structures (with endless mutations) to choose from:

- Centralized: A single and centralized IT organization provides these services to the SBUs.
- Dispersed: Independent IT organizations provide these services to designated SBUs.
- Integrated: Independent but coordinated IT organizations provide these services to designated SBUs.

For each considered alternative macro design, centralized, dispersed, integrated, or mixture, it is necessary to consider the following four basic questions:

- How many IT organizations will the corporation have? Will each SBU have its own or will they share IT service providers?
- What will be the roles and responsibilities of each IT organization? Table 6.1 shows a simple taxonomy of information systems. Which cells is each IT entity responsible for, and are they responsible for development and/or operations? A similar mapping must be done in terms of allocation of databases.
- Will the IT entities be separate from the SBUs they serve or will they be entities within the business units? If they are

Table 6.1
Roles and Responsibilities

Domain of System	Type of System				
	Transaction Processing	Information Analysis	Information Sharing	Workgroup Productivity	Individual Productivity
Corporate Shared SBU SBU Divisional Department Personal					

apart, what will be the economic rules for exchanging goods and services?

- How will multiple IT entities be governed? For issues of common concern such as architecture, corporate communications networks, and human resource polices, what governance mechanisms will be deployed to maintain synergy?

In this way, you design a macro IT organizational structure of centralized, dispersed, integrated, or mutated for both development and operations that aligns itself with the macro SBU structure and union/multistate strategy of the business.

The Micro Problem of IT Organizational Structure

The micro problem of IT organizational design starts where the macro problem ends. For each IT entity that will exist, it is necessary to design an internal structure that will deliver operations and/or development in a fast, flexible, and friction-free manner. If the internal structure does not become a strategic configuration of power, then all efforts to make IT maneuverable will fail because it will not be possible to mobilize the IT resources in an effective and efficient manner.

While there are endless mutations and variations, there are six basic micro designs structures to choose from as follows:

- Functional structure (Figure 6.2): Employees are grouped strictly vertically based on functional skills and expertise.
- Matrix structure (Figure 6.3): Employees are grouped in a gridlike structure with multiple chains of authority.
- Product structure (Figure 6.4): Employees are grouped into self-contained product-driven structures that are end-to-end responsible for a given family of products.
- Geography structure (Figure 6.5): Employees are grouped into self-contained structures that deliver all products and services to a geographical region.
- Front-end/back-end structure (Figure 6.6): Employees are grouped into customer-facing functions that serve customers and use products and services developed and supported by back-end functions.
- Process structure (Figure 6.7): Employees are grouped into horizontal teams that deliver products and services by process.

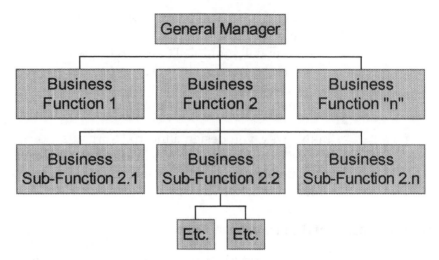

Figure 6.2   Functional structure. Design is founded on business
function.

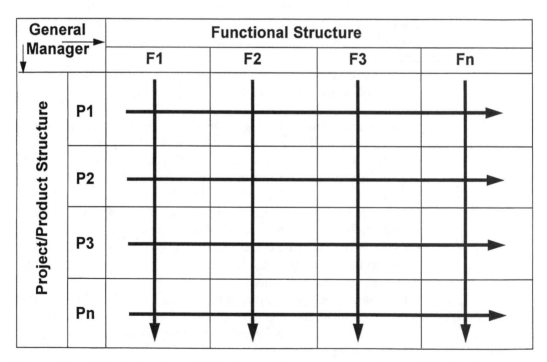

Figure 6.3   Matrix structure. Multiple reporting arrangements are defined to integrate
vertical function with horizontal processes.

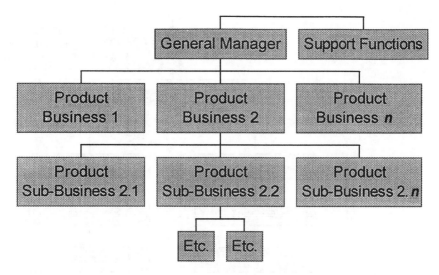

Figure 6.4   Product structure. Design is driven by end product.

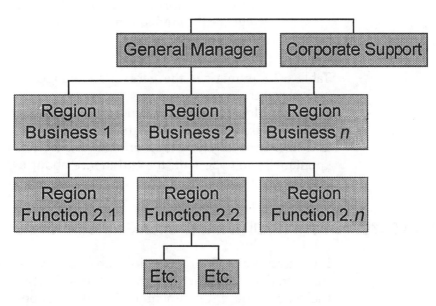

Figure 6.5   Geographic structure. Design is driven by geography.

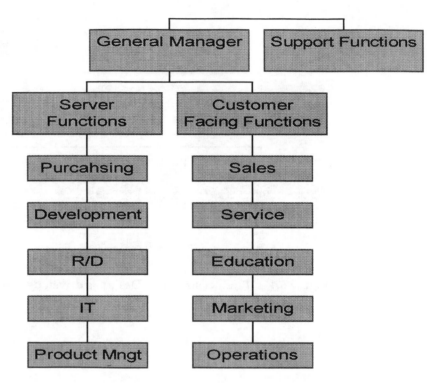

Figure 6.6   Front-end/back-end structure. Design is divided between those who face the customer and those who develop and operate the products and services that the customers buy.

Table 6.2 summarizes the generic advantages and challenges of each structure.

The problem for the information age IT organization is to define a structure that balances conflicting needs. While we need stability and formality for short-term efficiencies, we need flexibility and spontaneity to cope with the turbulence about us. We need to be organic rather than bureaucratic.

THE PROBLEMS WITH TRADITIONAL IT ORGANIZATIONAL DESIGNS

Most traditional IT organizations are a structural combination of functional and product design structures. MVS people supported the mainframe environment while UNIX people supported the UNIX environment. Operations people supported specific techno-

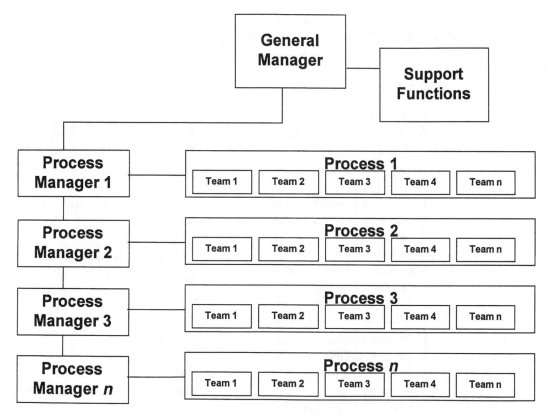

Figure 6.7   Process structure. Design is a function of business processes.

logical smokestacks. Developers were organized by product teams to serve specific customers. Figure 6.8 illustrates this structure, which made reasonably good sense during the industrial age of IT. Since the IT technology platforms were vertically segregated, functional centers of excellence to achieve stability and efficiency were a good choice. Each functional unit could strive to optimize its individual environment for the welfare of the customer and the corporation. There was little need for cross-environment collaboration, coordination, and information flow.

Two things have gone wrong with this model. First, the technology that we wish to deploy, that is, interactive multimedia across distributed and heterogeneous computing environments, is horizontal in nature. To make it work requires extensive horizontal collaboration and coordination across functional specialties. The traditional

Table 6.2
Advantages and Challenges of Micro Organizational Design

Organizational Structure	Advantages	Challenges
Functional	1. Efficiency 2. Centers of excellence 3. Focus 4. Ease of management	1. Efficient decision making 2. End-to-end accountability 3. Functional loyalty 4. Lack of flexibility
Matrix	1. Provides attention to multiple dimensions of organization design 2. Coordination 3. Considered allocation of resources 4. Horizontal communications	1. Difficult to implement and manage 2. Power battles 3. Delineation of authority 4. Costs of communication
Product	1. Product/customer focused 2. Accountability 3. High product-level coordination 4. Decision making at product level	1. Cost inefficiencies 2. Horizontal product coordination 3. Responsiveness to local needs
Geographic	1. Market sensitivity 2. Decision making and authority at market level	1. Cost inefficiencies 2. Cross-geographic 3. Local loyalties
Front End/ Back End	1. Single customer interface 2. Customer responsive 3. Promotes many to many relationships	1. Linking front ends to back ends efficiently and effectively 2. Cost allocations 3. Decision making
Process	1. Efficiency 2. Customer focus 3. Productivity	1. Process leadership 2. Cross-process coordination 3. Functional expertise 4. Process fiefdoms

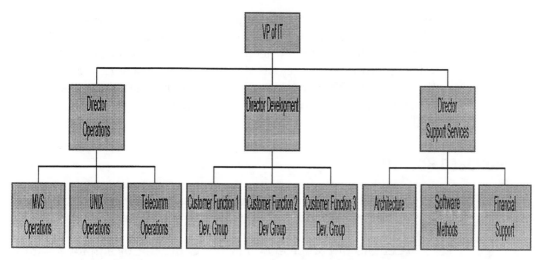

Figure 6.8   Traditional IT organization design. The traditional IT organization structure was a combination of functional and product structures.

IT hierarchical smokestack structure is not only inappropriate for this, it also actively works against it as employees are loyal to their specific vertical technological environment rather than cross environment needs.

Secondly, the traditional smokestack IT organization was designed for stability and predictability. Its structure was designed to preserve rather than change. During the mainframe era of the industrial age, change was very slow and predictable. The smokestack structure took on a mechanistic and bureaucratic flavor as it would ponderously introduce or experiment with new technologies. Change was routinely viewed as a threat rather than an opportunity.

The problems with the traditional IT structure does not therefore require elaborate or extensive debate. Its shortcomings are dual.

- It was designed to optimize, through economies of scale, the delivery of vertical IT products and services.
- It was designed not to change but to preserve.

The result of this is obvious to everyone in our field. IT organizations are viewed as slow, inflexible, and a business obstacle to be overcome. They are not strategic configurations of power because their inherent micro organizational structure is misaligned with the horizontal technological needs of the information age. They are misaligned because they create tremendous friction to change for the business. They cannot cope with continual change and the rapid horizontal introduction and utilization of gregarious information technologies.

THE PROPOSED SOLUTION

The proposed solution to this problem is to design a new micro IT organizational structure built on three interrelated ideas:

- Centers of competency (COC): Grouping of employees into logically related sets of skills.
- Process: All work gets done through processes.
- Internal marketplace: An internal marketplace is established in which centers of competency buy and sell products and services to each other.

We will develop the proposed micro organizational design structure by building on these ideas as follows:

1. Centers of Competency (COC)

A center of competency is a group of employees with a logically related set of skills. It is often also refereed to as a center of excellence or a knowledge center. The center of competency provides an administrative home for employees, provides a place to learn skills and receive specialty mentoring, and a facility to investigate and develop best practices.

A center of competency is a minibusiness, a boutique service provider. As shown in Figure 6.9, it provides a group of services to other IT centers of competency. Its manager or coach is the business manager and is responsible for developing the center of competency so that its employees can find work. The coach/manager, like any other business person, owns capabilities and must find utilization opportunities for them. So a center of competency is a minibusiness. It is not unlike an SBU. It has products to sell, a marketplace, the need to earn revenue, and the need to continually upgrade its products and services to maintain its customer base.

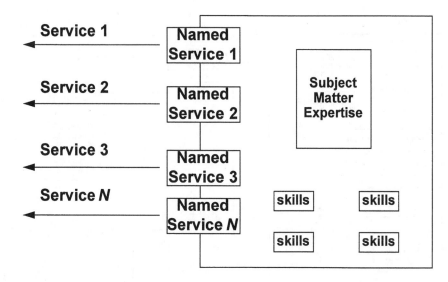

Figure 6.9   Center of competency. IT employees are grouped into centers of competency.

2. Process

All work is the result of executing processes. Process owners hire individuals from centers of competency and form teams to develop processes. Product managers, marketing/sales managers, and senior management hire members of the centers of competency to execute processes. Figure 6.10 shows how a team is formed. The buyer hires individuals with the necessary skills from each center of competency.

3. Internal Marketplace

As shown in Figure 6.11, the IT organization runs on the model of an internal marketplace. The marketplace works as follows:

- Senior management negotiates budgets with product managers, marketing/sales, and process owners.
- Centers of competency are minibusinesses who need to earn revenue. They do not receive a budget. They have a cost and earning projection.
- The economy runs by the four centers with budgeted money, that is, product managers, marketing/sales, process owners,

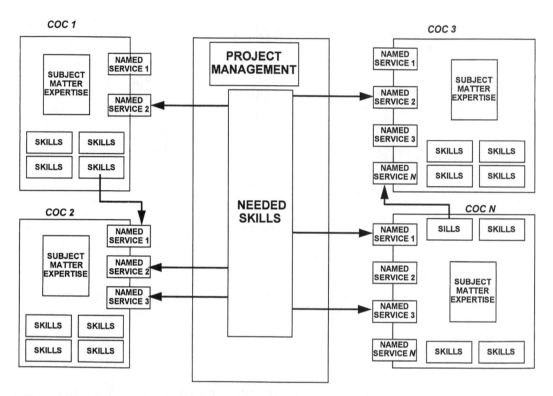

Figure 6.10 **A team. A team is formed by selecting appropriate members from the center of competency.**

and senior management, buying products and services from the centers of competency. This would generally involve the hiring of a project manager who would, in turn, shop for desired services in the internal marketplace. Centers of competency, in turn, also buy products and services from other centers of competency.

What we have now done is turn the traditional hierarchical, mechanistic, and bureaucratic IT organization into a vibrant and dynamic economic entity where there are buyers, sellers, and a sustainable strong motivation to cooperate and continually improve products and services.

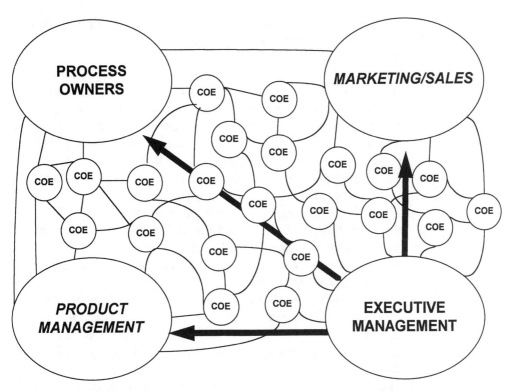

Figure 6.11 A team. A team is formed by selecting appropriate members from the center of competency.

Why is creating an internal marketplace built on boutique centers of competency a desirable structure for the information age IT organization? I would suggest the following reasons:

- The IT organization is no longer shielded from the marketplace realities. It also feels the day-to-day pressures to continually upgrade its products and services. If a center of competency wants to stay in business, it must continually improve its products and services to other centers of competency.
- The core structure for execution is a horizontal team. This team is formed using marketplace mechanisms.
- The normal marketplace mechanism of how you spend your money is used to foster alignment. As management, product

managers, marketing, and process owners shift their spending patterns, the centers of competency must respond or they will lose revenue.

- The structure lends itself to spontaneous reorganization. As spending patterns shift or centers of competency develop new products or services, it naturally adjusts to the new realities. You do not blow a whistle and say reorganize. Reorganization in the internal marketplace is occurring dynamically as some products and services win and others lose.
- The structure is very scalable. Successful centers of competency can be grown, shrunk, or replicated as needed.
- There is a marketplace. Centers of competency will only thrive if they can find buyers for their services. Product managers and marketing will only thrive if they employ processes to deliver products and services that SBU customers want. Everyone has a customer.
- Customers can evaluate, measure, and negotiate terms and conditions of purchase. Suppliers need to continually refine their offerings to maintain satisfied customers. Members of a center of competency work for their customer, not their vertical boss.
- The structure lends itself to virtual structures or, if desired, outsourcing. In both cases, one would decide which service offerings are better performed by noninternal providers, but those services must be designed into the overall internal economy.
- Centers of competency have extreme motivation to cooperate with each other. Only through horizontal collaboration on customer-focused team are they able to accrue revenue.
- Centers of competency improve value for buyers by integrating products and services across centers. Buyers can buy basic products and services or more finished goods.

The traditional IT organizational structure suffers from a gross inconsistency. The external customer-facing business units have to cope with the marketplace everyday. They have to be adaptive and fast. The mechanisms that cause concern for speed, flexibility, service, value, and quality are the marketplace mechanisms of choice and selection. Traditional IT organization units have functioned bureaucratically in the comfort of entitlement. They delivered products and services but did not have to win the business. The boutique structure of centers of competency integrated with the notion of an internal marketplace addresses this shortcoming.

CONCLUSION

The problem of designing an information age organizational structure for the IT organization is a problem of coordination. How do you design the micro IT organization so that horizontal products and services can be delivered rapidly, flexibly, and without friction? I propose that the best mechanism to do that is an internal marketplace based on center of competency boutiques that are subject to normal marketplace mechanisms. If you want speed and agility, you must submit the IT organization to marketplace pressures.

Specifically, the proposed design addresses the pressing design issues as follows:

- Heightened collaboration: The unit of delivered work is the team. Centers of competency only remain viable if they can work together on successful teams.
- Speed in everything: The internal marketplace rewards efficiency and speed. Centers of competency are motivated to continually improve their offerings with speed being a prime buying factor of purchasers.
- Responsiveness: Centers of competency earn their living. As any supplier in a marketplace, urgency in meeting customer needs is critical.
- Flexibility: Centers of competency are adaptive to meet the current needs and emerging needs that buyers will pay for. The problem for the center of competency is not what do I want to provide but what will a customer pay for?
- Innovation: Centers of competency are rewarded for constantly upgrading and innovating by the growth of their center.
- Permeability: There is little advantage to maintaining the status quo. Centers of competency search for new ideas and ways to remain prosperous.
- Leverage: Centers of competency mentor and teach their preferred skills to others. Processes are reused and tuned to promote efficiency in execution.
- Execution: Execution is accomplished through the unit of the team. Noncooperation is rewarded by replacement.

- Spontaneity: The design lends itself to spontaneous self-reorganization. As money and opportunities are made available, entrepreneurial centers of competency hustle to the new opportunity.
- Accountability: Buyers are accountable for what they buy.
- Authority: Buyers make informed purchase decisions.
- Control: Management can expand contract, or reposition the internal economy, at will, based on how it changes its spending patterns.

I submit that the internal marketplace structure is superior to the other six structures (Figure 6.2–6.7) that we have discussed in this chapter. It is superior because it is fast, flexible and removes friction. It is superior because it repositions the IT organizational structure as a strategic configuration of power.

7

Anatomy of an Information Technology Guru

"Mirror, mirror on the wall, who is the greatest IT Guru of all?"

GURUS

As was illustrated in Figure 1.29, periods of rapid change create fertile markets for advice givers. As counsel about information technologies has never been as important as it is now, who are these advice givers? What makes an advice giver a guru worth listening to? These are important questions. The difference between those who use IT wisely and those who don't is widening. Whom we lean on for sage advice will make a profound difference to our success.

The IT industry is inhabited by a significant number of people who have earned or aspire to earn the prized title of *guru*. The title of guru bestows upon the individual a community recognition that the person has demonstrated exceptional and durable thought leadership in our field. It is not the only possible signature of thought leadership stature, that is, people with a lot to say, for better or worse, are also referred to as pundits, oracles, soothsayers, academic experts, published authors, futurists, and market researchers, but none is quite as desirable, alluring, accomplished, and coveted as the very exceptional designation of guru.

The IT industry provides especially rich and fertile soil for growing gurus because of the incredibly dynamic nature of the industry. Since the IT field is constantly in motion, the focal point of intense innovation and entrepreneurship, and is of ever-increasing crucial importance to the competitive advantage of all information age companies, the need for excellent advice is always in vogue. Most IT executives find themselves with unprecedented needs for both conceptual IT ideas and the means to apply those ideas to build, sustain, and compound competitive advantage for their companies. Gurus meet the continuing and urgent customer priority for highly competent and far-sighted advice.

As shown in Figure 7.1, as we pass through the halfway mark of the 1990s, IT management finds themselves caught in a seemingly inescapable three-way pincer squeeze:

1. They are under tremendous pressure from the business users to reduce costs and add value. All strategic initiatives require the novel use of IT and the business insists that IT deliver.

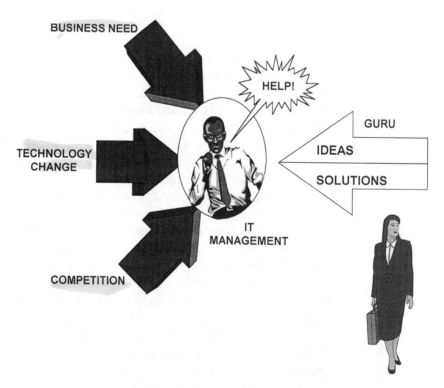

Figure 7.1   **Help!!! IT executives are finding themselves caught in a three-way pincer squeeze.**

2. They are the victims of a massive technology paradigm shift from host-centered to network computing, which is dating skills and causing a requirement for massive transition assistance. While keeping the legacy systems running, it is necessary to reengineer the IT organization to be able to integrate a whole plethora of emerging technologies into the IT portfolio.
3. They are experiencing outsourcing and systems integration competition from able and agile competitors. The IT organization is losing its internal monopoly status as the sole supplier of IT services and must aggressively compete for the business.

Gurus who can provide ideas and solutions are not merely welcomed, but aggressively sought after by harried IT executives searching for an escape from the closing pincer.

In the remainder of this chapter, we would like to perform a generic analysis of gurus. Like any other subject, IT gurus are subject to in-depth study and analysis. By understanding guruism better, you are better positioned to evaluate the advice you are given and select your advice givers with improve efficacy. As Glinda, the good witch of the North in "The Wizard of Oz" would say, we need to know, "Are you a good guru or a bad guru?" In this way, we gravitate to winning advice, advice that is deep and far-reaching and do not waste time with losing advice, advice that is shallow and nearsighted.

WHO ARE THE GURUS

Anybody can become a guru. It is the most democratic of institutions in that entry is solely a function of profound merit. The marketplace decides who is and who is not a guru by whose advice it seeks and whose advice it follows. While an individual can certainly be temporarily hyped, over time, the IT community is quite adept at distinguishing whose advice is deep and far-reaching and whose advice is shallow and nearsighted.

A guru is generally distinguishable from other public IT figures by the following seven attributes:

1. *Breadth of ideas:* The guru is able to provide highly competent advice on a wide range of related IT subjects. The ability to perform synthesis analysis is a key trait.

2. *Depth of ideas:* The guru's thinking is layered and deep. The ideas may be expressed simply but, with reflection, reveal themselves to have graduated and deep strategic roots.
3. *Coherence of ideas:* The breadth and depth of ideas are horizontally coherent. There is a remarkable consistency, synergy, and integration laterally across thoughts.
4. *Durability of ideas:* Both the individual ideas of the guru and the guru herself are durable. The ideas have lasting power and the guru is able to developing a stream of innovative and thought-provoking ideas over an extended time period.
5. *Impact of ideas:* The guru is able to influence decision makers. Not only do people who make decisions listen to the guru, they act on the guru's ideas and the ideas have a measurable positive impact in driving business results.
6. *Size of following:* The guru is well known by name, reputation, and sight. A large audience is willing to attend events simply because the guru is speaking.
7. *Loyalty of following:* A large body of people are students of the guru. Over an extended period of time, they seek out advice from this individual and will present and strongly defend her ideas to others.

It should be obvious from this list that it takes accumulated knowledge, experience, a prolonged period, foresighted thinking, and perseverance to become a guru. Also, to be a guru, the individual must provide counsel to senior IT or business management executives. Only by winning the admiration and loyalty of senior management can the impact attribute be achieved.

As is common in reaching the peak in any field, there are a number of well-recognized rungs that precede guru status. Typical jumping off positions for guru status may include:

- *Hero executive:* A senior executive in a user or vendor firm who has achieved wide notoriety. In the former case, the executive shares her experiences of managing her IT organization. In the latter case, the vendor executive provides unique insights into the direction of the industry.
- *Legendary technologist:* A technical individual who has acquired wide fame for her expertise with an emerging and exciting technology. Unless the individual can broaden her subject mat-

ter and audience, this is often a deadend position as the advice is often too technical for executive management.

- *Partner consultant:* A senior partner in a well-respected consulting firm who, by virtue of her expertise in applying IT technology, has earned the respect of multiple clients.
- *Market researcher:* A market research analyst for a leading market research firm. By virtue of the individual's research, analysis, and sharing of that research with the firm's clients, the individual wins respects for her insights of market directions. This role provides excellent access to decision makers.
- *Academic:* An individual from a prestigious university whose research, writings, and lectures on IT have made her sought after for advice. Academics always risk the charge of being "too theoretical" and often have to overcome skepticism that their ideas are not actionable.
- *Author/writer:* An individual who has written books and articles that have had industry influence. This category may include editors and journalists within the IT media community.

These roles are certainly not exclusive. It is quite common for aspiring gurus to concurrently execute many of these roles or sequentially move between them. While there is nothing wrong with achieving any of these plateaus and the individuals in these roles often give exceptional advice, they are accurately described as second-tier roles. Until the consultants, authors, academics, and so on achieve, through market acceptance, the seven attributes listed earlier, they remain supporting actors with the guru commanding center stage.

THE DIMENSIONS OF THOUGHT LEADERSHIP

Gurus compete in the thought leadership marketplace. The products they sell are ideas. Their role is especially relevant to the information age (Figures 1.3 and 1.4) where information and knowledge rather than land, labor, or capital provides the source of value for customers. The idea business is especially wonderful because it has a quality of nondepletion: You have it, you sell it, and you still have it.

As shown in Figure 7.2, there are three dimensions to thought leadership: the ideas, the thought leader, and the marketing of

Figure 7.2   Thought leadership. Thought leadership is a function of the ideas, the thought leader, and the marketing of both the ideas and the thought leader.

both the ideas and the thought leader. Each will be discussed separately.

1. The Ideas

The ideas that gurus present may normally be partitioned into four broad and overlapping classifications:

- *Complex business phenomena:* The ideas explain complex business or technical phenomena. The thought leader reveals mysteries and, in so doing, permits the listener to be a member of a restricted club that exclusively understands.
- *Out of the crisis:* The ideas provide a way out of a serious or chronic problem. The ideas provide a path to salvation and escape from a most pressing issue.
- *Fire and brimstone:* The ideas severely criticize actions and behaviors that are being executed. The ideas urge you to cor-

rect your corrupt ways before the day of reckoning and justice inevitably arrive.

- *Vision:* The ideas paint a glowing picture of a highly desirable future. If you will but follow the ideas, you can share in the nirvana to come.

Again, an idea may span classifications or a guru may present a portfolio of ideas that emphasize different themes. One may understand the four types of ideas as respectively addressing different audience needs for revelation, salvation, judgment (damnation), and hope.

Regardless of which type of idea, pure or hybrid, is presented, to flourish, the idea must be dressed with a rich collection of the following accessories:

- *Timely:* The idea addresses, in a clear and powerful manner, a pervasive and serious problem of the age. There is a very receptive and eager market for the idea. The idea is in perfect harmony with the times and circumstances of the potential adopters.
- *Understandable:* The idea is readily understood by the potential adopters both in terms of the absolute meaning of the idea and how that idea directly solves their problem. The adopters of the idea can quickly recognize the relevance and benefits of adopting the idea and how the idea ends their search for a solution.
- *Exciting:* The idea is more than interesting; it is exciting. The excitement is contagious and creates a self-sustaining momentum for the idea. The adopter feels that this is not business as normal and if they adopt the idea, they will participate in a special event.
- *Distinct:* The idea is unique and clearly superior to alternative ideas. Implementing the idea makes you a member of a very, very special community.
- *Simple yet complex:* The idea can be grasped at a simple level but there is considerable depth to it. As the layers of the idea are peeled away, it continually reveals more insight and power. Potential adopters are awed as the depth of the thinking is revealed in its totality.
- *Acceptable:* The idea is ethically, socially, and politically acceptable. The idea can therefore have appeal to a broad market. In

this way, a predictable set of strong resistance to adoption is avoided.

- *Signature:* The idea has a simple and appealing logo that communicates the essence of the idea. The logo becomes a strong symbol for the idea.
- *Broad application:* The idea addresses the needs of a large and diverse marketplace. The idea must therefore be adaptable to the specific needs of different users and industries.
- *(Pseudo) scientific basis:* The idea includes formulas, notations, acronyms, and jargon that gives the idea a rational scientific flavor. At least a day of technical education is required to fully comprehend the underlying theory of the idea.
- *Incomplete:* The idea is not quite complete as presented. Consulting help, implementation support, and education is required to get it to work.
- *Individual action:* A potential adopter can see how she, as an individual, can apply the idea and how she, as an individual, can directly benefit from applying the idea. There is personal benefit to be derived from executing the idea.
- Group action: Potential adopters can see how they, as a work community, can all benefit from implementation of the idea.
- Anxiety-reducing: The potential adopter can understand how this idea will relieve the pressures and problems that are confronting her. Control, order, stability, and safety can be restored to her environment. The daily anxiety of having to live with ambiguity, chaos, and fear of failure can be alleviated.
- *Customizable:* The adopter can add value. They can implement the idea in a personalized manner and therefore become a "thought leader" themselves.

Obviously, the raw merit of an idea is inadequate to assure its marketplace success. Considerable packaging is required to assure market acceptance. The acme of success for an idea is to become the *dominant logic* (Table 2.2) of an era. Dominant logic, as we previously discussed, means that the idea has accrued such widespread acceptance and implementation that it becomes a standard and unquestioned way of both understanding events and formulating actions. In recent times, Total Quality Management and business reengineering have achieved this status. It is worth noting that being the originator of a dominant logic is what often finally makes someone a guru rather than having become a guru, one then creates a dominant logic.

2. The Thought Leader

The thought leader is in the personal services business. People are not only buying the ideas, they are buying the person who has created and is selling the ideas: A successful thought leader must include in her persona the following attributes:

- *Untainted:* The thought leader is a step removed from the daily market mayhem. They are untainted by overt commercialism and their ideas transcend immediate products and profits.
- *Teach/explain/share:* The thought leader is teaching, sharing, and explaining; she is not selling. There is no overt sales motion in progress and the thought leader is successful by virtue of having gotten the potential user to consider her thoughts.
- *Showmanship:* The thought leader is both entertaining and interesting as well as knowledgeable. The thought leader can hold the attention of an audience for an extended period. The thought leader realizes that the idea business is very much part of the entertainment business.
- *Presentation skills:* The thought leader can communicate through a variety of communication media.
- *An expert authority:* The thought leader is a recognized expert. Books, articles, speaking engagements, academic credentials, references, professional society memberships, work experiences, projects, and so on all contribute to giving the thought leader the critical credential of "expert."
- *Trustworthy:* The thought leader is someone you can trust. She has an obvious passion and commitment to her ideas and is wholly believable. The thought leader cares deeply and personally about the success of each client.
- *Personable:* The though leader is friendly, has a pleasant sense of humor, is wise, interested, and concerned about each client.
- *Accessible:* The thought leader makes herself accessible for direct contact with clients and is easily approachable.

Gurus are selling themselves as much as they are selling their ideas. Without these attributes, they will never become gurus and, having achieved the coveted title, they will lose it if they forget to maintain a deep and pervasive personal concern for their clients.

3. Marketing

Regardless of innate merit, all products and services must be marketed. The ideas that a guru peddles are a product and must be marketed with the same intensity as any other service. To be successful, the following must be remembered:

- *The idea is a product:* the idea is understood to be a "product" in every sense of the word. It is produced and sold to the marketplace with a carefully designed value proposition.
- *Distribution channels:* The idea can be and is packaged to be presented in an engaging way through multiple media including seminars, courses, audio/video tapes, books, articles, white papers, and followers.
- *Audience/market:* The thought leader speaks to, writes for, and touches decision makers. If your audience is not decision makers, whatever you are, you are not a guru.
- *Reference marketing:* Reference marketing is used to provide testimonials and proof of concept. It is an honor to be a client who is asked to be a reference.
- *Personable delivery:* The thought leader always attempts to appear personally at speaking opportunities. Every audience is special and she would, of course, not send an associate.
- *Pricing:* The services that the guru offers must be premium priced. The pricing reflects the superior value of the ideas.

So a successful guru must, like any other business person, be very concerned with the Ps of marketing: what is the product they are selling, how will they promote it, how will they place and distribute it, and, of course, what will its price be.

Summary

The material in this section on the three dimensions of thought leadership could be but should absolutely not be interpreted cynically. While one could read this material and conclude that gurus are being mechanistic in formulating and delivering their services with a complete absence of sincerity, it is exactly the opposite that is true. A guru who is disingenuous will be a short-lived guru. Only those gurus with complete sincerity and concern for their clients will be able to achieve the coveted state and sustain it. So the preceding analysis of the dimensions of thought leadership should be interpreted not as a cold prescription of behavior for a shaman who is engaged in a sophisticated scam but a description of what sincere and dedicated people must do to earn market share in the fiercest of all marketplaces: the thought leadership marketplace.

THE VALUE CHAIN

As has been presented, a guru is in the idea business and, being in a business, the guru needs to have a value chain to deliver her products to the marketplace. Figure 7.3 illustrates a composite

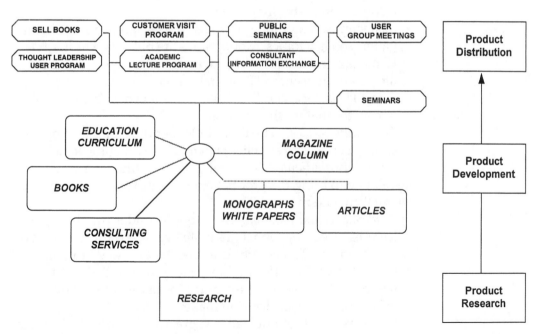

Figure 7.3   The value chain. The thought leader delivers her ideas through a carefully engineered value chain.

value chain for an imaginary and very prolific guru. The value chain consists of three levels as follows:

1. *Research:* The guru alone or with help from associates does research into the IT field and the emerging interests of IT decision makers.
2. *Product Development:* The guru and associates develop a rich set of products to offer to clients. Typical products would include the following:
   - *Books:* The thought leader publishes books on topics of immense concern to IT decision makers. In some cases, the guru is editor of a series. Books include tear-out marketing information cards or other reach information. Books are published in multiple languages.
   - *Articles:* The thought leader publishes articles in leading industry media. Articles are converted to marketing reprints after publication. Advertising for products/services in the journal is coordinated with publication of articles.
   - *IT magazine/web column:* The thought leader has a column in a respected industry magazine.
   - *Monographs:* The thought leader writes monographs (white papers) on key topics. Monographs are published as inserts in IT magazines and journals, given to customers as marketing literature, and sent to IT journals as basis for news stories.
   - *Education curriculum:* The thought leaders develops a catalog of courses that teach the ideas.
   - *Consulting services:* The thought leader develops a set of consulting services to aid clients in implementing the ideas.
3. *Product Distribution:* A rich set of distribution channels are developed to bring the products to market. Typical distribution channels would include:
   - *Academic lecture program:* The thought leader provides guest lectures at leading global graduate business schools as part of an "Academic IT Thought Leadership Exchange Program."
   - *Consultants information exchange program:* The thought leader has periodic sessions with other industry consultants who influence customer decision makers.
   - *Sell books:* The thought leader aggressively supports the sales of her books. As a number of books are published, they are referred to as a *collection.* Books are packaged into discount packages that include marketing material.

- *Customer visit program:* The thought leader is a guest speaker at customer internal IT learning events.
- *Industry public seminars:* The thought leader is a keynote speaker at industry seminars. Speaking is coordinated with bringing traffic to exhibition hall display by having book signing and giving away reprints, monographs, and so on.
- *Seminars:* The thought leader has periodic public speaking tours. Customers are given books, article reprints, monographs, and so on.
- *User group meetings:* The thought leader is keynote speaker at user group meetings. Private "executive-only" invite sessions are held.
- *Thought leadership group:* The thought leader leads a thought leadership group for customers. The members provide lists of topics of interest and the guru develops research to address the itemized needs.

So being in the guru business is like being in any other business. Ideas must be transformed into products and products must be brought to market. How else could it be?

THE INTRACTABLE PROBLEM OF CURRENCY

The dynamics of the IT industry creates an interesting paradox. On one hand, it is the source of the never ending need for gurus. Confronted with a relentless onslaught of innovation and change, decision makers have a continual and pressing need for strategic advice. So the dynamics of change fuels the need for an elite cadre of gurus to make sense and bring order to the incomprehensible daily marketplace mayhem.

On the other hand, the continual upheaval in technologies and associated methodologies challenges the ability of even the most gifted guru to stay current. Like everyone else, the guru's experiences and knowledge base are finite. In most cases, the guru has a heritage in a particular technology domain, such as database, transaction processing, human interfaces, application development methodologies, and so on. While the guru may be unusually knowledgeable and have insight, it is still quite a challenge to ceaselessly have to analyze rampant change and be able to put deep and far-reaching spins on it for a demanding and often fickle audience. So the same cause, the swirling dynamics of our industry, both creates gurus and destroys them.

This industry dynamic is best understood within the previously reviewed framework of technological substitution and diffusion S curves (Figures 2.12–2.15). The guru is consequently presented with a number of related challenges as follows:

1. Clients will want an analysis of each successive technological generation. They will want to know the impact of newly announced releases and what can be expected to follow in future generations.
2. Clients will want an analysis of the attack by the replacement technology (Figure 2.13). They will want to know if the substitution attack will be successful and when, if at all, they should jump to the new technology. They will also want to know if the attack will be a complete replacement attack, in which case the defender will become obsolete, or a complementary attack, in which case the two technologies will work together.
3. For the above two items, they will expect the analysis to be horizontal across multiple technological S curves and to be insightful. They will want a synthesis, not a analytical decomposition.

Besides the obvious challenge of doing this, we must remember that a guru, like everyone else, has a finite background.

Consider the S curves for human interfaces as illustrated in Figure 7.4. Assuming a guru was an expert in ergonomics for command mode and block mode human interfaces, why would the same individual automatically be equally gifted in understanding and analyzing multimedia or virtual reality? S curve attacks are not necessarily evolutionary; they might be revolutionary and, in fact, the more revolutionary they are, the more that decision makers will seek advice and the more difficult it is for the guru to be an expert on the newly emerged attacker.

So currency is a major problem for gurus just as it is for clients. As decision makers seek advice on new technologies, they must periodically ask themselves if their favorite guru is still special or is coasting on past glories. Consider, as a fictitious example, the gurus who became famous during the early part of the structured programming revolution for mainframe computing some 25 years ago. Many are now giving advice on object-oriented development for client/server computing. That is quite a shift of S curves. Is

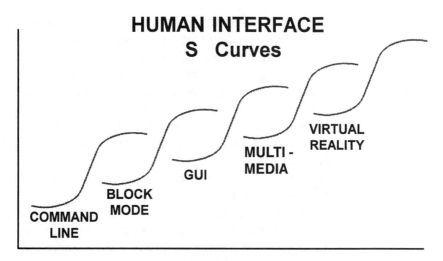

Figure 7.4   Human interface S curves. The evolution of interactive human interfaces can be understood as a series of S curves.

their advice still deep and far-reaching, or are they coasting on yesterday's reputation? So every now and then, you have to be like Glinda, the good witch of the North, and ask yourself, "Is she still a good guru or a has-been guru?" Gurus, like S curves have limits and it's the guru's problem to keep jumping S curves with the changes in information technologies while it's the client's problem to decide when that doesn't happen and the guru has reached her limit. At that point, you need to jump "G" curves to a new guru.

A problem complementary to the dated guru is the intimidating guru. Gurus routinely offer superb advice; they must or their market will quickly abandon them. Nevertheless, they are but human and can make gross mistakes. The problem is that due to their revered status and intimidating posture, few are willing to stand up and tell the emperor that *this time* they are naked.

An excellent example of this occurred with regard to the now-fading debate over the comparative cost of client/server computing and traditional monolithic host-based computing. A number of gurus wrote cost studies that irrefutably proved that client/server was anywhere from .7 to 14.3 times as expensive as host-centered computing (of course, this wide range of *scientific* results would make any reasonable person suspicious). While the reports were extremely influential and silenced many client/server advocates, the studies were, in truth, not even good nonsense.

The problem with all of the ones that I saw was that they uniformly engaged in the logical fallacy of contradiction. At some point in the study, they would say something, overtly or covertly, to the effect that *even though client/server and host-centered computing are not functionally comparable, we will ignore that and cost-compare them anyway.* For example one report said: "In practice, the nature of mainframe and PC/LAN interactions was qualitatively different" while another said: "The two systems are not functionally equivalent." What they were saying is that client/server and host centered are not functionally the same thing and they are functionally the same thing. Stated simply, they admitted that they were going to compare apples and oranges, ignored such, and proceeded. What they did was no different then stating that they were going to compare the cost of living in a teepee with the cost of living in a modern four-bedroom house and ignore all the differences. Yes, they would get the result that the 100 sq. foot teepee is cheaper then the 5,000 sq. foot house with all the modern amenities, but we would all see through the fallacious comparison of apples (teepees) and oranges (modern houses). Comparing mainframe environments with client/server environments without either down functioning client/server to operate at the more primitive level of the mainframe or providing enough resources so that the mainframe can do what client/server does, is just more apples and oranges.

To a person who understands the rules of logic, after the point of contradiction, all bets are off and a person concerned with seeking the truth will read no further. They will read no further because once you permit contradiction, you can prove anything is true; that is why it is a fallacy of reason. Their arguments, past the point of contradiction, could just as well have been used to prove that Monday is a mammal, a tuna fish sandwich is General Motors, or airplanes are kangaroos.

A priori admitting that you are going to deliberately commit a fallacy to prove your argument does not grant absolution; it just makes the reader wonder why you are doing it and why you need to do it when you know better. Once a fallacy is discovered in an argument, the argument is declared fallacious and no deduction may be drawn from it. The guru client/server cost studies do not prove that client/server is more expensive nor do they prove that they are less expensive. They do prove that with contradiction you can, once again, prove anything. They also prove that as good as a guru may be, there is no substitute for your own critical review of their arguments.

THE GREATEST GURU OF ALL

In the first act of Andrew Lloyd Webber's dazzling musical "Sunset Boulevard," the aging heroine, Norma Desmond, sings her great solo, "The Greatest Star of All." Of all the wonderful stars of the silent movie era, Norma's star shone the brightest. We live in the foremost era of IT gurus. Who is our Norma? Where are you, Norma? Who is the greatest IT guru of all?

This is a very American question. In all areas of our lives, defining who is the winner is paramount. All sports have most valuable player awards, the movies have the Oscars, television has the Emmys, and Broadway has the Tonys. These questions are endlessly argued in public and private debates. So we bring the question to the province of guruism. Of all the IT gurus, who alone stands above all the rest?

I will pass on giving my opinion as I am terribly partial in this matter. I believe that the marketplace decides this question and this chapter has provided the necessary tools for you to structure an evaluation. Choose your candidates carefully and evaluate each honestly against the following seven questions:

1. Does the guru offer superior advice on a wide range of important subjects?
2. Are the guru's ideas deeper and more far-reaching than others?
3. Is there a unique coherence across ideas?
4. Does the guru and her ideas demonstrate unusual staying power?
5. Does the guru have exceptional influence with decision makers?
6. Does the guru have a large following?
7. Are the guru's followers unusually loyal?

Table 7.1 provides a worksheet to engage in guru comparison.

Don't expect a unanimous answer if you do this with your colleagues. The answers to these questions represent judgments and opinions. I argue forever with my friends over who is the greatest ballplayer to ever play center field and we can never even come

Table 7.1
Guru Evaluation

	Candidate Gurus			
	Guru 1	Guru 2	Guru 3	Guru *n*
1. Does the guru offer superior advice on a wide range of important subjects?				
2. Are the guru's ideas deeper and more far-reaching than others?				
3. Is there a unique coherence across ideas?				
4. Does the guru and her ideas demonstrate unusual staying power?				
5. Does the guru have exceptional influence with decision makers?				
6. Does the guru have a large following?				
7. Are the guru's followers unusually loyal?				

close to an agreement. I imagine the same will be true in trying to answer the guru question, but it is not a futile effort; it is a fun effort.

CONCLUSION

Is it good or bad that we have an industry that is inhabited by so many gurus? Is it a blessing or an infestation, is it beneficial or harmful? I think the answer to that question needs to be framed by suggesting that it is not so much that it is either good or bad as it is instructive. As shown in Figure 7.5, as an industry moves from the craft stage to the engineering stage, from art to science, it is dominated in the early stages by gurus and later, as science enters the

ARTISAN TO ENGINEER

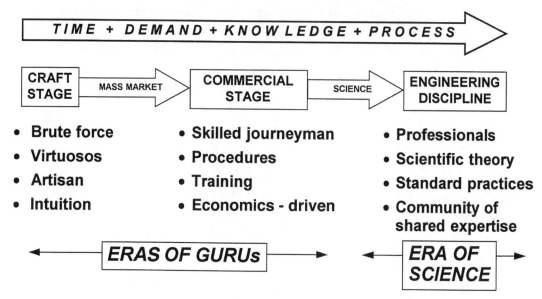

Figure 7.5   Engineering evolution. Engineering disciplines start out as crafts and progress to a basis in science.

picture, by scientists and engineers. A guru-driven industry is not good or bad, but reflects the relative immaturity of our industry. As our understanding of software engineering matures in the next decades, the popularity and importance of gurus will diminish as opinions will have to be replaced with facts.

EPILOGUE

Recall that Sun Tzu said:

> What everyone knows is what already has happened. What everyone knows is not called wisdom. What the aware individual knows is what has not yet taken shape; what has not yet occurred. If you see the subtle and notice the hidden so as to seize victory when there is no form, this is really good. A leader of wisdom and ability lays deep plans for what others do not figure on.

Perhaps this is why we are always in search for a truly great guru. Truly great advantage will accrue to those who are *aware* and know what has not yet taken shape. To foresee victory before it exists is the most remarkable and rare of abilities. Of course, this is not easily done and exceptional gurus are few and far between.

8

Epilogue:
The Way of the IT Warrior

PROLOGUE

One of the simplest yet most powerful frameworks for doing strategic analysis is called root cause analysis. As shown in Table 8.1, the root cause technique, borrowing from medical diagnosis methodology, divides problems into three hierarchical layers of causation:

- *The symptoms:* The most external presentation of the problem.
- *The illness or problem:* The malfunctioning part that is responsible for causing the symptoms.
- *The etiology or root cause:* The fundamental (underlying) first cause of the problem.

Table 8.1
Root Cause Analysis

Definitions	Root Cause Analysis	Treatment Plan
The external manifestations of the problem	Symptoms	Temporary relief
The malfunctioning part	Illness or problem	Cure for this episode
The first cause	Etiology or root cause	Eradication

When you treat symptoms, you get temporary relief but the problem persists. When you treat the problem, it is eliminated but may return. When you treat the root cause, you eradicate it.

When I think about the information age and apply root cause analysis to it, my layered results are as follows:

- *Symptoms:* The turbulence and instability of our times.
- *The problem:* The strategic paradox of coming together of opposites. Our IT inheritance has played a cruel joke on us. That which made us strong and powerful is now unable to cope with the turbulence and instability of the times. Our grand IT legacy, subjected to conflict, has become an albatross about our necks. Our dominant logic IT skills and approaches for the industrial age are dated and are growing increasingly irrelevant to mastering the information age.
- *The root cause:* The information age. The shift between epochs has changed the rules for creating societal wealth.

I believe that the advice in this book is worth your careful consideration because it provides a treatment plan at the root cause level. Many of the advice industry prescriptions fail to deliver the claimed efficacy because they provide treatment only at the symptom level. The problems are temporarily covered up but the relief is short-lived. They inevitably return, even more virulent than before. They are prescriptions that stop your coughing for but a few hours.

The strategy we have outlined in this book treats our conundrum at the level of etiology. A strategy of potentiality positions us to deal with the realities of the new epoch. Strategic configurations of power provide the means to create an IT organization that can maneuver without the fatiguing resistance of friction. Opportunistic strategies of actuality exploit the strategic configurations of power to build advantage where and when needed in a timely fashion. This is a treatment plan in harmony with the new order of the information age.

BODY

Sun Tzu established the enduring formula for winning 2,500 years ago:

> In ancient times, those known as good warriors prevailed when it was easy to prevail. Their victories were not flukes. Their victories were not flukes because they positioned themselves where they will surely win, prevailing over those who have already lost.

The way of the modern IT warrior is to prevail by creating strategic configurations (positions) of power.

Many IT leaders have lost the hunger for prevailing. They abrogate their leadership responsibilities and seek the easy way. Instead of struggling for advantage, they adopt shallow and nearsighted strategies such as mindless cost cutting, morale-destroying downsizing, management by fear, raising the bar of performance without providing any means of achievement, imploring the masses to work harder and faster, magical thinking (if I think it, it will happen), noncritical reliance on gurus, outsourcing the problem rather than solving the problem, executing strategy salads, fad surfing, launching wandering and aimless empowered teams, and encouraging diversity without providing for unity. This is not the way of an *aware* individual; it is not the way of an IT warrior.

At my seminars, sooner or later, I am asked the inevitable question, What exactly should we do now? My answer is that leadership means erecting a set of strategic configurations of power. My strategic logic is as follows:

- The information age ushers in a new era of unprecedented hyper-competition.
- The convergence of information technologies creates entirely new ways to compete and serve customers.
- The battlefield shifts from the marketplace to the marketspace as bits replace atoms as the basis for wealth creation.
- The information age erodes sustainable competitive advantage because barriers to entry are easily breached. Continuous and overlapping temporary competitive advantages become the way to competitive superiority.
- Information technology is elevated to a core competency.
- Superior management of IT demands the application of deep and far-reaching strategic thinking. Strategic thinking is your first core competency and your only truly sustainable competitive advantage.
- The IT response to the information age is a strategy of potentiality.

- A strategy of potentiality is realized by crafting a portfolio of strategic configurations of power. Strategic configurations of power permit you to win through limitless adaptive maneuver.
- The implementation of strategic configurations of power is managed through strategic planning.
- A starting set of configurations of power are IT architecture, the economy, human resource architecture, governance, and organizational structure. These configurations of power lubricate your business and eliminate the restraining effects of friction and drag.
- Strategies of actuality exploit the configurations of power to create endless tactical IT-based temporary competitive advantages.
- Perfect IT to business alignment is achieved. For the first time IT is able to align because it can continuously revise itself in harmony with the changing business requirements.

This strategy is built on classical strategic thinking. It is the way of an *aware* individual, an IT warrior who intends to prevail. The underlying idea of this strategy is to win. What is your information age strategy?

CODA

Some people are critical of my approach to strategic thinking. They suggest that it relies too much on *dated* classical strategy. How can you craft modern IT strategy based on the potentiality/actuality ideas of Miyamoto Musashi or the strategic configurations of power ideas of Sun Tzu? Shouldn't we follow the contemporary thought leaders on the seminar circuit? Nothing could be in greater opposition to the path to success. The teachings of the masters transcend time. They transcend time because they are abstract and represent a deep and far-reaching understanding of the eternal inner nature of strategic conflict. Following modern pied pipers who offer shallow and nearsighted fads is what will bring you to ruin. Strategic thinking must be judged on its efficacy; not its origin. Strategic thinking is about imagining a future and how you will win in that future. The teachings of Sun Tzu, Musashi, and other classical strategists are simply better guides to strategic thinking than that offered by modern pundits.

When I consulted in Australia for the first time, I had a most instructive experience. After breakfast, I went into the hotel's lobby store and asked for today's *Wall Street Journal.* The store manager smiled at me, apparently Americans did this all the time, and said that she could not give me any of today's newspapers from the states; *today had not happened yet.* She was absolutely correct. Australia was 16 hours ahead of the East coast and the East coast was still ticking away on yesterday. Today had not happened yet.

I am often asked if I can provide definitive evidence in support of all the ideas presented in this book. My answer is no, my ideas are not about yesterday. As you will recall, Sun Tzu said: *"What the aware individual knows is what has not yet taken shape; what has not yet occurred."* An aware individual is, metaphorically, 16 hours ahead. Most IT organizations are still ticking away on yesterday; today has not happened yet for them. What I have presented is for consideration, reflection, and action by aware individuals. It has not happened yet, but it will. It will take shape and it will occur. The question for your IT organization is when? When will you be prepared to compare in a marketspace where there is just you, them, and 1s and 0s?

Appendix A

An Information Age Bibliography

If you are interested in understanding the nature and implications of the information age in greater detail, I would suggest that you consider reading the following excellent books.

1. *The Information Society*, H. Dordick & G. Wang, Sage Publications, 1993.
2. *The Digital Economy*, D. Tapscott, McGraw Hill, 1996.
3. *In the Age of The Smart Machine*, S. Zuboff, Basic Books, 1988.
4. *Being Digital*, N. Negroponte, Alfred A. Knopf, 1995.
5. *Post Capitalist Society*, Peter F. Drucker, Harper Business, 1993.
6. *The Telecommunications Information Millennium*, R. Heldman, McGraw Hill, 1995.
7. *Global Paradox*, John Naisbitt, W. Morrow, 1994.
8. *Powershift: Knowledge, Wealth, and Violence at the Edge of the 21st Century*, Alvin Toffler, Bantam Books, 1990.
9. *Frontiers of Electronic Commerce*, R. Kalakota & A. Whinston, Addisson Wesley, 1996.
10. *The Monster Under The Bed*, Stan Davis & Jim Botkin, Simon & Schuster, 1994.

Appendix B

Mandatory Reading For Strategists

If you are going to maximize your strategy and strategic thinking skills so that you can respond creatively to the information age, you will have to become a student of strategy. As strategic acumen is the most fundamental competence required for all aspects of business, as well as information technology, becoming a lifelong student of strategy is an extremely worthwhile endeavor. As your career develops and your responsibilities grow, you will have greater and greater opportunities to apply your strategic wits to address deeper and more far-reaching business and IT problems. You prepare yourself through study, experience, and being mentored.

The following annotated bibliography is a list of the books that I have found most helpful in learning about strategy. These are not books that you read; they are books that you study. The books convey their messages in proportion to your readiness to understand. As you reread these books over and over again, you will never ceased to be amazed how you receive new insights from the exact same source due to your increased receptivity.

1. *The Art of War,* Sun Tzu (See Appendix C). The greatest work ever written on strategy. It is an order of magnitude better than the next work. The book has flourished as the par excellence source of strategic teaching for 2,500 years because of its insights into the essential nature of conflict. Appendix C provides an expanded list of *Art of War* references. If you plan to study only one book on strategy, this is the book. The most famous quote from *The Art of War* is the paradoxical and insightful "It is best to win without fighting."

2. *The Book of Five Rings*, Miyamoto Musashi, translated by Steve Kaufman, Charles E. Tuttle Company, 1994 (Numerous other translations available). A strategy classic second only to *The Art of War* in its wisdom. Of particular value is its emphasis on preparation, lifelong learning, focus, and the will to win. It is often referred to as the Japanese *Art of War*. Musashi summarized his entire philosophy of strategy in the simple but profound statement "The underlying idea of my way of strategy is to win."

3. *The Prince*, Niccolo Machiavelli, translated by Bruce Penman, The Gurseney Press Company, 1981 (Numerous other translations available). *The Prince* is an invaluable reference on political strategy. Though the book is routinely criticized as being immoral, it is not so much moral or immoral as it is amoral. What is particularly valuable to the aspiring strategist are the examples of strategic assessment and reasoning that Machiavelli demonstrates. The first rule of strategy is to see things as they are in truth, not as you would wish or prefer them to be. While some of Machiavelli's prescriptions are extreme for our modern-day sensibilities, he is an exceptional teacher of clear strategic thinking. Machiavelli also writes a great deal about the need to proactively anticipate and quickly react to change. These skills are, of course, at a premium in coping with information age turbulence. Regarding change, Machiavelli said:

> Some princes flourish one day and come to grief the next without appearing to have changed in character or in any way. This I believe arises because those princes who are utterly dependent on fortune come to grief when their fortune changes. I also believe that those who adopt their policy to the times prosper and that those whose polices clash with the times do not. This explains why prosperity is ephemeral. If time and circumstances change, he will be ruined if he does not change his policy. If he changed his character to the times and circumstances, then his fortune would not change.

If we are not to be ruined, we must change our character and actions to be in harmony with the new times and circumstances of the information age.

4. *Warfighting*, US Marine Corps, Doubleday, 1994. This succinct, crystal-clear book describes the military doctrine of the US

Marine Corps. The doctrine that it espouses is maneuver. Though the context of the book is war, its philosophies and prescriptions are easily mapped to the business equivalent situations. Many commentators dismiss military strategy as being inappropriate to business strategy. For example, in *Fad Surfing in the Boardroom* by E. C. Shapiro, Ms. Shapiro said: "War—A metaphor for business from which the customer is unaccountably left out." This commentary misses four important points:

1. The essence of both problems is coping with psychological, political, economic, social, and physical (in the case of war) conflict.
2. The ultimate objective of both is exactly the same. As Sun Tzu taught, the height of success is to win without fighting.
3. The objective of strategy is to satisfy customers but the reason for strategy is competition. If there wasn't competition, strategy would reduce to a bureaucratic problem of administration. It is always prudent to attack a problem at its roots.
4. The simple truth is that, in general, military strategic thought is much deeper and more far-reaching than business strategic thought. The reason for this is that it really matters. If you doubt this, read a typical business or IT strategy book and than read *Warfighting*. Which provides a much more penetrating strategic analysis? If a business fails, everybody picks themselves up and gets another job. If a country loses a war, its entire way of life and freedom are compromised.

Table B.1 illustrates four points of focus that you may take in preparing strategy. It seems to me that a market focus is the

Table B.1
Strategic Focus

		Competitor Focus	
		High	**Low**
Customer	High	Market Focused	Customer Focused
Focus	Low	Competition Focused	Internally Focused

most productive. Read *Warfighting* as a metaphor for how to engage in conflict situations and win through the use of a maneuver strategy.

5. *Strategy*, B. H. Liddell-Hart, Meridian books, 1991. This book consists of two parts. The first part consists of a history and analysis of warfare. While instructive, it may prove tiring if you are not interested in the histories of the major wars of the last 2,000 years. The second part called "Fundamentals of Strategy and Grand Strategy" is a wonderful abstraction of the first part. Mr. Liddell-Hart proposes a general theory of how to engage in conflict that is entirely applicable to business. His concentrated essence of how to deal with conflict is as follows:

    1. Adjust your end to your means.
    2. Keep your object always in mind.
    3. Choose the line (or course) of least expectation.
    4. Exploit the line of least resistance.
    5. Take a line of operations that offers alternative objectives.
    6. Do not throw your weight into a stoke while your opponent is on guard.
    7. Do not renew an attack along the same line (or in the same form) after it has once failed.

    These excellent maxims are as suitable for developing business and IT strategy as they are for military strategy.

6. *Strategy*, E. Luttwack, Belknap Press, 1987. This is a book about nuclear strategy. As a nuclear confrontation is perhaps the ultimate conflict, it provides the definitive explanation of strategic paradox. *The Art of War* and *Strategy* by B. H. Liddell-Hart also cover the subject of strategic paradox but this book completely explains the phenomenon. After reading this book, it will make perfect, though paradoxical, logical sense that as the world gets smaller, small companies get bigger and big companies get smaller.

7. The books of Michael Porter. Michael Porter is a business school professor at Harvard University. His books on strategy, which include *Competitive Strategy*, *The Competitive Advantage of Nations*, and *Interbrand Choice, Strategy, and Bilateral Market Power*, focus on building, compounding, and sustaining competitive advantage, and have demonstrated enduring value. This is a nontrivial accomplishment as most books on business and IT strategy are normally faddish and offer only fleeting

value. He is the creator of concepts such as The Five Forces, The Value Chain, and Strategic Groups. His work is very applicable to understanding how to use IT to build competitive advantage in any age.

8. *Hypercompetition: Managing The Dynamics of Strategic Maneuvering*, A. D'Aveni, The Free Press, 1994. An excellent analysis of the need for successful businesses to engage in maneuver market strategies. It completely develops the logic of hyper-competition that characterizes the information age and recommends a maneuver response. The books explains the demise of sustainable competitive advantage and the need to breed an endless stream of overlapping temporary competitive advantages. It is because of the arguments brilliantly developed in this book that IT must support the business with a strategy of potentiality.

9. *Thinking Straight*, A. Flew, Prometheus Books, 1977. This is a book about how to think logically. It teaches the rules of inference, syllogisms, fallacies, deduction, inference, and so forth. The ability to think logically is important to a strategist from two perspectives:

    1. You have to be able to analyze the arguments of others. Are the arguments presented to you good sense or nonsense? Arguments that are persuasive are often fallacious and arguments that we would prefer too reject are often valid. We must be masters of the skills of logic to distinguish between the two.

    2. You need to be able to develop cogent arguments in defense of your positions. If you develop fallacious arguments to support your ideas, not only will you be subject to embarrassment if exposed, but worse, if not exposed, you will lead your business into a new situation even worse then the one they had hoped to escape from.

    This book, as well as many others like it, are valuable in improving your reasoning skills. Once you have mastered the rules of logic, you will be appalled at how much of what is routinely presented in the IT media channels does not even qualify as good nonsense.

10. *Strategic Thinking*, B. Nalebluff and A. Dixit, Norton, 1991. This is a book about game theory. It views strategy in terms of games of moves and countermoves. This is very applicable to engaging in a strategy of maneuver as it emphasizes the impor-

tance of anticipating an opponent's response. The book is also fun to read because of the choice of examples.

As I am sure that you have noticed, none of these strategy books focuses on IT strategy. This is because, as was stated in the Foreword, I too believe that IT strategy is 90% strategy and 10% IT. To be a good IT strategist, it is first necessary to learn strategy and then apply those skills to the subject area of IT. Most of the people that I meet in the IT profession know IT very well but they have little formal education or preparation in strategy and even less in strategic thinking. This list will provide assistance in alleviating that shortcoming.

Appendix C

An Art of War Bibliography

If you are going to be the best strategist that you can be, then you must be a student of *The Art of War* by Sun Tzu. The following is a list of readily available books and articles that will help you interpret the definitive classic work on strategy and strategic thinking.

TRANSLATIONS OF *THE ART OF WAR*

1. *The Art of War*, Sun Tzu, translated by Thomas Cleary, Shambhala Dragon Editions, 1988.
2. *The Art of War*, Sun Tzu, translated by Samuel B. Griffith, Oxford University Press, 1963.
3. *The Art of War*, Sun Tzu, translated by L. Giles, Luzac & Co, 1910.
4. *The Art of Strategy*, Sun Tzu, translated by R. L. Wing, Dolphin Press, 1988.
5. *The Seven Military Classics of Ancient China Including The Art of Strategy*, Sun Tzu, translated by R. D. Sawyer, Westview, 1993.

BOOKS ABOUT *THE ART OF WAR*

1. Donald Krause, *The Art of War for Executives*, Perigee Books, 1995.
2. Wee Chow Hou, *Sun Tzu: War and Management*, Addison Wesley, 1991.
3. Chin-Ming Chu, *The Asian Mind Game*, Rawson Associates, 1991.

ARTICLES ABOUT *THE ART OF WAR*

1. "For White Collar Warriors," Andrew Sherry, *Far Eastern Economic Review,* July 21, 1994.
2. "Strategic Management Thought in East Asia," Rosalie L. Tung, *Organizational Dynamics,* Spring 1994.
3. "Sun Tzu's Strategic Thinking and Contemporary Business," Min Chen, *Business Horizons,* March/April 1994.
4. "Sun Tzu's Art of Stock-picking," Louise Lucas, *Asian Business,* March 1994.
5. "Honda and the Art of Competitive Maneuver," Benjamin Chris, *Long Range Planning,* August 1993.
6. "The Art of War and the Art of Management," Raymond E. Floyd, *Industrial Management,* September/October 1992.
7. "The Gospel According to Sun Tzu," Joseph J. Forbes Romm, December 9, 1991.
8. "Adjusting to the Job of Strategist: Tactical Advice from an Old Soldier," Cloud Avery, *Computerworld,* July 23, 1990.
9. "From Battleground to Marketplace," Wee Chow Hou, *Asian Business,* April 1995.
10. "A Convergence of Western Marketing Mix Concepts and Oriental Strategic Thinking," Sui Pheng Low, *Marketing Intelligence and Planning,* Vol. 13, No. 5, 1995.
11. "Sun Tzu's Art of War," Wee Chow How, *International Review of Strategy,* Volume 5, John Wiley & Sons, 1994.
12. "A Game Theoretic Interpretation of Sun Tzu's Art of War," Peter Ordershook, *Journal of Peace Research,* May 1994.

Index